SUPERVISING CONFLICT

A Guide for Faculty

Cultivating respectful and productive academic relationships is a priority within higher education. What can faculty do when conflict disrupts research progress and strains the supervisor/student relationship?

Supervising Conflict offers practical advice and tools to help faculty identify and actively respond to the most common grad school concerns – the "everyday" conflicts. Drawing on data collected over four years at a large research-intensive university in Canada, Heather McGhee Peggs provides faculty with a map to where issues are likely to emerge based on hundreds of coaching conversations with faculty and students.

While ideally every campus would have a dispute resolution office and a graduate peer support team to help individuals navigate conflict, the reality is that faculty are often managing complex and difficult situations on their own. This unique resource combines negotiation and fair complaints-handling principles with insights from a multidisciplinary graduate peer team and highlights the critical role that equitable, restorative, and trauma-informed approaches can play in the prevention and resolution of conflict. This book includes opportunities for self-reflection, real-life case studies, and activities for professional faculty development. *Supervising Conflict* guides administrators seeking to address graduate concerns earlier and more effectively at a systemic level.

HEATHER MCGHEE PEGGS is a lawyer and former manager of the Graduate Conflict Resolution Centre at the University of Toronto.

In view of the complex, individual, and specific nature of graduate school issues and resulting or potential conflicts, this book is not intended to replace professional legal or other advice or institutional resources and supports that are available for members of a university or college community. The information in this book is intended for general informational purposes only. Readers should use their own good judgment in applying the recommendations, practicing the strategies, and asking the questions contained in this book. The author and publisher expressly disclaim any responsibility for any liability, loss, or risk, personal or otherwise, which is incurred as a consequence, directly or indirectly, of the use and application of any of the contents of this book. The references and links provided are current as of the date of publication.

Supervising Conflict

A Guide for Faculty

HEATHER MCGHEE PEGGS

UNIVERSITY OF TORONTO PRESS
Toronto Buffalo London

© University of Toronto Press 2023
Toronto Buffalo London
utorontopress.com

ISBN 978-1-4875-4901-5 (cloth)   ISBN 978-1-4875-5728-7 (EPUB)
ISBN 978-1-4875-5186-5 (paper)   ISBN 978-1-4875-5428-6 (PDF)

All rights reserved. The use of any part of this publication reproduced, transmitted in any form or by any means, electronic, mechanical, photocopying, recording, or otherwise, or stored in a retrieval system, without prior written consent of the publisher – or in the case of photocopying, a licence from Access Copyright, the Canadian Copyright Licensing Agency – is an infringement of the copyright law.

___

Library and Archives Canada Cataloguing in Publication

Title: Supervising conflict : a guide for faculty / Heather McGhee Peggs.
Names: McGhee Peggs, Heather, author.
Description: Includes bibliographical references and index.
Identifiers: Canadiana (print) 20230136583 | Canadiana (ebook) 20230136605 | ISBN 9781487551865 (paper) | ISBN 9781487549015 (cloth) | ISBN 9781487554286 (PDF) | ISBN 9781487557287 (EPUB)
Subjects: LCSH: Conflict management. | LCSH: Graduate students – Supervision of.
Classification: LCC HM1126.P44 2023 | DDC 303.6/9–dc23

___

We welcome comments and suggestions regarding any aspect of our publications—please feel free to contact us at news@utorontopress.com or visit us at utorontopress.com.

Every effort has been made to contact copyright holders; in the event of an error or omission, please notify the publisher.

We wish to acknowledge the land on which the University of Toronto Press operates. This land is the traditional territory of the Wendat, the Anishnaabeg, the Haudenosaunee, the Métis, and the Mississaugas of the Credit First Nation.

University of Toronto Press acknowledges the financial support of the Government of Canada and the Ontario Arts Council, an agency of the Government of Ontario, for its publishing activities.

To the G2G

Contents

From the Author   xi

Acknowledgments   xv

Who Wants to Talk about Grad School Conflict?   3
    What Types of "Conflict" Are We Talking About?   7
    How Conflict Impacts Us   10
    Has COVID-19 Changed Grad School Conflict?   11
    What Impact Do Current Events/Movements Have on Grad Conflict?   14
    What Time of Year Does Grad Conflict Emerge?   16

Why Do Grad Students Avoid Conflict?   21
    Fear and Uncertainty (Risk and Reputation)   22
    Assumptions and Previous Experiences   23
    Isolation and Feelings of Inadequacy   24
    Complexity and Time Required   25
    Psst … Faculty Avoid Conflict Too   26

Why Is Conflict Something Faculty Should Manage?   28
    Poorly Managed Conflict Can Be Costly   28
    Effective Conflict Management Can Be Beneficial   30
    Avoidance Isn't the Only Option   32
    Are We Escalating Conflict Unintentionally?   37

What Does Grad Conflict Management Involve?   40
    What Makes Conflict Resolution Unique in Higher Education?   41
    What Is the "Secret Formula" for Resolving Conflict?   44
    Conflict Management Influencers   45

viii   Contents

Interests and Positions	45
Managing Conflict Fairly	50
Identity, Intersectionality, and Individual Experience	53
FACILITATED CASE STUDY: The Silent One	57
Focusing on Early Resolution and Conflict Prevention	58
Integrating Trauma-Informed Approaches	60
Restorative Approaches	63
TIP SHEET: Trauma-Informed Restorative Questions	67
Responding to Conflict Online	68
TIP SHEET: Email Best Practices (for Emails You Send)	71
Resolving Conflict Informally	72
TIP SHEET: Pitfalls and Better Practices for Informal Meetings	78
If It's Not My Conflict, How Can I Help?	**79**
Listen to Words and Clarify Meaning	81
Expect Emotions and Be Trauma-Informed	83
Make Effective Referrals	87
QUIZ: Where Do I Refer This Grad?	91
What Are the Grad Conflict Hotspots?	**93**
CONFLICT #1 – Supervision	**95**
Looking beyond Positive Graduate Survey Results	98
Supervisors and Grad Students Flag Similar Sources of Conflict	99
Power, Pressure, and Personalities	101
CONFLICT #2 – Grad School Challenges (Miscellaneous)	**107**
CONFLICT #3 – Escalation and Appeals	**110**
Taking a Leave from Grad School	112
Processes for Escalating Conflict within Universities	113
CHECKLIST: Taking a Leave from Grad School	114
CONFLICT #4 – Interpersonal Conflict (Not Supervisory)	**115**
ROLE PLAY: Dumped and Ignored	117
When Storms Hit Grad Group Work	119
TIP SHEET: Nine Steps to Approaching Campus Conflict	124
CONFLICT #5 – Research and Thesis	**125**
FAQ: Intellectual Property and Authorship	129
ROLE PLAY: Publishing Letdown	130
CONFLICT #6 – Academic Progress	**132**
Family/Financial + Academic Progress	134

Grad School Challenges + Academic Progress	135
Health/Wellness + Academic Progress	135
Supervision + Academic Progress	136
Research/Thesis + Academic Progress	137
TIP SHEET: Five Ways to Deal with Negative Feedback	138
TIP SHEET: Five Ways to Move from Rejection to Resilience	139
CONFLICT #7 – Family and Personal	**141**
SKIT: Family Priorities	144
Roommates and Housing	146
Grief and Loss	148
CONFLICT #8 – Health and Wellness/Accessibility	**150**
CONFLICT #9 – Laboratories	**157**
TIP SHEET: Brainstorming How to Prevent Lab Conflict	160
SKIT: Lab Workload Overload	163
CONFLICT #10 – Career and Work	**165**
Work Placements and Internships	168
SKIT: Career Collision	170
What Can Supervisors Do to Prevent Conflict?	**173**
Start Thinking about Conflict on Day One	174
TIP SHEET: Supervision Early Days	175
FACILITATED CASE STUDY: Storm on the Horizon?	178
Clarify What "Effective Supervision" Means	180
Manage Expectations (Roles and Responsibilities)	183
SKIT: Time to Prioritize	188
Considerations for Remote/Virtual Supervision	190
Maintain Boundaries	193
TIP SHEET: Setting Boundaries	196
Include "Light Touch" Interventions in Supervision	197
What Can Supervisors Do to Resolve Conflict?	**200**
Be "Open" to Resolving a Conflict …	201
… And Be Okay if It Doesn't	202
Acknowledge (Faculty) Power and Take the Lead	203
Listen to Get More than Information	206
TIP SHEET: Six Critical Listening Tips from the FBI and MIT	208
Answer More Often with a Question	209
ROLE PLAY: Reflective Questioning	211

    Reframe as a Joint Problem to Solve   212
    Focus on the Future   213
    Move beyond "Difficult"   214
    Exercise Cognitive Flexibility   216
    Switch to a Bigger Picture View   217
    Consider Timing   218
    Acknowledge Complexity   218
    Use Positive and Negative Messaging   220
    Keep Process Top of Mind   223
    Negotiate in a Way That Is Respectful and Inclusive   223
    Self-Evaluate: What Could I Do Better …   225
    … And What Am I Doing Well? (Be Kind to Yourself)   227

What Can Departments or Institutions Do to Support Conflict Management?   **228**
    Encourage Training and Other Professional Development   230
    Build a Faculty Coaching Team   232
    Consider Peer Support   234
    Know When to Bring in an External Third Party   239
    Look at Online Guided Conflict Resolution Pathways   241
    Live Up to Institutional Promises   242

What Do We Do When Conflict Isn't Resolved?   **244**
    Advice Doesn't Always Lead to Resolution   244
    There Needs to Be a Different Process   245
    It Is Simply Time to Move On   246
    It Can Make More Sense to Agree to Disagree   246
    ROLE PLAY: Switching Superstar Supervisors   248

Notes   251

Index   279

About the Author   287

From the Author

I once said to a colleague that after hearing hundreds of alarming accounts of conflict in graduate studies I would rather write a book than complete a PhD ... and here is proof!

My perspective on conflict in higher education is that of a former litigator and a grad school outsider (LLB not PhD), who worked as a university insider, managing conflict and complaints at two large universities in Toronto, Canada. As a junior litigator, I learned quickly that clients wanted us to take action – to advise them about how to proceed based on the facts, the law, and the realities of a given situation. When I was hired by the University of Toronto in 2015 to bring an idea for a conflict resolution center for graduate students to reality, I also knew action was required. The university was keen to support students navigating challenging supervisory (advisory) relationships – an issue that had already been flagged as a key concern in various surveys, reports, and by graduate student working groups.[1]

I recognized that the scope of graduate conflict was likely much greater than supervision based on my experiences reviewing hundreds of student complaints with a fairness lens in an ombuds office ("an ombuds" is also referred to as an ombudsman or an ombudsperson). I saw potential for this new office to wrap support around, and develop capacity throughout, the graduate community. The resulting Graduate Conflict Resolution Centre (Grad CRC) included a diverse, multidisciplinary, graduate student peer advisor team. Training for the graduate peer advisors was intensive and comprehensive, and I extend my profound gratitude to colleagues who shared their time and expertise with the team – their involvement enhanced skills and profoundly impacted the team year after year.

Over four and a half years we pushed the uncomfortable reality of grad school conflict into the open – challenging the graduate community to strategically engage with, rather than avoid, conflict. We provided confidential conflict resolution coaching and facilitated dispute resolution training for students, faculty, and staff. While a third of our conversations were related to supervision, the remainder touched upon a wide range of issues from the personal to the professional – examples are included throughout this book.

We helped individuals to self-advocate, to navigate supports and resources, to escalate concerns appropriately, and to develop the practical skills, strategies, and confidence to engage actively and proactively with conflict. It therefore came as a surprise to the whole team when senior administration decided to close what was viewed by students and faculty as an effective and trusted service. The decision of senior administration to close what was viewed by students and faculty as an effective and trusted service was perplexing and difficult for me and the graduate peer team – as a student or as a faculty member, navigating conflict in grad school is more challenging than ever.

A student-centered conflict resolution model, with informal, front-line allocation of resources (including paid grad student staff!), confidential data collection, and sharing data insights with the university community, is a best practice in graduate conflict management.[2] However, it isn't necessary to wait until a conflict management center like the Grad CRC is developed or to hire and train a peer advisor team – there are ways faculty (as supervisors/advisors, principal investigators [PIs], mentors, and administrators) can take action right now to manage conflict more effectively. I encourage readers to use this book for DIY (Do It Yourself) professional development and as a guide for how to deal with conflict in small, everyday ways, even if your first instinct is to avoid, deny, or delay taking action to resolve an issue. Here are some strategies I include in this book:

- A unique overview of grad school "hotspots" to help you identify where graduate conflict may be flaring.
- *What you can do* practical recommendations for how to manage graduate school conflict individually and across the institution, tips and suggestions for further learning (links, videos, articles), and questions for self-reflection or for use in group faculty professional development.
- Mini-case studies based on hundreds of real conversations that the members of the Grad CRC team had with PhD/master's students, faculty, and staff that are designed to illustrate a conflict hotspot topic with questions to highlight and practice specific conflict management strategies.

- Practical resources and engaging training activities including tip sheets, checklists, quizzes, case studies, role plays, and skits (because engaging faculty as actors is an entertaining path to great discussion and learning).

Effective and early conflict management helps to build capacity, reduce time to completion, and enhance the graduate experience. Conflict management is in the doing, using simple tools and strategies to manage conflict daily, and planting the seeds of early resolution that can take hold at a systemic level.

It was my professional privilege to have worked with each of the thirty-four curious, kind, and insightful doctoral and master's students who were part of the grad-to-grad "G2G" peer advisor team (2016–20). I am extraordinarily grateful to everyone in the U of T graduate community who shared with us their stories of challenge, hope, and resilience – their willingness to talk openly about the realities of graduate school conflict is one of the reasons why I wanted to write this book. I extend a special thank you to the Grad CRC staff, partners, and champions for helping us highlight how conflict can be an opportunity in graduate school.

To my husband Mike, who truly understands how important it was for me to write this book, I could not have done this without your love and support before, during, and after the book was finished. Thanks to my two sons who motivated me with enthusiastic hugs and demonstrations of brotherly conflict resolution. My heartfelt appreciation is extended to Lynie Awywen (MI, Library and Information Science) for her valuable assistance, to Dr. Nana Lee for her comments on early drafts to Sharon Sutherland for inspiring me with her creativity and commitment to ADR, and to Rebecca Hazell (MPhil, MEd) whose support paved the way for me to translate the work of the Grad CRC into a book to help faculty manage conflict.

The challenge of navigating conflict on campus is as much of a concern today as it was when the Grad CRC was first imagined. The need for graduate conflict prevention and enhanced communication and self-advocacy skills to resolve graduate conflict, is greater than ever. This is about more than getting along – it is about accountability, mental health, fairness, equity, and safety on and off campus. I hope that these real-to-life insights into graduate school conflict will help you to manage challenging issues in your supervisory relationships, and that you will spend less time suffering the consequences of unmanaged grad school conflict by engaging proactively to resolve conflict earlier and more effectively.

Heather McGhee Peggs, BA (Hons.), LLB

Acknowledgments

I would like to acknowledge the essential connection that existed between the work of the Graduate Conflict Resolution Centre (Grad CRC) and the land on which the University of Toronto operates. For thousands of years this has been the traditional land of the Huron-Wendat, the Seneca, and the Mississaugas of the Credit. Toronto is home to many Indigenous people from across Turtle Island. I am incredibly grateful to the original stewards of this land and for the opportunity to live, work, and learn in Toronto.

I have included in this book material related to the Grad CRC that was created or compiled in the course of my employment with the University of Toronto (2015–20), and with the support and funding of the University of Toronto. The case studies, examples, and excerpts from coaching conversations are based on actual conversations with graduate students, faculty, and staff between 2016 and 2020, with edits and compilations made to protect confidentiality and for illustrative purposes. The Grad CRC program partners were the School of Graduate Studies, Student Life (St. George), and the Graduate Students' Union (UTGSU) representing more than 19,000 graduate students on three campuses.

I have made every effort to indicate when included materials were written by or in collaboration with the Grad CRC graduate peer advisor team. Quotes and reflections from the peer advisors have been edited for length, spelling, and grammar and are otherwise their own words. Where available I have included the peer advisors' first names and the graduate degree they were enrolled in at the time they worked at the Grad CRC (most now graduated!), in other cases they are cited as "peer advisor" or as "we." I ask for their forgiveness for any errors or omissions.

SUPERVISING CONFLICT

Who Wants to Talk about Grad School Conflict?

Conflict is a shameful reality of higher education and is the hidden cost of pursuing a graduate degree. Left unchecked and unexamined, conflict can undermine research productivity, destroy academic relationships, and negatively impact student, faculty, and staff health and wellness. However, when properly managed, conflict can also be a catalyst for positive change by providing institutions with valuable information about the impact of their processes, decisions, policies, and priorities and by giving individuals an opportunity to reflect upon and refine their own approaches to challenging situations.

My experiences managing a conflict resolution center at a large, urban, research-intensive Canadian university, illuminated the fact that there is a collective desire by members of the graduate community to learn how to self-advocate and engage in conversations to resolve differences. Faculty as well as students are eager to understand options for managing conflict, including how to resolve or escalate concerns while preserving critically important academic relationships; they are "starved for the tools and knowledge of conflict resolution" (Nelson, MSc Institute of Medical Science).

The hundreds of graduate students, faculty, and staff who sought the Grad CRC's confidential conflict coaching services, plus thousands of participants in our conflict management skills training, are proof that members of the grad community really want to talk about conflict! Between January 2016 and June 2020, we engaged in 732 conversations with graduate students, 86 with faculty or staff, plus 95 conversations with undergraduate students, postdocs, community members, parents, and individuals who did not provide identifying details to our team.[1] By providing a low-barrier service, including multiple drop-in locations across a large tri-campus urban university, we were reaching more graduate students as well as others who might have been just curious about the service, or who were looking for information about the university or graduate school, or who were wanting to talk about a conflict in their lives. For these individuals, the peer advisors would use their discretion about whether to engage, redirect, or refer to our mandate to explain why they were not able to assist.

Over the years we found the day-to-day connections with the Grad CRC office were like making popcorn – a few slow conversation "pops" here and there, then perhaps no conversations for a day or so ... but then a number of "pops" in quick succession. Therefore, it was important to collect data to assess our impact over the longer term, and so that we could use aggregate data to improve our service and to relay information about conflict "hotspots" back to our partners and to the various campus graduate supports. Staff tracked details of our coaching conversations in an anonymous way, and stored the information in a secure, password-protected database. Our collection of data was user-driven: We did not ask anyone to answer questions or provide specific information (e.g., names, student ID, program or department, year) to access our service, instead we listened and recorded what we heard from users.[2]

In this book, faculty will find many of the conflict management tips and strategies we used in our conflict coaching sessions as well as recommendations for grad specific support, training, and DIY materials that may be useful for professional development or for enhancing capacity to manage conflict at a departmental or administrative level. I was surprised by the breadth of issues that students, faculty, and staff across all disciplines, departments, and years of study wanted to discuss off the record under the umbrella of "graduate conflict resolution" and the unexpected commonality of experience related to conflict among graduate students from different disciplines, programs, departments, and years of study. For example:

- "I haven't talked to my supervisor in months."
- "I'm not getting guidance from my supervisor about what I'm supposed to be doing."
- "My supervisor/PI isn't supportive of me taking any time off for personal reasons."
- "My advisor told me I should be working every weekend!"

The experience of doing graduate research and working with a supervisor can be as rewarding as it is overwhelming. Not surprisingly, more than 33 percent of our discussions included supervision issues – the complex relationship where academic personalities, perspectives, power dynamics, and pressure (university "culture of excellence") combine to varying success. "During my role I've also gained an appreciation of the complexity of issues that students can encounter during their graduate education which can often be exacerbated by power dynamics, cultural differences, mental health issues, systemic barriers and the 'culture of excellence' at the University" (Rachel, MSc Institute for Medical Science).

Faculty supervisory concerns often paralleled those raised by students:

- "My [student/supervisor] hasn't responded to my emails."
- "My [supervisor/student] responded poorly to what I said in our last meeting."

It is important to note that even though most of the individuals who reached out to our "conflict resolution center" wanted to discuss a "conflict," at times we heard from faculty and students about excellent and productive supervisory relationships and from a few individuals who seemed blissfully unaware that there might be conflict in their department. In addition, as a result of talking with fellow students about concerns, many of the peer advisors were able to implement preventative strategies for their own relationships and had come to appreciate their own academic relationships: "[Today's conversation] made me appreciate how great the supervision in my life is" (Manaal, PhD Social Work).

In our office, we were observing the flip side (negative) of positive survey findings. For example, a 2019 Canadian national graduate survey found that close to 89 percent of doctoral and master's students ($n = 63,077$) were satisfied with their academic experience, describing their experience as "excellent," "very good," or "good."[3] Similarly the results of this survey for our particular institution, found a 91 percent satisfaction ($n = 6,041$).[4] From my conflict management perspective, I am more interested in the respondents who did not answer positively (i.e., the 7,127 grad students across Canada who ranked their experience as "fair" or "poor"), because this can offer insights into what might be needed to prevent conflict.

Here are four additional ways that these same national survey results can provide insights into potential sources of graduate conflict:

- *Declining satisfaction of doctoral students year over year*: First-year doctoral students had 90 percent satisfaction with their program, third-year students had 85 percent, and fifth-year students had 80 percent.[5]

- *Ambivalent or negative feelings about the faculty/student relationship*: When asked to rank the relationship between faculty and graduate students as "excellent," "very good," "good," "fair," or "poor," 13.3 percent of graduate students ranked the relationship as only "fair" or "poor."

- *Poor opinions about overall supervisor performance*: Graduate students were asked to comment on whether their advisor "Overall, performed the role well" on a scale of "strongly agree," "agree," "disagree," and "strongly disagree," 11.8 percent disagreed or strongly disagreed.

- *Conclusions that supervisor feedback is not constructive*: Over 8 percent of graduate students responded "disagree" or "strongly disagree" to the statement "My advisor gave me constructive feedback."[6]

While the topic of conflict in graduate school is not a new one at academic conferences or for campus workshops,[7] the focus is often on how students can take steps to resolve supervisory (interpersonal) disputes, rather than what faculty or administrators can do to prevent or manage common concerns.[8] I cannot promise that by using the strategies or approaches in this book all graduate conflict will be prevented or resolved; however, I am confident that these insights will help faculty to identify opportunities to build trust and to move conversations forward in productive ways. Grad students want to feel that their supervisors and departments "have their backs" and that the academy is committed to addressing any disputes or issues that might arise fairly and with consideration for the student point of view.

WHAT YOU CAN DO

! Are you ready to get faculty colleagues thinking strategically about conflict in grad school? Consider these questions:

Q1. Do we acknowledge that supervisory conflict exists within our department?

Q2. What information do we have about how students are feeling about their supervision and their graduate experience (e.g., participation in surveys, working group observations, anecdotal information)?

Q3. When do we hear about current conflicts? When do we (if ever) learn about past conflicts?

Q4. How can we identify and acknowledge conflict earlier? Is conflict "welcome" in our department?

What Types of "Conflict" Are We Talking About?

Within a highly competitive, diverse, and hierarchical environment such as post-secondary education, conflict can emerge, "when disagreements, differences, annoyances, competition, or inequities threaten something important."[9] Throughout this book, I share insights into what grad students told us was important to them and into ways to prevent, resolve, or manage the much wider range of real-to-life concerns that grads identify as conflict. As peer advisor Rachel (MSc, Institute of Medical Science) noted in her year-end reflection, "Quite often, students yearn to be heard, understood, and have their feelings validated. This can often be difficult when communicating with supervisors, faculty, or other individuals in leadership positions due to underlying power imbalances or fear of judgment."

For example, imagine a PhD student and their advisor are discussing whether the student's thesis is ready to defend. Whether this conversation will become a conflict depends if there is "something important" at stake, and if yes, for whom and why. If neither person's interests are threatened, a difference of opinion about timing for a defense might be resolved by the student saying, "I'll take some time to rework things based on your comments," or the supervisor confirming, "I agree with your proposed defense timeline."

Consider how this conversation might change if the student is under financial pressure to finish quickly, or if the supervisor needs to expand an element of the student's research to benefit a larger body of research. There is now potential for conflict to emerge. Power imbalances and miscommunication are just two factors that can fan the flames of conflict.

Looking across 800+ coaching conversations with graduate students, faculty, and staff who provide support to graduate students, we identified these potential sources of graduate conflict:

- supervisory relationship (communication, feedback, roles, and responsibilities)
- realities and challenges of doing a graduate degree (motivation, scope, and isolation)
- escalating concerns or appeals (policies and processes)
- interpersonal conflicts – not supervisory (group work)
- research and writing (thesis, publishing, and intellectual property)
- academic progress (time to completion)
- personal issues and family obligations (housing and roommates)
- health and wellness; accessibility (disability) and accommodation concerns
- lab concerns
- career and work (future, references, practicums, placements, and internships)

This is by no means an exhaustive list of what we talked about over the years – although as peer advisor Michael (PhD Neuroscience) noted after his second year in the role, graduate student issues reappeared in cycles which for his department included: "i) academic issues with graduating/professorial issues, ii) broke up with significant other and can't focus, iii) not sure about the future and nervous, iv) financial concerns."

Some of the issues that didn't make the Top Ten include concerns about funding and finances (e.g., awards, bursaries, and scholarships), disappointment with facilities (e.g., library, study spaces, or office allocations), and general questions about conflict resolution training or off-campus services (e.g., community mediation services, options for advanced dispute resolution skills training). The case studies and examples in this book are intended to illustrate the complexity and the overlap of these graduate hotspots.

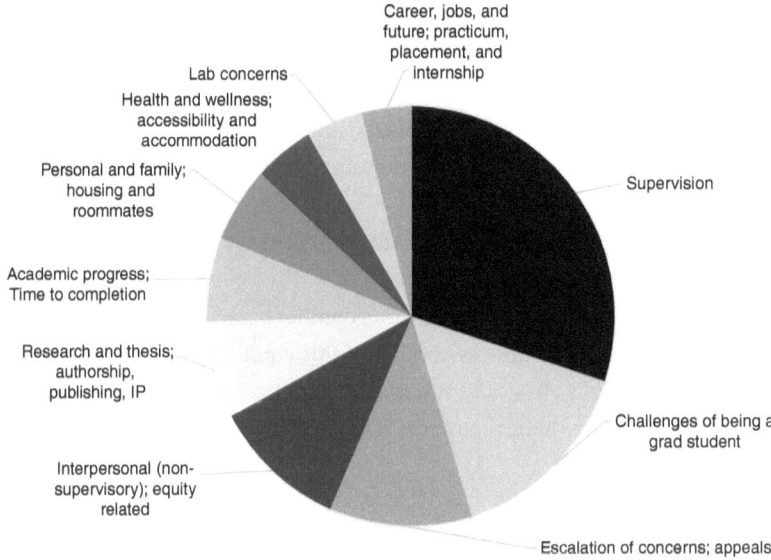

Figure 1. Top 10 graduate issues brought to Grad CRC, 2015–20

WHAT YOU CAN DO

❗ Grad CRC peer advisor Safa (MSc Medical BioPhysics) used her conflict management training to support her department's mental health and wellness committee.[10] From conversations and surveys with the department's grad students, the committee identified "grad school-related stressors" and developed "MBP Faculty Tip Sheet," including:

- *Work-life balance*: "Remind students to measure their productivity in terms of their research output, rather than the hours of work that they put in per week."

- *Pressure to succeed*: "When your students hit a roadblock in their research, remind them that this is a common and necessary part of the process. Relate to them with a personal story of your own roadblocks as a grad student."[11]

How Conflict Impacts Us

We saw time and again how people were impacted on several levels by conflict: raised voices, scowls, clenched fists, tears as well as vivid descriptions of how these individuals were experiencing the conflicts in their lives.

Brain We will respond intellectually to conflict as we try to make sense of what is happening.

Heart We will respond emotionally to a conflict based on our own prior experiences and how we feel about this conflict.

Body We will react physically when we experience conflict, such as that knot in your stomach, tightness in your chest, or catch in your throat.

Reacting to a situation that is unexpected is normal. Many authors have examined our individual tendencies to fight, flight, or freeze in non-life-threatening interactions like the conflicts discussed in this book.[12] It takes practice to PAUSE and override instinctive and involuntary responses. While a PAUSE can seem very long in the moment, we only need seconds (i.e., the time it takes to take a few slow breaths) to recognize that we are poised to react, to appreciate the information that these initial reactions give us, and to think about how we might respond rather than react.

Members of the graduate community told us that they felt "calmer," "less stressed," "relieved," "more confident/prepared," and "better" after a coaching conversation. The peer advisors observed changes in the demeanor of fellow students before and after conversations, including, "a sense of hope reflected in students' eyes when they receive tools that they believe they can apply to their situations to achieve desired results" (Melissa, PhD Developmental Psychology and Education). One grad student said they were "motivated and inspired" to take steps to address the conflict that had brought them to our service, and faculty told me they were gratified to have found somewhere on campus to get advice and talk through the stressful situation they were experiencing.

WHAT YOU CAN DO

! Reflect on the ways you might experience or respond to conflict differently (more/less intensely) at work than in your personal life, including on emotional, physical, and intellectual levels. Recall a recent disagreement with a grad student or colleague at your institution.

Q1. Try to recall what you were thinking and feeling (emotional and physical)?

Q2. Were you able to tell or can you guess what impact this disagreement might have had on the other person?

Q3. Did this experience change how you interacted with this person (or others) afterward?

! Breathing can help you PAUSE when you are poised to react. It can be as simple as taking a few slow breaths in and out through your nose[13] or trying more structured techniques such as "box breathing." Controlled breathing is like "meditation for people who can't meditate."[14] To learn more, watch these two short YouTube videos: "Reducing Stress Through Deep Breathing" (Johns Hopkins) and "Box Breathing Relaxation Technique" (Sunnybrook Hospital).[15]

Has COVID-19 Changed Grad School Conflict?

While the effects of the COVID-19 global pandemic were not felt uniformly or entirely negatively by all members of the campus community,[16] connections and communication between faculty and students, among students, and between students and campus, and between campus and the community, changed dramatically as a result of campus shutdowns and impacts of the pandemic locally and around the world. Before March 2020 we heard from grad students that they felt isolated and anxious about their graduate experience, and now they are living in "a society that has become used to unprecedented isolation and social anxiety," and the cultivation of community and connection on campuses has been aggressively and intentionally broken by the COVID-19 response."[17]

How did COVID-19 impact our service? When university campuses shut down in March 2020, our conflict coaching and training moved to online formats. Grad students (new and returning) continued to reach out for these services. Between March and June 2020, 66 percent of our conversations (phone or video chat) were 45 minutes to 1 hour 15 minutes long.

What is perhaps surprising is the fact that the pandemic had relatively little impact on the types of issues that were raised with our office. COVID-19-related concerns were only a reason for connecting in about 10 percent of conversations, with the remaining 90 percent related to the familiar hotspots outlined above – with a slight increase in the number of supervisory concerns. COVID-19 examples included:

- Grads were feeling (more) isolated because they were no longer physically present on campus.
- Grads expressed concerns about safety and the availability of personal protective equipment for return to campus.
- Some grads were worried they might need academic extensions because of additional COVID-19-related responsibilities, both personal and professional.

According to an October 2020 online survey of 502 university students and 2,208 faculty, the pandemic negatively impacted both faculty and students.[18] The survey found that the top negative impacts were isolation/lack of communication with professors (student perspective), and not as effective/engaged/no interaction (faculty perspective). While the survey didn't ask about the impact that COVID-19 was having on campus conflict, the findings regarding the pandemic's impact on faculty/student communication, engagement, and interaction are relevant both as potential sources of conflict and as challenges for conflict resolution.

For months students lost any opportunity to engage in person with other students or with faculty in a supervisory/academic capacity, and just as importantly from a conflict management perspective, as people. Engaging with others in ways that are not subject to assessment, grading, or for academic and professional development gives us the opportunity to see (and remember) someone in a context that is different to the one in which we are trying to resolve a conflict.

So, has COVID-19 changed grad school conflict? I have heard from ombuds colleagues that, in some instances, the movement to online interactions facilitated greater collaboration and increased communication within academia.

I suspect that avoidance is still the default approach and so many unresolved graduate conflicts are bubbling beneath the surface. The greatest impacts of COVID-19 on grad school conflict are perhaps yet to come – we won't know until these simmering issues emerge over the coming months and years what the impact of avoidance in the context of a global pandemic has been (mental health and wellness, academic progress, interpersonal relationships), and how people will respond. I recommend using the approaches and resources in this book to prepare for more intensity and greater challenges in resolving concerns given lingering COVID-19 side effects of anger and frustration.[19]

WHAT YOU CAN DO

! Be aware of the signs of secondary stress or "compassion fatigue" (i.e., where the stress of others becomes our own). In her blog, "Advice for Faculty Members in a Turbulent Time," psychologist and professor Mindi Thompson (University of Wisconsin) has six strategies to help faculty focus on health and wellness, including ways to "focus on select responsibilities and goals" and set "boundaries around consumption of media, social media, email and text messages."[20]

Q1. Consider, how do you take care of yourself so you can support students?

Q2. What might help you "walk the talk"? Are you talking to your grad students about self-care but failing to practice it yourself?

! Communicating with someone who is frustrated or angry is often an uncomfortable interaction and our first inclination (after run away!) is to try and get the person to calm down. One of the best response strategies is to ask open-ended questions or make open-ended statements: e.g., "How can I help?" "Tell me more about that."[21]

> **!** Remember – you don't have to hang on to an angry encounter, especially if it is just one of many other positive or neutral encounters with someone. A piece of advice from the Mayo Clinic for managing anger more effectively is: "Don't hold a grudge."[22]

What Impact Do Current Events/Movements Have on Grad Conflict?

Social movements and global events not only influence the types of conflict that can emerge on campus, they also impact how those conflicts are experienced by faculty, staff, and students, and expectations for resolution and prevention of future conflict. One example is the calls from students and faculty to the University of Toronto's administration in late 2019 to halt the practice of campus police arresting and handcuffing students experiencing mental health distress related to an on-campus incident. By the summer of 2020 (in the wake of the murder of George Floyd that spring in Minneapolis, Minnesota), there was a broader call to defund and abolish campus police, and in December 2020, there was an incident on U of T campus involving graduate students related to the #CopsOffCampus movement.[23]

For educational institutions, being responsive to social movements and global events and responding through appropriate conflict management mechanisms is both an opportunity and a responsibility. In 2020–1, the Chief Commissioner of the Ontario Human Rights Commission wrote two letters to Ontario college and university presidents and principals about student concerns related to the duty (unmet) of institutions to "create safe and inclusive places to study, and to remove systemic barriers to participation."[24] As post-secondary institutions begin what is likely to be a lengthy post–COVID-19 recovery, "institutional integrity and accountability and the importance of recognizing the role higher education plays in advancing social equity will be key."[25]

In some of the workshops and training we facilitated, participants would bring up examples related to current events (on and off campus) and highlight issues of race, intersectionality,[26] power, and privilege. The peer advisors were also talking to each other and to fellow students about their own and other students' experiences as Black, Indigenous, and racialized grad students.[27] In early 2020, several peer advisors mentioned to me that the conflict management skills that they had developed as part of our program were helpful for navigating conversations with colleagues, families, and friends about anti-Black/anti-Indigenous/anti-Asian racism,[28] the Black Lives Matter (BLM) movement, and COVID-19-related issues such as social distancing and mandatory masking.

Reluctance to discuss a topic may indicate a different level of comfort or knowledge around engaging in conversations about experiences or identities that differ from their own rather than a lack of interest in resolving a concern or complaint. As the director of the Graduate Centre for Academic Communication told the peer advisor team in her training session, "Discomfort is information."[29] It may be that someone needs time to think or get more information, so they feel ready to respond in a thoughtful and informed manner, for example: "Before responding, I'd like some time to really think about what you just said/asked."

As part of the annual onboarding training for the peer advisors, the equity and inclusion office facilitated a session on how to engage in equitable conversations. I scheduled this session near the end of training so that the peers would have an opportunity to get to know each other and develop trust by engaging in learning together around other topics (communication, conflict coaching, facilitation, resources, policies, and processes) and feel comfortable asking questions and being self-reflective about their own biases in front of their teammates in the session.

The various front-line conflict management strategies outlined in this book can be significantly enhanced by on-campus expertise, including consultation and involvement of individuals or offices that specialize in equity work or having conversations about anti-racism.[30]

WHAT YOU CAN DO

! Create brave spaces for conversation. Brave spaces shift the focus from safety (which may be illusory) to courage, while still encouraging discussion around "ground rules or guidelines for conversations."[31] The University of California San Francisco Office of the Ombuds published "Brave Conversations: 5 Step Tip Sheet" that provides a good framework for developing brave conversation spaces. Examples include process-focused considerations such as:

- *Confidentiality*: How will outcomes of the conversation be memorialized or shared?

- *Facilitators*: If it makes sense to have someone guide the conversation, how do we ensure that they have training, support, and the trust of everyone involved?[32]

! Use curiosity to bridge the gap between your own discomfort and a critical conversation, and to ensure you are talking about the same thing:

- "I'm not familiar with the word/phrase you used – do you know where I can get more information about [*the word/phrase the speaker used*]?"

The other person may provide you with a definition or refer you to a resource (article/expert) you could consult for more information. Here is another example,

> Q: "I'm not that familiar with the term 'intersectionality' – do you know where I can learn more?"
>
> A: "Sure, the term was coined by a Professor of Law at UCLA named Kimberlé Crenshaw back in the late 1980s. She has a short video called 'What Is Intersectionality?' that does a better job than I would at explaining it."[33]

! If you aren't sure if there are supports on your campus to help faculty navigate equity issues, check if your institution has an ombuds who may be able to provide advice or a referral.

What Time of Year Does Grad Conflict Emerge?

While we sometimes had a seasonal wave of one particular issue, for example, a grad student "break-up summer" or a "winter of roommate woes," in general, conflict in grad school is a year-round possibility.

In 2018–19, our busiest month for conflict coaching was in March; however, the previous year, we had the most visitors in May, October, and November. Here are examples of the types of issues that grad students brought to our attention each month, selected to be illustrative of broader conflict themes that we identified from our data for each month.

SEPTEMBER (IMPOSTER FEELINGS, BOUNDARIES)

- PhD student had a close good working relationship with a fellow doctoral student which has deteriorated – wanting to repair relationship and set boundaries.
- Master's student feeling pressure and stress of grad school course load.

OCTOBER (GOAL SETTING, ROOMMATES)

- PhD student is concerned about how to complete their degree in light of changed circumstances and priorities.
- Master's student wants to find a way to deal with a loud and inconsiderate roommate and negotiate a schedule for studying and socializing.

NOVEMBER (EXPECTATIONS, GROUP WORK)

- PhD student is concerned because their thesis supervisor has been unresponsive for the past year and no longer seems interested in their research.
- Master's student doesn't feel their group is allocating work fairly.

DECEMBER (AVOIDANCE IS NOT THE ONLY OPTION)

- PhD student is feeling pressure to finish early for financial and family reasons; they are reluctant to talk with their supervisor about their personal circumstances.
- PhD student has been avoiding having conversation with supervisor and wants to learn communication strategies.

JANUARY (FEEDBACK, RESOLUTIONS)

- PhD student dismayed by comments they received at a recent committee meeting; they feel that their supervisor should have been more supportive (when trust has been broken, is it possible to get it back?).

- Master's student wants to find a way to get their advisor interested in their project.

FEBRUARY (MOTIVATION, RAISING CONCERNS)

- Graduate student shared concerns about patterns of unwelcoming behavior they (and a colleague) are observing in the department.
- Master's student feeling isolated and unmotivated to finish writing thesis.

MARCH (THE "MURKY MIDDLE," MANAGING UNCERTAINTY)

- Master's student is struggling to decide whether to finish their master's degree and stop, or continue to pursue a PhD; scared to have conversation with their supervisor.
- PhD student is concerned that they are nearing the end of an extension they got to complete their PhD and their supervisor has not been responding to emails.

APRIL (DIFFICULT CONVERSATIONS, COMMUNICATION SKILLS)

- PhD student is in a conflict with a lab staff member who they feel was overstepping their role; the student doesn't feel they are getting the support they need from their advisor.
- Master's student has had disagreement with instructor over a final grade and wanted to talk about options/resolutions proposed by instructor and the department.

MAY (COMPETING OBLIGATIONS, EXPECTATIONS)

- PhD student says they have a "very unsupportive and bullying supervisor"; they want to change supervisors and talk about how to approach potential new supervisors.
- PhD student is confused about their supervisor's expectations; they have very different communication styles and understandings of what supervision looks like.

JUNE (BUILDING A SUPPORT NETWORK, GROWTH)

- PhD student wants to talk about supervision styles and expectations.

- Master's student is looking for tips on how to ask questions about direction of their thesis and wondering about what campus supports are available.

JULY (SIMMERING SUMMER SITUATIONS)

- PhD student is wondering if they are in the right program; discussions with their supervisor are always tense because they seem to be working at cross-purposes.
- Master's student has issues with current supervisor and wondering about process for changing supervisors, or ways to make current supervisory relationship work.

AUGUST (GETTING THINGS BACK ON TRACK, RESTORATION)

- PhD student is worried about graduating and "what happens next"; how to ask for reference letter.
- PhD student is wondering about where to go with their research (stay in program?) given they feel they are "at odds" with their supervisor.

WHAT YOU CAN DO

! We found that graduate students tended to seek information "just in time"[34] or, more often, at the last minute. Effective conflict management will include traditional forms of training (e.g., workshops developed in advance and scheduled each semester) and just in time learning (e.g., pop-up "lunch & learns," or on campus digital screen/billboard updates). If you know the types of concerns which might be coming forward in August, it may make sense to plan for early interventions to provide information, tips, and support in May/June.

! Keep track of the types of graduate issues you are hearing about each month or each quarter in your department. Aim to share these within the department at regular intervals to give everyone a heads-up about possible emerging issues.

! Create a conflict calendar. We worked with the graduate student services office to put together a graduate calendar with themes (conflicts, concerns, challenges, stresses, happenings, and deadlines) for each month that we used for individual and joint workshop and event planning.

Q1. What support offices/resources are available for grads in your department or on your campus?

Q2. Are they available throughout the calendar year?

! Hire a graduate student to do an environmental scan or empower a grad student advisory group with a diverse and multidisciplinary composition to brainstorm ways to fill gaps.

Why Do Grad Students Avoid Conflict?

Overwhelmingly, we observed graduate students avoiding conflict related to their graduate experience. Often students had ignored (or tried to ignore) a difficult situation for months or years before reaching out to our service. Specifically, peer advisor Megan (MEd Counselling Psychology) noted, "One of the main barriers to coping and managing stressful situations is feeling shame, alone, or overwhelmed, making it hard to reach out and ask for help." Imagine a PhD student anticipating a heated conversation with their supervisor over inconsistent research results. The student's first instinct might be to simply get out of the way. They might hope that future results will be better, that their supervisor will get distracted by another issue or grad student, or they may hold out hope that someone else will talk to their supervisor for them.

While some conflicts dissipate as time passes and interests shift, in other instances relationships deteriorate. For example, we heard individuals describe avoiding offices or labs where they might encounter the other person, others who were asking about how to change supervisors or leave a program/lab, and a few who wondered aloud about whether to quit grad school entirely. Some of the key reasons why grad students avoid conflict include:

- fear (including risk to reputation or retaliation) and uncertainty
- assumptions and previous experiences
- feelings of inadequacy or isolation
- complexity and time required

Fear and Uncertainty (Risk and Reputation)

Most graduate students are high performers who would not want their supervisor thinking they are incompetent. Students told us they were afraid that speaking up might impact their reputation or put future positive references at risk:

- "I am afraid to talk to my supervisor." "Couldn't I end up worse off than I am now if I speak up?" What about retribution?"
- "Speaking up will damage my reputation. I'll be known as a complainer. I can't risk it – I need a great reference."
- "My department is very competitive. I don't want anyone to know that I have a problem."
- "If I talk to anyone in my department, my supervisor will find out. My supervisor is friends with the [chair/dean]."
- "Maybe I'm wrong about this and it isn't a big deal."

> **WHAT YOU CAN DO**
>
> ! Normalize having an uncomfortable or difficult conversation before you need to have one. One strategy is to outline how you normally bring a concern to a student's attention (i.e., model a respectful and thoughtful approach) and then ask the student questions like:
>
> - "What do you think of me using a similar approach if I want to bring an issue to your attention?"
> - "Anything you might want to do differently that might make it easier to bring an issue to my attention?"
>
> ! Remind students that experiencing a conflict and speaking up about a concern is not suggestive of poor academic performance. Flip the issue and ask: "If I brought a concern to your attention, would you automatically *think less of me* as a supervisor?"

Assumptions and Previous Experiences

In our coaching we heard things like:

- "I've tried to talk to my professor before and it didn't go very well so I'm not going to talk to them now."
- "Everyone knows that faculty member is difficult – they won't change if I talk to them."

The information we gather from interactions, perhaps accumulated over months or years, can reinforce assumptions about how someone will react or respond, which can create unseen barriers to resolution that may not be easy to overcome. In our coaching conversations we would acknowledge 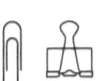 that it is possible that what happened in the past could happen again or that an assumption could be accurate, and we would also point out that it is possible that something else might happen – we could be surprised! By focusing on what the individual we were speaking with might do to create opportunities for change, we shift the focus from what we can't control (how other people act) to what we can control (how we will prepare for a conversation or respond in the moment).

> **WHAT YOU CAN DO**
>
> ! As you actively listen to someone explain why they haven't taken action to resolve a concern, acknowledge the impact of previous experiences and assumptions.
>
> - "I can see how you might not want to talk to your supervisor now if things didn't go well *last time*."
>
> ! Ask about patterns to determine whether a situation is a new or long-standing one.
>
> - "When did this start?"
> - "What was your relationship like *before*?"

> ! Encourage people to recall past successful strategies that might be useful to try to manage a current situation.
>
> - "Was there ever a time you disagreed with this person, and you were able to resolve your differences?"
> - "Is there anything you *did then that you could try now*?"

Isolation and Feelings of Inadequacy

Most graduate students feel like an imposter at some point in their graduate experience, and feelings of inadequacy and isolation are common.[1] We heard comment from students like:

- "People think you're smarter than you think you are."
- "I can't talk to anyone in my department about this – I feel so alone."

As part of the peer team onboarding training each year, I invited a staff member from the Student Life Academic Success team to talk about power and imposter phenomenon in graduate school. They noted that some grads might experience imposter feelings more profoundly because of their (intersecting) identities (e.g., racial, ethnic, disability, gender identity). Whether spoken or unspoken, and whether you are speaking to a student or a fellow faculty member (faculty and staff feel like an imposter at times too), how you feel in relation to your academic experience can impact how you feel about taking steps to resolve a concern within that same academic environment.

An important component of conflict management is figuring out ways to support individuals so that they feel (more) confident in speaking up and taking steps earlier, to address concerns. The peer connection was particularly powerful for graduate students who doubted their ability to manage conflict on their own. Although the peer advisors themselves experienced imposter phenomena while coaching – one saying, "I still find myself wondering if I have done/said the right thing sometimes," and another asking, "What value could I possibly offer to these highly qualified individuals?" – they recognized that these were normal feelings that helped them to relate in a deeper way to other grad students who were feeling like an imposter in grad school.

WHAT YOU CAN DO

! Watch an animated video that connects self-doubt and high performance and suggests ways to help students combat imposter feelings: "What Is Imposter Syndrome and How Can You Combat It?"[2]

! Consider how your students' experience of imposter phenomenon might differ from your own experiences as a grad student (or as a faculty member). Here are two insightful blogs for further reflection: "Imposter Syndrome: An Intersectional Approach" by Isabel Rodriguez,[3] and a blog from Graduate Women in STEM, "Identity in Academia: The Relationship between the Imposter Syndrome and Intersectionality."[4]

Complexity and Time Required

Untangling a conflict can be complex and time consuming. A student's current crisis or conflict might be having a "multi-layered impact on their lives ... not only impacting a student's academic experience but also their mental and physical health, and their academic and personal relationships." (Manaal, PhD Social Work)

Table 1. Number of coaching conversations held each year at the Grad CRC and the percentage that are over 30 minutes

Year	Total # conversations	30–60 minutes	Over 1 hour
2019–20	225	32%	24%
2018–19	160	48%	18%
2017–18	200	34%	23%
2016–17	205	55%	20%
2015–16	123	18%	22%

> **WHAT YOU CAN DO**
>
> ! Be realistic about how long it can take to problem solve. In our experience, conflict conversations needed forty-five minutes (or more) to get to the point of effective student-centered problem-solving.
>
> ! If you realize that a conversation will take longer than the time you have allotted (you have another meeting, pressing deadlines etc.), ask to reschedule for later in the day or week.

Psst ... Faculty Avoid Conflict Too

Avoidance is also a very popular conflict resolution strategy among faculty. One faculty member I talked with had been dealing with a simmering departmental issue for ten years!

Some faculty shared that they felt enormous pressure to try to resolve every issue themselves (especially if they were in an administrative chair/director role) and they were often overwhelmed when conflicts did not resolve easily. Academic conflict can be particularly tough to manage on top of other responsibilities (professional, personal, family) that are being juggled. It was helpful for faculty to hear that they might be taking on too much responsibility for solving a particular problem (are they part of the problem, or have they been drawn into the conflict?) and that they could refer students to relevant campus resources/policies and processes.

Imposter syndrome is not just a student phenomenon.[5] Faculty mentioned competitive department cultures and keeping up appearances (reputation) as deterrents to speaking up or admitting they needed help. In these circumstances, faculty were usually happy to confide in me because I wasn't in their department or a faculty colleague – that separation was helpful for them in reaching out for help to resolve a conflict. While uncertainty can have a paralyzing effect, so too can feeling that there are no realistic options for resolving a conflict. What happens if a faculty member is in a conflict with another faculty member and their "Plan B" would involve altering their current employment arrangement? Given specific research interests and requirements, where can they go? Another department or another university?

WHAT YOU CAN DO

! Examine your own thoughts and feelings (not just the nature of the conflict) and note whether you could reframe or reuse that approach in the future.

Q. In the past, what has caused you to step toward, or away from, a conflict?

! In circumstances where you might be avoiding a conflict because you don't know what to say or do, own your uncertainty.[6] Consider saying: "I'm not sure what we should do in this moment" and either commit to finding out and circling back or refer the student to someone who may be able to help them. For more insights into the phrase "I don't know," listen to the Freakonomics podcast, "The Three Hardest Words in the English Language."[7]

! When you sense there could be a problem (that you are trying to avoid addressing), instead of waiting, schedule a quick discussion with your grad student:

- "I'd like to get ahead of any potential issues – let's schedule a 15-minute call this week to check in on your research/opportunities for publishing/next steps for you after graduation [or whatever "hotspot" you think is relevant] and anything else that might be coming up for you."

! Brainstorm with a faculty colleague other ways to develop an active conflict management mindset.

Q. What can you do to get ahead of conflicts (that you might later want to avoid)?

Why Is Conflict Something Faculty Should Manage?

Two prime functions of a university include providing a community to foster and advance academic research and the instruction of students. These two functions create numerous opportunities for conflict to emerge.[1]

Having spent well over a decade in universities helping students and faculty navigate complaints and concerns, it certainly appears that "conflict is inevitable"[2] within institutions of higher learning. If conflict is simply an inevitability of graduate school, why should universities[3] pay attention to how they are managing conflict?

It starts by recognizing that conflict can result in both constructive (productive) and destructive (non-productive) outcomes.[4] For example, academic debate and intellectual opposition are expected and encouraged with academia, but personal attacks, disrespectful language, declarations of battle (picking sides, recruiting allies), labeling ourselves or others (victim/bully, good/bad) are unwelcome results of an interpersonal clash. As we found most often within the graduate community, a conflict may play out silently with people simply avoiding each other and suffering internally – again, not ideal.

Conflict is a signal that we need to listen, engage, examine, disrupt, or improve processes, policies, and approaches. It needs to be addressed as early as possible – "as soon as it is visible."[5]

Poorly Managed Conflict Can Be Costly

As institutes of higher education, universities are concerned with reaching for the highest possible standards in every aspect of education, and that should include their approaches to managing disputes. When universities sidestep or quietly sweep conflict into a dark corner, there is both a risk of escalating harm and incurring costs individually and institutionally, including:[6]

- lost time and productivity because of dealing with or being distracted by conflict, for example, research stalling, dissatisfaction, absences, "presenteeism"[7]
- loss of sense of purpose, belonging, trust, or community
- physical and/or mental unwellness
- financial costs related to escalation, for example, formal administrative processes, external review, legal action,[8] or media attention
- impact on reputations

When institutions work to ensure that interactions, decision-making, and conflict/complaint management processes are fair and equitable, the result will be decisions that are less likely to be challenged outside of the university grounds, legally and morally. As one Canadian director of student conduct observes, "If you have a clear, fair process and can show you have followed the process, it tends to stave off the lawsuits, as students feel that their concerns have been heard and they have received fair treatment."[9]

On an individual level, where conflict is managed inappropriately and conflicts are not addressed or resolved, researchers have found that this can result in "a gradual decline in the relationship, and could result in supervisees concealing their difficulties from their supervisors," and they also "found that supervisees engaged in censoring reports to supervisors and disregarded supervisors' feedback while appearing to comply."[10] Inauthenticity is a barrier to building a trusting, supportive, and respectful relationship between a supervisor and a supervisee.

Protracted unresolved conflict can make people increasingly pessimistic about options for managing or resolving the concern. The time and energy someone hopes to save by avoiding a conflict in the moment, isn't always a savings in the long run. I recall one faculty member who was so discouraged by a lengthy conflict with their graduate student that they stated emphatically: "Nothing can be done now."

It was extraordinarily difficult for me to help them see that there might be courses of action within their control.

> **WHAT YOU CAN DO**
>
> ! Next time a colleague shares a story about being in a conflict with someone, listen for mention of these costs:
>
> - "It took up my whole afternoon!" (Time)
> - "It ruined my day." (Productivity)
> - "I can't go back to the office/lab." (Belonging)
>
> ! As a first response, reflect back what you are hearing:
>
> - "Sounds like a really *time-consuming* situation."
> - "Seems like this probably affected what you had *set out to accomplish* today."
> - "If you don't want to go back to the office/lab, this situation must be having a big impact on how you *feel about your workspace*."

Effective Conflict Management Can Be Beneficial

Faculty and graduate schools have a lot to gain by openly acknowledging the inevitability of conflict in grad studies. Here are five reasons why early and effective conflict management approaches should be a priority:

1. Effective conflict management aligns with the pursuit of excellence and an appreciation of the importance of graduate student well-being.

Most graduate schools would say that their mission or purpose extends beyond the pursuit of excellence in academics and includes support for the (physical, mental, social, financial) well-being of a diverse student population. Effective conflict management can benefit these objectives. The peer advisors noted that after coaching conversations, the students seemed to have "moved from a place of no options, anxiety, and sense of being overwhelmed by their dilemma – to a place of possibilities, choices, and options" (Kimberly, PhD Social Justice Education).

2. *Effectively managing conflict preserves limited time and resources for academic pursuits.*

Helping individuals address conflict earlier within what are often complex university systems can avoid unnecessarily/prolonged stressful situations, save time and resources, and promote timely completion and research progress.

3. *Being actively involved in managing conflict enhances the positive experience of grad students.*

It can be empowering for graduate students (and faculty) to engage in conflict resolution, which in turn can strengthen resilience, build connections, and enhance positive (or reduce negative) feelings about the graduate experience. As a PhD participant in one of our supervisory workshops said, "I know what to ask my supervisor about at our next meeting!" Developing capacity within the institution for managing, resolving, and preventing conflict (for the next time) can address feelings of isolation and fear among graduate students with respect to resolving conflict. In addition, "research suggests that structured engagement with someone who holds divergent views can be transformative, even without a concrete resolution."[11]

4. *Building conflict management capacity cultivates trust within and beyond the institution.*

Conflict management involves trust. Trust is both a precondition to and an outcome of effective conflict management. Trust increases student and faculty/staff satisfaction and may have positive ripple effects on the reputation of the institution with internal and external stakeholders.

5. *Professional development for faculty can be enhanced by conflict management training.*

Dispute resolution/conflict resolution/ alternative dispute resolution (ADR)[12] skills are commonly sought in job descriptions and included in graduate professional development training. It is clear from attendance and feedback from our workshops that conflict management and communication skills development was something students (and faculty) were looking for as part of their professional development.

> **WHAT YOU CAN DO**
>
> ❗ Interested in learning more about the role of trust in doctoral supervision? Check out the learning resources (videos, reports, templates) for supervisors in Dr. Kay Guccione's book, *Trust Me! Building and Breaking Professional Trust in Doctoral Student Supervisor Relationships*.[13]
>
> ❗ In a situation where there is a lack of *interpersonal* trust (trust between people), one useful strategy is to have those involved start by collaboratively building *procedural* trust (trust in a structure or process). Getting agreement on the 'nuts and bolts' or 'housekeeping' elements of a negotiation can lay "the groundwork for effective substantive negotiations."[14]

Avoidance Isn't the Only Option

Faculty and grad students are often told that they should be attempting to resolve issues informally at the lowest level, but from our conversations we know that this suggestion was terrifying for some individuals. While we observed a clear preference for avoidance, this is not the only possible way to respond to conflict, and we encouraged people to be more strategic – if they are going to avoid a conflict, it should be because they have determined that that is the right approach for that conflict at that time, appreciating other possible approaches.

Consider a classic example of positions versus interests. Imagine two chefs in a restaurant kitchen fighting over a single orange.[15] Each chef says to the other, "I want the orange!" which is their position. However, they each need the orange for different reasons: one wants the peel for a citrus cake, and the other wants the juice to add to a special orange sauce. These are their interests. Unfortunately, since the chefs never get past stating their positions, they end up resolving their argument by splitting the orange in half. Each gets half of what they wanted/needed (i.e., half the juice and half the zest of the orange). If each chef had taken the time to try and understand the others' interests, they might have resolved their argument in a more mutually beneficial way.

What if in addition to compromising (i.e., accepting the stated positions and dividing the orange in half) or collaborating (i.e., determining interests and then one chef gets the peel and the other the juice of the whole orange), there were other possible ways to resolve the issue?

In our workshops, we asked participants which approaches were represented by each of the following images – keeping the chef-orange scenario in mind.

Q. What is your guess for each conflict resolution approach?

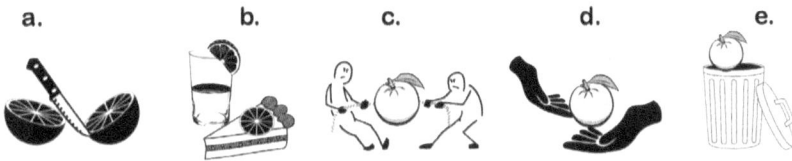

We engaged workshop participants in a discussion about the different ways that people approach conflict, using the five approaches set out by Kenneth W. Thomas and Ralph H. Kilmann in their conflict behavior instrument known as the Thomas-Kilmann (TK) model. The approaches (compromise, collaboration, competition, accommodation, avoidance) are located along two axes (assertiveness and cooperativeness).[16] Here is how the above orange images a. through e. might fall within this framework:

a. *Compromise.* "Let's cut the orange in half." Or, "I'll let you have the orange if you give me a chocolate bar."
b. *Collaboration.* "Let's talk about why you need this orange (juice or peel?)."
c. *Competition.* "I need this orange so I'm just going to take it or fight for it."
d. *Accommodation.* "I know this orange is important to you so you can have it."
e. *Avoidance.* "I'm throwing this orange away, so we don't have to argue about it anymore."

We asked participants if they thought they had a "default" or "go-to" approach that they used across all conflicts, or whether they used "different conflict styles at different times, even in the same conflict."[17] For example, we may normally *compromise* with our friends, *compete* with our loved ones, and *avoid* with colleagues.

This discussion was important for our message that our response to conflict should be a strategic choice; a choice that can impact academic, personal, and professional relationships. Each conflict approach will have advantages and disadvantages depending on the situation. For example, while principled negotiation makes collaborative approaches seem like the ideal way to resolve a dispute, collaboration can be time and labor intensive. As peer advisor Amika (PhD Health Informatics) noted, "What is most important is intentionality: selecting the conflict style that aligns best with one's situation and considers the resources, time, and stakes involved."

If intentionality is key for individual choices for approaching conflict, what matters from an institutional perspective? Institutional conflict management involves building capacity for responding to conflict (appropriately) at all levels within the organization as well as being able to identify where and when conflict is likely to emerge within the system (and at a deeper level, where conflict is being perpetuated at a systemic level). To be truly effective, Robyn Jacobson recommends that a university's policies, persons, and processes be "infused with the commonly held and acknowledged values, goals, and guiding principles of the institution" and that institutions have both (a) a conflict management center, and (b) a method of keeping an eye on potential conflict areas (i.e., an ombuds).[18]

The benefit of beginning to think strategically about which approach to conflict you are taking is that you can switch course and try another approach if that first one doesn't work. There is no prohibition on using more than one (or your own version) in a single conversation.

WHAT YOU CAN DO

! Recall a recent disagreement/argument with a student or faculty colleague. Try to categorize your approach/the other person's approach to the conflict using the TK model.

Q1. Do you think the discussion might have gone differently if you/the other person had taken a different approach?

Q2. Is the approach you used in this disagreement your default conflict resolution approach (at work or in general)?

Q3. If you are currently working with a graduate student, do you have a sense of whether they have a go-to conflict management approach?

MINI-CASE STUDY: APPROACHING CONFLICT – PART 1

Read the following scenario and circle the response that is closest to the response you might have. Answer according to your first instinct (rather than what you think is the "best" answer).

You supervise a PhD student who has been taking your feedback on their writing very personally over the past year. They never make any of the recommended changes, and as a result you are concerned that the student's work is not up to standard. You booked a video chat with them to discuss "resources available to you on campus to help you to improve your latest draft." During the call the student suddenly and loudly blurts out: "You have no idea how aggressive and insensitive your feedback is!"

Your response is:

A. "I don't think that continuing this conversation is a productive use of our time." Then end the call as quickly as you can.

B. "My feedback might be interpreted as aggressive and insensitive, but it is important that you work on getting your writing up to the departmental standard."

C. Pause, then ask the student, "What do you mean by 'aggressive and insensitive'?"

D. "My feedback isn't the problem; your writing is the problem."

E. "My latest email didn't come across as I had intended, and I promise to provide more constructive comments with the next draft."

MINI-CASE STUDY: Approaching Conflict - Part 1 Interpretation of Responses Using the TK Model and Questions

A. *Avoidance.* Sometimes hitting "pause" can be a strategic choice to defer a conversation for a later date (i.e., to get more information).

"I think it makes sense for us to stop for now and reconvene next Monday after we have both taken another look at the latest draft and my comments. How does that sound to you?"

B. *Compromise.* Authenticity is key – do you acknowledge that the feedback was harsh? Following a statement with a "but" may invalidate the first statement for the listener.

"I want to talk to you about your writing and explain my feedback. What if we start with the feedback?"

C. *Collaboration.* This approach can be time-consuming and particularly challenging when emotions are running high, or one participant isn't in the right frame of mind to problem solve.

"I want to understand your concerns and make sure we have enough time to talk through the feedback and next steps. How do you think we should proceed?"

D. *Competition.* When our instinct is to respond to verbal attacks in kind, it can help to reframe a response as a question.

"You mentioned feedback. What part of your draft do you think would be most helpful to talk about first?"

E. *Accommodation.* Consider what happens if you make concessions but the student does not.

"One of my responsibilities as your supervisor is to provide you with feedback that is constructive. What would be most useful for you at this time?"

Are We Escalating Conflict Unintentionally?

We observed a phenomenon whereby an individual (A), instead of talking (or emailing) directly to the person with whom they were having a conflict (B), would talk with (or email) another person (C, or multiple people) about the conflict. In my experience, this is a common university work-around for addressing conflict and avoiding uncomfortable conversations.

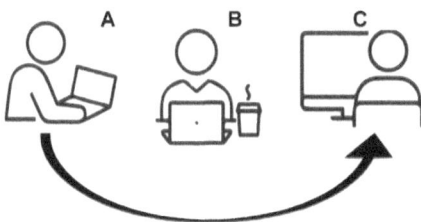

Sometimes A has legitimate reasons why they do not want to have a direct conversation with B (e.g., in the past, A brought a similar concern to B directly and B refused to engage with them, and so now they are choosing an indirect route through C to see if C can help with the current issue). In such cases, A is normally aware of the fact that involving another person (C) may have the effect of escalating or appearing to escalate the matter from B's perspective or the institution's perspective. This is different from a situation that results in an "unintended escalation."

This happens when A simply skips (or avoids) having a potentially uncomfortable discussion with C in favor of having a discussion with C. In such cases, A hasn't considered the larger impact on the conflict of their inaction (with B) and action (with C), although in many cases they hope that C will take their side against B or intervene to resolve the conflict for them. Here is the crux of the problem with this approach. When I go around you (or over you) instead of going directly to you, I may feel relieved. Indirect means I don't have to deal with the issue directly – I can avoid it. Whew! But ... when you go around me, instead of coming to me directly with a concern, I may feel upset, embarrassed, or betrayed. The matter is now bigger and more widely known than it needed to be, from my perspective. The result? Unintended escalation.

While this approach seems to align with the power structures of the institution (including grad student perceptions of powerlessness), it is far more complex. For example, sometimes grad students assumed before talking to us that their department chair or graduate school vice dean was their supervisor's "boss" with the ability to "make them" do or stop doing something. When we talked with students about how it might seem to a supervisor if their student was talking to a faculty colleague (albeit one with administrative responsibilities) about a concern as opposed to them directly, the shift in perspective would often pave the way for a deeper discussion around how to escalate a concern (processes, policies, supports), to whom (roles, responsibilities, impact of involving C), and when (timing) to escalate their concerns, so they did not also have to manage unintended escalation.

WHAT YOU CAN DO

! If you are talking to a student who asks, "Should I go and talk to Person C about my conflict with Person B?" then ask them this question:

- "If someone had a problem with you, would you rather they came to talk to you about the problem or went and talked to *someone else* about it first?"

! Be respectful and kind. If the student responds to the above question that they would rather someone talked to them directly about an issue rather than someone else, encourage them to reframe the situation in their mind:

- I'm going to talk directly to Person B about my concern because it is respectful and is the right thing to do, and I'm going to assume that they will be happier that I came to them with my concerns instead of going to talk to Person C.

MINI-CASE STUDY: APPROACHING CONFLICT – PART 2

Reread Mini-Case Study: Approaching Conflict – Part 1 on page **35** *about supervisor feedback and the student's response during a video call. After the meeting, you carefully craft an email and send it to the student:*

From: SUPERVISOR
To: STUDENT

I want to follow up on our call yesterday. Satisfactory academic progress in graduate school is related to many factors, including writing. I am concerned because my latest feedback has not been incorporated into your recent draft. See, for example, my comments on pp. 6 and 31: [QUOTE]. I would like us to review the [INSERT LINK] to guideline about standard of writing/academic progress] and then speak next Monday or Tuesday afternoon (1–4 p.m.) to discuss your latest draft and next steps. Many grad students find 1:1 consultations at the university's writing center [INSERT LINK] helpful or their online resources [INSERT LINK]. Please confirm your availability.

The student sends you the following email response:

From: STUDENT
To: SUPERVISOR

I have serious concerns about your feedback on my latest draft and previous feedback. I want to be making progress with my writing and I would like to talk to you about what you meant by comments such as [QUOTE] and [QUOTE]. I feel that these comments and the overall tone was quite harsh. I would be able to have a call next Monday or Tuesday afternoon (1–4 p.m.) to discuss. Please let me know.

Q1. How would you feel about the student's response?

Q2. How would you feel if you found out the student went to the graduate chair about the situation instead of responding directly to you?

Q3. Reflecting on your answers above, would you change your response to the student after the video call? If yes, in what ways? Edits to the email? Different approach?

What Does Grad Conflict Management Involve?

 Conflict management is a broad concept that recognizes the importance of looking at conflict not only at an individual level (puzzle pieces) but also across the institution (the puzzle). Within higher education, an effective conflict management approach will include preventative strategies as well as a range of informal dispute resolution approaches; although, pathways to the courts or to tribunals may also be contemplated. I prefer the term "conflict management" to "conflict resolution" to recognize that it is not always practical, desirable, or possible to resolve a conflict (or dispute)[1] either in the moment or for the longer term. Instead, we may need to:

- take time to get more information/assess possible approaches
- figure out a way to work across our differences
- refocus our time and energy on other priorities
- find ways to escalate our concern within the institution

For many individuals who connected with our office, effective conflict management was simply a way to try to improve their academic relationships and get on with their research. People might start a coaching session by saying something like: "I'm not sure if you are the right person to ask but," or "I don't know if I would call it a 'conflict' but there is this situation with my supervisor/student." We would reassure people that no issue is too small to talk about with our team. Giving people permission to talk about the small issues can be a gateway to them talking about larger conflicts. Feeling empowered to tackle a smaller matter can also build confidence and skills to manage larger and more complex disagreements.

Our conflict management office was part of a large campus support system which included student counseling services (employee assistance programs for staff), equity and inclusion offices, sexual violence prevention and support office, community safety office and campus police. We helped connect people to appropriate supports and supported individuals who were referred to us by these other services. While at times the issue being discussed might have seemed relatively inconsequential to us, we provided a non-judgmental and tailored approach that respected an individual's interests, interpretations, and experiences of a situation.

As peer adviser Amika (PhD Health Informatics) noted, we considered the individual's "readiness to pursue certain options" amid the range of supports available, and we helped them to see their options more clearly by "break[ing] down situations into manageable components." We helped students, faculty, and staff to focus on what they could control about a situation, including what skills they might develop/strategies they might employ, to bring them closer to their desired goals, and, as Amika further noted, to see "conflict as an opportunity to strengthen relationships and understand areas requiring clarification or explicit expectations."[2]

A comprehensive conflict management approach will give members of the institution opportunities for learning (skills, strategies, and approaches). Having opportunities to change our minds, to have our minds changed, and to hear each other's perspectives and ideas can enhance the graduate experience.

What Makes Conflict Resolution Unique in Higher Education?

In universities or colleges, the resolution of disputes takes place either via well-worn formal avenues or informal pathways. It is largely up to individual institutions to determine how to manage complaints and concerns and how to ensure processes to resolve issues are fair and equitable; although, in certain circumstances there may be a legislated policy framework, for example, with respect to sexual violence and harassment matters.[3] This means informal and formal policies and processes differ from institution to institution.

On the formal side there are complex policies, procedures, and guidelines that set out how the quasi-judicial processes work and for what types of issues, and the role and responsibility of various decision-makers, committees, and tribunals. Grade appeals, academic misconduct, and non-academic conduct matters are often dealt with through formal processes. Some institutions have internal ombuds offices and/or conflict management offices with mandates that can informally intervene and/or formally investigate complaints about unfair processes or decisions.[4]

Within the spectrum of informal resolution individuals must rely "on their own efforts or on some person in some position who may be willing, and may have some dispute resolution skills, to provide a solution to their problem."[5] Notwithstanding department or faculty handbooks that might contain "what to do if" scenarios or "how to approach a difficult conversation" flowcharts, there are myriad of "'unwritten rules' and expectations [that] can confuse or trip up students, especially those who may be more isolated than others based on gender, race, ethnicity, socio-economic, or other cultural or demographic characteristics."[6]

At an institutional level, conflict management involves building capacity across an organization to prevent and manage conflict earlier and more effectively, as well as identifying trends and systemic issues that need to be addressed at the institutional level such as changes to policies and processes. Many times, we heard from individuals that they were as interested in making sure that a concerning situation didn't happen to anyone else, as they were in having the situation resolved for them personally. Conflict management involves turning a critical eye inwards, while recognizing that conflict can emerge from all directions.

> **WHAT YOU CAN DO**
>
> ! If you are open to talking about small concerns, try to recall if you have explicitly invited your grad students to bring issues to your attention. How might a formal and specific invitation ("I would like you to talk to me about the small issues and any concerns") make a greater impression than a vague statement ("My door is open"), considering the supervisor-supervisee power imbalance?[7]
>
> ! Be specific about how you want students to connect with you about concerns – phone, email, text, or in person. Specify whether they can connect "at any time," with advance notice ("Please send me an email with a heads up about

what you want to talk about"), or some variation ("Tuesday afternoons I'm normally free to talk about any issues – call any time between 1 and 5 p.m.").

Q1. Do you expect students to manage small concerns independently and only come to you as a last resort?

Q2. Is there (or could there be) a designated senior student, faculty or staff member, or team in your department who can triage smaller concerns from students?

! Grads often turn to fellow grad students for information and support on problem-solving. Are there ways for you/your department to tap into existing informal and diverse peer channels to amplify and clarify information about conflict resolution and campus supports?

! The 2021 Graduate Calendar at the University of Guelph includes a section that describes formal and informal dispute resolution paths with flowcharts for four types of graduate conflict: (1) interpersonal conflict between the student and the advisor; (2) dispute about evaluation of progress, qualifying or oral examination; (3) disruptive, abusive, or destructive behavior on the part of the advisor; and (4) disruptive, abusive, or destructive behavior on the part of the student.[8]

Q1. Is there anything similar at your institution to help guide graduate faculty and students through common sources of conflict?

Q2. The Guelph calendar refers to "informal mediation" and "informal complaint." At your institution, is there guidance for informal resolution of graduate concerns?

Q3. What questions do you have about how to engage in an informal process? (See discussion at page 72.)

What Is the "Secret Formula" for Resolving Conflict?

People have asked me if there is a universal strategy or a secret formula that can be applied to any conflict to come up with a resolution. I believe they were looking for me to help them to define an equation that would look something like this:

$$A \text{ (my problem)} + B \text{ (universal strategy)} = \text{RESOLUTION}$$

Unfortunately, there isn't a simple solution to every conflict. Indeed, to be fair, we want to review each conflict on its own merits and find resolutions or strategies to manage situations that consider the interests of the individuals, their relationship and the particular context. It helps to flip and reframe the problem as follows:

$$A = \text{my UNIQUE problem}$$
$$B = \text{a CUSTOMIZED conflict resolution strategy}$$
$$A + B = \text{the RESOLUTION that considers my unique circumstances and my interests}$$

In other words, we appreciate that a customized conflict resolution approach might be necessary when it is applied to our own problems. When we say we want simple and generally applicable strategies for resolving disputes, we are really thinking about resolving other people's problems. For our own problems, we want others to appreciate what makes our problem and circumstances unique – we want more customization.

While I believe there is an important place in conflict management for "if A, then B" guided pathways (as I discuss on page 241), a better question is, "If A, how do we determine B (the appropriate conflict resolution strategy), in order to move toward resolution?" Such pathways can, and should, be used to pave the way for self-reflection and to build confidence to bring concerns forward.

WHAT YOU CAN DO

! The real benefit of effective conflict management is that you may find out what is actually going on beneath the surface with graduate students and your faculty colleagues. Conflict and complaints serve a purpose. This means:

- Be prepared to experience discomfort with some of what you are hearing as you listen. Complaints may be opportunities, but they are not compliments.

- Help students to distinguish between options for resolving a particular situation (where the focus is "How do I resolve X problem?"), and options for effecting systemic change (where the desired outcome is "How do I make sure no one else has to go through what I went through?").

Conflict Management Influencers

As a conflict resolution practitioner, I have been influenced by interest-based negotiation theory and the guiding principles of administrative fairness, equality, and equity. A fair, equitable, and relationship-centered approach, with a focus on early resolution and prevention, resonated with the individuals I worked with, perhaps because such an approach can be reconciled with or enhanced by the academic theories and concepts they were engaging with in graduate studies. Here I've provided some insights into these influencers with brief summaries of key elements and examples from the graduate context.

Interests and Positions

In the early 1990s, Roger Fisher, Willliam Ury, and Bruce Patton of the Harvard Negotiation Project wrote a popular guide to principled/interest-based negotiation called *Getting to Yes*.[9] One of their key and oft-cited recommendations is that negotiators try to "separate the person from the problem."[10] They distinguish between a person's "positions" (fixed or specific ideas that someone has about how to resolve a situation) and their "interests" (the underlying needs or motivations that underlie why someone has taken a particular position – the "why?" beneath the positions). In practice, positions and interests are informed by an individual's experience, identities, background, and the system in which they are being articulated.

Let's examine interests and positions in relation to a simple supervisor/student dispute:

STUDENT: Let's have a video chat this Tuesday.
SUPERVISOR: I think we should talk on the phone next Friday.

The positions as articulated by the student and the supervisor seem incompatible: The conversation can either happen on Tuesday over video or next Friday over the phone, but not both. Now try to guess, what are the interests buried beneath the stated positions? Perhaps the student has personal news they would prefer to share face-to-face or needs to share a document or image from their computer. Perhaps the supervisor is busy or finds video calls distracting.

An interest-based approach might look more like this:

STUDENT: Let's have a face-to-face video chat this Tuesday.
SUPERVISOR: That may not work for me – are there reasons why you suggested a video chat?
STUDENT: I really want you to have a look at some of the data I've been working with – I can easily share my screen when I need to on a video chat.
SUPERVISOR: Okay. Tuesdays I'm out of the office most of the day, so we need to look at another day to do a video chat. How about this Thursday or Friday early afternoon?

Grad school, more so than undergraduate education, is about relationships – especially relationships between doctoral and master's students and their supervisors/committee members. Principled negotiation emphasizes the importance of relationships and proposes that negotiation does not have to involve one person winning and the other person losing; but rather, that by considering everyone's underlying interests, there may be opportunities to seek "win-win" outcomes that meet mutual interests.

Principled negotiation has faced criticism over the years, including that it can be difficult and time-consuming to apply in practice, and because the focus is on determining "interests," the potential value of "positions" may be lost. On the latter point, positions often provide information about "underlying issues, about individual and group values (e.g., internal unity) and ways of seeing the world (e.g., religion/doctrine),"[11] and about that person's understanding of a particular situation (e.g., what they believe might be possible as outcomes).

Here is an example of the importance of positions for how a discussion unfolds: A PhD student who comes to you for advice and says: "I need a new supervisor who will support my research."

The position taken – changing supervisors – gives the listener a sense that (a) the situation is serious, (b) the student thinks changing supervisors is relatively easy, and (c) that changing supervisors will result in more support for their research.

Instead of responding with a reality-check comment like "You know that changing supervisors is really difficult," the position taken points us in the direction of questions that might help us (and the student) determine underlying interests and start working toward solutions that meet everyone's interests:

- "What do you hope will happen when you get a new supervisor?"
- "Tell me more about the research support you are looking for. And what else are you looking for?"

I note that with this example, there may be situations where a change in supervisor meets the interests of both the supervisor and the student!

The most important takeaway from interest-based negotiation theory might be that discussions will have top layers (positions – what people say they want) as well as underlying layers (interests – what people may not say that they need), and this differentiation remains incredibly useful for conflict resolution in the higher education context.[12]

WHAT YOU CAN DO

! Before you start a conversation, reflect on your own underlying interests, as well as the other persons'.

! During the conversation – ask questions. If someone says "I want A," or "I think that A is what we should do," (their position), instead of responding with your own solution B (your position), ask a question.

! "Why?" is often a good question to uncover interests, however, it can sometimes be interpreted as overly blunt. (No one likes to feel they are being interrogated!) Alternatively, try:

- "Tell me more about A." [A is the stated position.]

- "What are some reasons why A is important to you?" (Note: A possible response is, "A isn't important," which can lead to a discussion of what is important.)

- "When you say A, it seems to me like you value X – is that right?" [X is a guess at the interest behind A.]

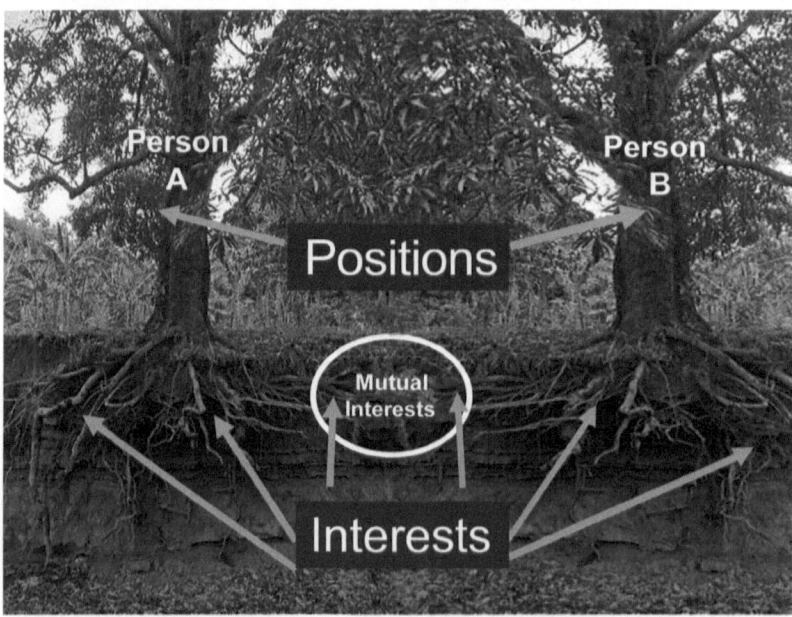

Figure 2. Position trees and interest roots (R. Hazell, 2019)

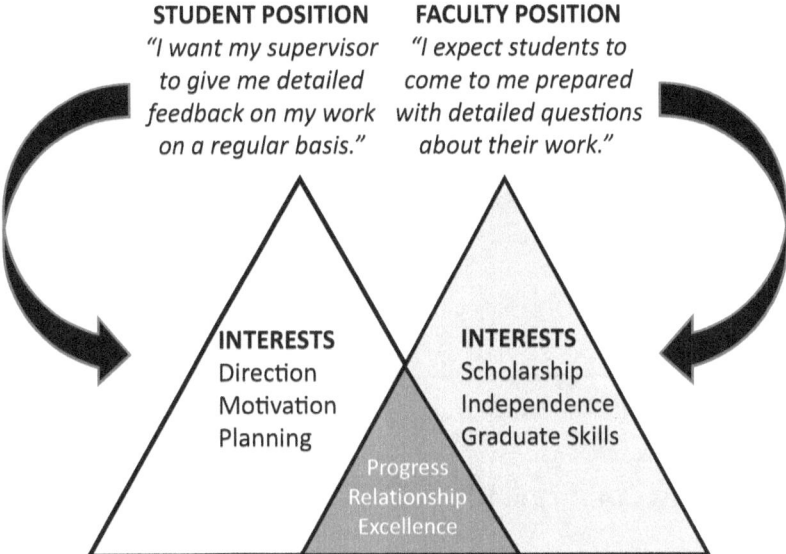

Figure 3. Student/faculty positions and interests

MINI-CASE STUDY: DO POSITIONS = INTERESTS?

For each of these grad student concerns and requested solutions, underline positions (the ask) and guess what the speaker's interests might be (motivation behind the ask). What questions (2 or 3) might you ask the student to see if you are correct?

1. "My supervisor doesn't support my research, so I need to change supervisors."

2. "I am really anxious about meeting with my committee, and I need to see a counselor."

3. "I need an extension to rewrite my paper – my supervisor's comments were brutal!"

MINI-CASE STUDY: Possible Positions/Interests

1. *Position?* Change supervisors.
Interests? To feel supported; to finish quickly; to get help with research questions.
2. *Position?* See a counselor.
Interests? To feel supported; to protect mental health; to get more time to prepare for the meeting.
3. *Position?* Extension to rewrite the paper.
Interests? To write well; to feel that the supervisor understands them.

Managing Conflict Fairly

Our internal sense of fair/unfair is the product of "our moral development from teen years to adulthood."[13] Most of us "know it [fairness] when we see it" and feel like we can act fairly. We accept that certain individuals are granted the role of arbiter of fairness: referees make calls about fair play in sports, judges are responsible for making fair legal decisions. Within many institutions of higher education, there are ombuds who can assess and uphold the principles of fairness and offices mandated to support equity, diversity, and inclusion (EDI), and human rights.[14]

Fairness sets the standard for the way we should treat one another, for the way we should make decisions, and for the decisions themselves. Within an organization like a university, fairness ensures that policies are easy to find and understand, that processes are clearly outlined, that there are opportunities for participation and clarification, and that reasons are given for all decisions. From the beginning ("getting it right") to the end ("putting things right") and beyond ("seeking continuous improvement"), fairness matters.[15] There is research to suggest in contexts where individuals have a strong need to belong, as I would suggest is the case with university students who may have a profound sense of affiliation with their university, program, or department, procedural fairness will likely matter even more.[16]

In terms of graduate conflict management, it is important to examine how people are understanding and articulating their expectations and experiences as individuals and as members of a particular graduate community. What choices were made? What actions (or inactions) were taken (or not taken)? What was the outcome and what were the impacts on the individuals involved?

To assess fairness and determine "Is this situation fair?," most post-secondary ombuds have adopted a form of the Ombudsman Saskatchewan's fairness triangle, which looks at these three elements of fairness:

- *Relational.* Members of the graduate community (students, staff, and faculty) should be treated fairly with consideration of identity, social location, and intersectionality.
- *Procedural Fairness.* All decisions that impact members of the graduate community should be made through a fair process.
- *Substantive Fairness.* The decisions should be fair.[17]

Though sometimes relational fairness and *equitable fairness* are used interchangeably,[18] equitable fairness may also be seen as an overarching consideration impacting how people are treated, how processes unfold, and how decisions are made.

For conflict prevention, a decision-making process that is fair will have legitimacy in the eyes of participants, often regardless of whether the outcome is in their favor, and will stand up to scrutiny (internal and external). People care about fairness not simply because a fair process is likely to benefit them directly (i.e., that within a fair process one will be able "to control one's own outcomes") but also because of a value placed on relationships and memberships in particular communities. This may include a sense of belonging to a department, a faculty, a research group, or an identity group. Fair processes are one way to ensure that one's voice will be heard by others, and thus fulfill a deeply human need to belong.[19]

Here is an example of the interplay between equality, equity, and fairness in relation to a potential graduate conflict:

Equality requires consistency in how policies and rules are applied and in how decisions are made; processes and outcomes should not be arbitrary.

- A department requires all PhD students to meet with their full advisory committee at least twice a year or they will be flagged by the department as failing to make satisfactory academic progress. (POLICY)

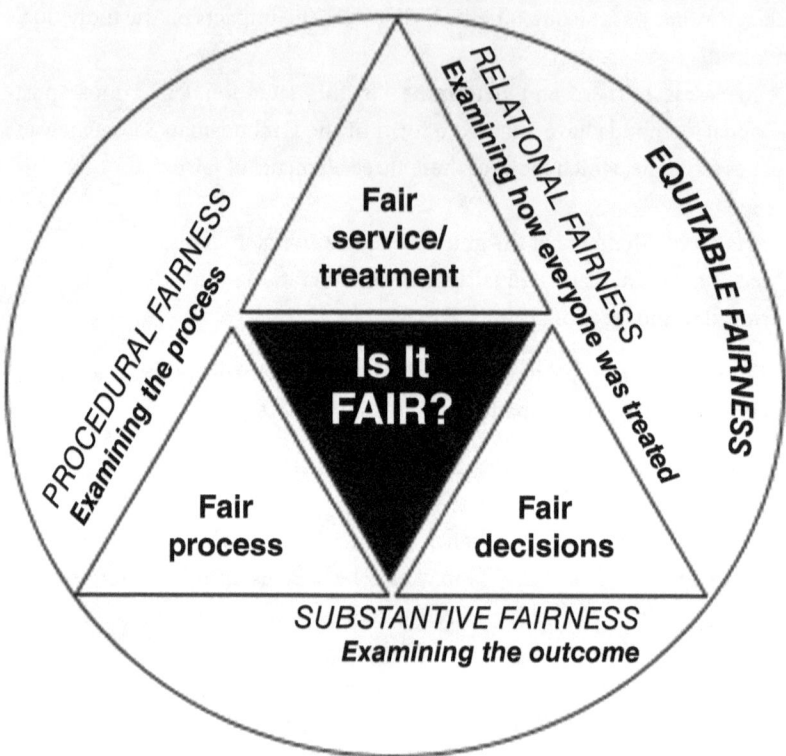

Figure 4. Fairness triangle – modified from the Ombudsman Saskatchewan fairness triangle

Equity recognizes that individuals and groups of people have different experiences, histories, resources, and opportunities (at individual and systemic levels), and they may need to be treated or supported in different ways to achieve equality.

- A PhD student with a chronic illness and family obligations has been unable to schedule the required second advisory committee meeting this year. Equity asks us to consider how might this student need to be supported or treated differently to be on an equal footing with the rest of their PhD cohort with respect to this departmental requirement. (SITUATION)

Fairness shows us how to make decisions and exceptions in a principled way within a system of institutional rules and processes. It requires us to be impartial and just, to consider all perspectives, and to be reasonable, timely, and accurate in consideration of specific situations and among situations, including with regard to students in similar circumstances.

- Before the PhD student is flagged as failing to have made satisfactory academic progress for not having met twice in the year with their full advisory committee, fairness asks us to consider if there is a way for them to share their circumstances as part of a decision-making process? How are exceptions made and communicated? How are students supported? (OUTCOME)

WHAT YOU CAN DO

! How do you know if you are being fair? What is your process for fair decision-making? To learn more about fairness and fair decision-making, watch the TEDxNashvilleWomen video, "The Neuroscience of Decision-Making: Are We Foul or Fair?,"[20] and listen to the *This American Life* podcast, "No Fair: Fan Perceptions of Referee Impartiality in Professional Basketball."[21]

! As a decision-maker, you can keep fairness in mind by using a checklist or a self-assessment guide, such as the "Administrative Fairness Checklist for Decision-Makers"[22] from Ryerson University (now Toronto Metropolitan University) and the "Fairness by Design: An Administrative Fairness Self-Assessment Guide" from the British Columbia Ombudsperson.[23]

Identity, Intersectionality, and Individual Experience

When asked who was using our services, I noted that we talked with more doctoral students than master's students and that 1 in 10 conversations were with faculty or staff.[24] In some years, where numbers were sufficient to protect confidentiality, I was also able to share information about faculty affiliation. For example, in 2018–19, the top three faculties (each representing 11 percent of conversations) were Arts & Science, Applied Science & Engineering, and Medicine.

What people really wanted to know, however, was whether the graduate students who used our services identified as members of racialized and other minority/underrepresented groups (and as a related question, whether that was reflective of the diversity of our institution's graduate student body).

At our bi-weekly team meetings, the peer advisors described connections with a diverse group of grad students; however, we didn't have reliable quantitative data. This shortcoming can be traced to (a) the data we chose to collect, (b) the priority we placed on confidentiality and informality, and (c) our data input in practice. Based on advice from the university's equity and inclusion office, we did not assume or assign identities to anyone as part of our data collection – we only recorded self-identified identities. In addition, I only wanted to collect data that was relevant to our office's mandate (conflict resolution), so only if someone told us their concern was related to their identity (e.g., Black, Indigenous, racialized, female, LGBTQ2S+, international, mature student, having a disability) were such details to be recorded by the team.

What I found over the years was that in practice, some peer advisors were making assumptions about identities or recording a self-identified identity which was unrelated to the conflict that had brought the individual to our service. Most years, in addition to these data shortcomings, the data set was too small to report on and ensure confidentiality (or perceptions of confidentiality).

For one year, 2017–18, I was able to provide some limited insights into identity, because in over half of the coaching conversations we had that year the person described a particular characteristic as being relevant to what brought them to speak with us: 28 percent self-identified as "international," and 23 percent as living with/having a "mental or physical health/disability."[25] When I looked closer at the issues discussed in these two identity groups, three sources of conflict were at the top: Supervision, Personal/Family, and Interpersonal (non-supervisory). Further, Personal/Family was raised much more frequently as a source of conflict for international students (22 percent) and students living with/having a mental or physical health or disability (15 percent), than they were across all conversations (6 percent). This is just one illustration of the complex and multifaceted nature of conflict, and the potential for sources of conflict to impact some identity groups more than others.

WHAT YOU CAN DO

! Discuss with a colleague: Conflict often includes several interconnected issues and the individuals involved will have varied and multiple identities. In other words, conflict is often multi-layered and complex, just like the individuals involved in the conflict. Challenge each other to describe how you might demonstrate respect for an individual's perspective and experience of a conflict.

! Race and intersectionality can be complex and passionate topics of discussion. Conversations or learning may benefit from skilled facilitators who can encourage productive and respectful discussions. Ijeoma Oluo has written a book to help people have conversations about race entitled *So You Want to Talk about Race*.[26]

Q. *What have you read, listened to, or watched that might be informing your comfort levels and approaches to discussions about identity, individuality, and intersectionality?*

MINI-CASE STUDY: NOT WELCOME IN THE MEETING

Imagine you are your department's chair, and a PHD student has sent you this email:

Dear CHAIR,

I am writing to you about a situation that has been bothering me for some time. As one of the few non-white PhD students in this department, I don't feel welcome at departmental meetings. In the past when I have tried to speak up about my observations about anti-Black racism, I've been silenced by white students and faculty, even though my comments are never directed at any person in our department.

Considering the department's Statement of Solidarity Regarding Anti-Black Racism,[27] I would like to know what you are going to do to challenge the status quo and foster "the systemic development of an institutional culture of anti-oppression" in the department as described in the statement. I want to ask you as Chair to reflect deeply on the dominant department culture which makes these meetings deeply alienating spaces for anyone who identifies as Black Just because there are now a few racialized students, staff, and faculty in this department, doesn't make it inclusive. Sincerely, STUDENT

Q. *Assuming you will be having a conversation with the student and want to identify the student's interests and understand what they mean by "alienating", "silenced," and "inclusive," what questions might you want to ask?*

MINI-CASE STUDY: INTERNATIONAL AND MORE

Imagine you are in a graduate administrative role and both a graduate student and their supervisor have separately shared their views with you on a potential conflict.

"I'm an international STUDENT in my last year of my PhD. Because of a change in my family's circumstances, I have to return home a few months earlier than expected, but I can't get my supervisor to commit to an earlier defense timeline."

"I am a SUPERVISOR to four PhD students, two of them who are scheduled to defend shortly. Now my third PhD student (an international student) wants to defend earlier than planned! I can't figure out how to make this work with my own family responsibilities."

Q1. *Can you identify identities, positions, and interests?*

Q2. *What assumptions might you be making?*

Q3. *Who did you relate to more reading this – the student or the supervisor?*

Q4. *How might you try and get each person to see the conflict from the other person's perspective?*

FACILITATED CASE STUDY: THE SILENT ONE

The original case study was written by peer advisor Hifza (MSc Immunology) for a conflict resolution/equity workshop for women in the sciences. Her co-facilitator was a staff member working to support EDI (equity, diversity, and inclusion) on campus.

Time Required. 15 minutes

Instructions. As you read the case study, reflect and jot down answers to the discussion questions at the end. After 5 minutes, the facilitator will lead a discussion with the larger group (10 minutes).

Case Study. Imagine overhearing the following comment in a conversation between two faculty members:

"I have a student who doesn't seem to understand what I am trying to teach them. I mean, I appreciate that English isn't her first language, but still … I spend extra time explaining things multiple times and she never says anything! On top of that, she makes mistakes and won't ask me any questions when she clearly needs help. I'm so frustrated and don't know what to do with her. You're so lucky though! I saw one of your students present at the last group meeting and it was excellent! His English is so clear, and he seems so confident – it is incredible what he is accomplishing."

Questions for Individual Reflection:

- What equity issues can you identify in this case study? Other issues that the female student might be dealing with?
- Can you identify the speaker's position? Their interests?
- Are there any campus resources that might be appropriate to refer the female student to? Resources for the faculty member?

Discussion Prompts (for Facilitators):

- Unconscious bias
- Intersectional identities
- Roles/responsibilities
- Unlawful discrimination/harassment vs. "unacceptable behavior"

Focusing on Early Resolution and Conflict Prevention

When organizations empower well-trained frontline staff, with the discretionary authority to resolve issues with a focus on creativity and flexibility, this can enable earlier resolution of complex issues.[28] In a university context, when faculty and students (those individuals who interact on the "front line" of academia) appreciate that they have the power to resolve conflicts, to develop the training/tools to be able to do so properly (fairly), and to escalate appropriately when necessary, this sets the stage for early resolution of conflict.

"Conflict coaching" is one early resolution tool. It is a way for a trained "conflict coach" to transfer specific dispute resolution skills, tools, and knowledge to a person who is experiencing a conflict (or looking to prevent a potential conflict), so that they can more effectively self-advocate and engage with contentious situations.[29] Coaching gives individuals tools they can keep in their conflict management toolbox for the next conflict. Conflict coaching is respectful, collaborative, encouraging, and forward-looking. It can also be consuming emotional work: In our office, we would often spend over an hour with someone or have multiple conversations to really understand all their concerns.

Listening to someone describe a conflict can be like being presented with a tangled ball of string. The conflict coach's job isn't to untangle the mess for the person (just like a swim coach's job isn't to swim the race for the swimmer), but to work with the person to help them:

- Find the string ends within the tangle that they want to grasp at this time.
- Figure out the best ways of pulling these ends out of the tangle.

With the string metaphor, professional counseling might be more appropriate for someone who wants to understand how or why the string got tangled, and perhaps work over time to untangle the entire tangled ball of string. The objective of coaching is not to delve into someone's *past*, but to explore what is happening in the *present*, including any "obstacles," in order to "discover new options and possibilities that can be implemented … in the *future*."[30]

For example, if a graduate student shares with you a story about their conflict with their supervisor or committee member, consider if any of the conflict coaching questions we used might help you to focus on supporting the student, rather than trying to resolve their problem for them:

- *"What brought you in to talk to me?"* PAST: Keeping the person and their experience of the conflict at the center of the discussion.

- *"What are you hoping I can help you with?"* PRESENT: Identifying interests, goals, and priorities. Brainstorming options, resources, and policies/processes.

- *"How would you like things to turn out?"* FUTURE: Emphasizing a strategic approach (pros /cons) and doing a reality check re: context and other perspectives/interests.

- *"Would you like to role play how things might unfold?"* PRACTICE: Keeping a focus on the other person and avoiding being drawn into solving a problem *for* the other person is not easy.

Peer advisor Matt (PhD Drama, Theatre, and Performance Studies) noted after one such conversation, "It was very difficult to hold back from offering advice, and I probably didn't do this enough. But the meeting calmed him down and allowed him to leave with a plan."

WHAT YOU CAN DO

! Reflect on being a faculty mentor and learn about coaching styles for leaders. For more insights, read Nirmala Hariharan's blog, "The Faculty Series: What Does It Take to Be a Mentor,"[31] and Herminia Ibarra and Anne Scoular's article, "The Leader as Coach" (Harvard Business Review).[32]

Q1. What makes a great coach?

Q2. Is there someone you think is a great coach? Why?

Q3. How does a coach differ from a mentor?

! Here are 5 quick tips for confident conflict coaching that I shared in faculty training:[33]

1. Ask yourself, whose problem is it? (Hint: It may not be yours!) Be clear about what you can/can't do for the student.

2. Listen and respond more often with a question than a comment.

3. Assess whether the student is ready to problem solve. Sometimes more listening and understanding is necessary, sometimes that is all that is needed.

4. Share information and offer a range of possible resources/supports and be clear about "what next."

5. Have the student summarize the conversation – do they understand their options, priorities, and next steps?

Integrating Trauma-Informed Approaches

When we engage in a discussion to resolve an issue/concern or to help someone determine their options for resolving a conflict with someone else, we want to avoid making things worse. This can be even more important when interacting with individuals who distrust administrative processes because of past trauma[34] or previous negative experiences, or because they are navigating conflict within a university structure that has a colonialist history (e.g., Indigenous students).[35]

A trauma-informed approach involves: "knowing, understanding, acknowledging, and validating that a person ... has suffered trauma from their lived experiences, including intergenerational trauma."[36] It is not about diagnosing or treating trauma. Context and history are relevant considerations for conflict management, resolution, and restoration (i.e., moving forward after a conflict).

Here are some of the trauma-informed strategies that we used in our coaching:

- *Be present.* In the moment, remember that it can take an enormous amount of courage/energy to talk about a difficult situation or to reach out for help, so being there 100 percent matters.

- *Show genuine interest in and respect for the individual's story and their perspective/interpretive angles on their experiences.* Consider that simply through the act of being listened to, individuals have the opportunity to listen to themselves more carefully. Saying things aloud can sound different from what we say to ourselves in our own heads.

- *Keep the other person at the center of the conversation*: Try to power individuals to take steps to resolve their conflicts; make sure you are not overpromising about your role in resolving the conflict. We found that we might have to clarify our mandate several times over the course of a conversation.

- *Be accurate*: If you don't know something or make a mistake, say so. For example, "I'm not sure what forms you need to submit – I'll have to get back to you."

- *Be consistently firm about boundaries*: If the time allotted to a conversation runs out, say so, and be clear about what happen next. Be explicit if language (e.g., swearing, unacceptable words or phrases), tone, or actions (e.g., yelling, thumping table) are inappropriate. For example, "I am not comfortable with the language you are using, and we can't continue this conversation if you continue to use these terms." A deeper discussion about the importance of boundaries in conflict management starts at page 193.

It can be helpful to think of trauma-informed approaches as a form of "universal interpersonal design." When we infuse all of our interactions with trauma-informed principles, such as safety (bravery), trustworthiness, transparency, collaboration, empowerment, voice, and choice,[37] we improve interactions for everyone without having to make individual determinations of whether someone has or hasn't experienced/is or isn't experiencing trauma.

> **WHAT YOU CAN DO**
>
> ! When someone remains in a state of anger or agitation, one option is to offer to reschedule the appointment to a different time and location,[38] because:
>
> - The delay/disruption can provide time for the individual to calm down, reflect, and regroup: *"I think we should end our conversation and reconnect in a few days. Can we compare calendars to find a time/date that works?"*
>
> - A change of location can sometimes set a different tone – we sometimes forget that location plays a role in our interactions; for example, the power inherent in meeting in a supervisor's office in contrast to meeting in the department's graduate student lounge: *"When we meet next – do you have a preferred location?"*
>
> - By focusing on the discussion process (rather than the substance of the discussion) and coming to a mutual agreement on something as simple as the time or place for the discussion, can set a positive tone for the next part of the conversation: *"Do mornings work? Before or after 10 a.m.?"*
>
> ! Know when to keep others informed.
>
> *Q1. Who do you talk to about concerning student (or faculty) situations?*
>
> *Q2. When are you supposed to loop them in?*

MINI-CASE STUDY: DOUBLE GRAD TROUBLE

Two graduate students have come together to talk to you and get some advice since you are known as a "friendly faculty member" in the department.

The two students tell you that they have been working collaboratively on a large research project under the same supervisor. Both students acknowledge that they have had difficulty working with their supervisor since the beginning of the project: They mention their supervisor is "very disorganized" and "unpredictable." Both students tell you they feel "abandoned" by their supervisor. During the conversation, one of the students seems extremely angry and uses profane language to describe how the supervisor recently took a lengthy vacation without letting the students know. The other student looks more like they are about to burst into tears and lets the other student do most of the talking. The students tell you that they have composed an email to their supervisor but haven't sent it yet.

Q. How could you use trauma-informed strategies to approach this situation and respond to the students?

Restorative Approaches

Restorative approaches (also referred to as restorative practices) have been practiced in Indigenous communities in Canada, New Zealand, South Africa, and other parts of the world for centuries. "Restorative justice," or RJ, may be the most widely known form of restorative practice[39] because it has been incorporated into the criminal justice system in Canada[40] as well as in other jurisdictions. RJ can be understood more broadly as a "philosophical perspective on justice and how it can be obtained by the people who have been impacted by criminal acts."[41] RJ places an emphasis on accepting responsibility for harms, and centering the "role of victims, wrongdoers, and the community in facilitating the restoration of relationships."[42]

Broadly speaking, restorative practices, including affective statements and questions, restorative circles, and community conferencing[43] have been incorporated in a very limited way in the post-secondary education context – primarily in relation to residence disputes or student conduct issues.[44]

In my view, universities have a responsibility to be moving more purposefully in a restorative direction in relation to the management of campus conflict. The commitment of Canadian universities to take up the calls to action from the Truth and Reconciliation Report (TRC Report) issued in 2015[45] and the 2021 discovery of unmarked graves at residential school sites in Canada[46] underscore the importance of moving beyond words into action in terms of Indigenous reconciliation. Several of the calls to action in the TRC Report speak directly to the importance of learning about the history of Indigenous peoples, including "skills-based training in intercultural competency, conflict resolution, human rights and anti-racism" and the integration of "Indigenous knowledge and teaching methods into classrooms."[47] One way to do this is for universities to consider how incorporating restorative practices might enhance campus conflict management or to provide viable alternatives to the semi-judicial colonial dispute-resolution processes that were originally "baked into" the institution.

Restorative approaches can be used both in response to a live conflict or after an incident has occurred (reactive) or preventatively (proactive) to engage  a community in conversation. Restorative objectives include mutual learning and support by bringing people together to identify the impact/harms, to accept responsibility, and to rebuild relationships, trust, and connections that may have been damaged between individuals, while also considering the impact on the larger community.[48]

In identifying issues and trends in graduate conflict, I was increasingly seeing reasons why restorative approaches might be well suited to resolving supervisory and lab issues. This is because restorative approaches examine the impact of conflict not just on individuals but also on the members of their community (e.g., student, supervisor, department; students, principle investigator (PI), lab group). In many ways, labs are mini communities within the institution where conflict can have profound ripple effects.

Imagine a conflict on an interdisciplinary research team between several graduate students: They have been arguing about which theoretical approach to apply, and comments have become increasingly personal and heated. There is potential here for the entire project to be derailed by the conflict, and for faculty supervisors or others (postdoctoral/undergraduate students) to become involved, or as we often saw happen, for individuals to withdraw from this awkward and tension-filled situation.

Like conflict coaching, which involves working with someone to help them resolve an issue, rather than solving the issue for them, restorative justice is about decisions/outcomes being made with the participants, rather than to (or for) the participants.[49]

While one criticism of restorative practice is that it is time consuming and administratively complex, there are myriad ways to engage restoratively, from small shifts in language and approach to large community-based restorative processes. Once a university has developed internal restorative capacity, they have the ability to assess when and how to approach a conflict restoratively, and the question becomes, "Which restorative process/approach is appropriate for this situation/these circumstances?" A 2017 independent review of a number of Restorative Justice/Restorative Approach (RJ/RA) processes that had taken place at Dalhousie University (Canada) concluded that with "skill and leadership of [the] internal practitioners ... RJ/RA does offer value and positive change for individuals and their communities and can assist in behavior change in students, staff, and faculty."[50]

Another example of a restorative approach is the two-month long community engagement process that the Standing Strong (Mash Koh Wee Kah Pooh Win) Task Force at the Toronto Metropolitan University (formerly Ryerson University) engaged in to review concerns associated with the university's namesake Egerton Ryerson. The process was "represented as a circle with no one above, no one below, no one ahead and no one behind."[51] A 2019 review of a restorative facilitation initiative at a hospice in England found three potential benefits to using restorative practices as part of their institutional conflict management:

- There was a more supportive and positive culture.
- Time was saved because of fewer formal grievances.
- There was a happier and more productive workforce because issues were being discussed as they arose, and staff were able to "have direct, honest conversations with each other without fear of retribution."[52]

WHAT YOU CAN DO

! Think about how you can you increase your knowledge and familiarity with restorative concepts. Are there Indigenous communities or individuals on or off campus that you can consult or collaborate with? Seek out restorative resources, training, and workshops, especially those led or developed in collaboration with experts from the Indigenous community.

! Interested in engaging in a virtual circle? Here are two articles to help guide your process: "Q&A Facilitating Circles Online" by Linsey Pointer, PhD,[53] and "During the COVID-19 Crisis, Restorative Practices Can Help" by the International Institute for Restorative Practices.[54]

! Here are four ways that I included restorative practices in our work that you might try:

1. Arrange team meetings in a *circle* with chairs but no tables. Invite participants to contribute in ways that are authentic to each individual – talking (in turn) or remaining silent.

2. Try an interactive *land acknowledgment activity* instead of simply reading the university's statement. At the outset of our 2019 peer advisor training, everyone was invited to share their own connection to the land on which the university stands and to the university as an institution. I am just starting to learn about the significance, protocol, and responsibilities associated with territorial acknowledgments,[55] yet I felt that participating in this territorial acknowledgment activity, the group (myself included) had a greater sense of purpose and belonging to a shared experience from the outset, than peer team groups in earlier years.

3. Reframing issues to highlight impact, ways of making things right, and rebuilding *trust*.

4. Thinking about the *impact* that our actions (as conflict coaches and trainers) might have on the larger university community, and how our service fits into the larger circle of support for graduate students.

! When you talk with a graduate student or a fellow faculty member who is experiencing a conflict, here are some restorative questions you might want to ask:

- "What impact has this conflict had on you?"
- "Who else has been impacted by this situation?"
- "What needs to happen to make things right/better/to rebuild trust?"

TIP SHEET: TRAUMA-INFORMED RESTORATIVE QUESTIONS

Framing conflict coaching interactions in a trauma-informed way and asking appropriate trauma-informed, restorative questions takes practice. *Consider some observations about common questions and examples of restorative alternatives.*[56]		
Questions	**Observation**	**Restorative Questions**
"What's wrong?"	Question is framed in the negative – something is "wrong."	"What happened?"
"Start from the beginning and tell me all about your experience."	Invasive question that asks for too much information about an experience that may have been difficult/painful.	"What did you think (at the time) when this happened?"
"Sounds like a terrible situation but aren't you glad you changed supervisors?"	Question may seem dismissive. Assumes the situation (with the new supervisor) is better.	"What has been the hardest thing for you?"
"That was a long time ago – aren't you ready to move on?"	Question seems to discount impact and assumes "time heals all wounds."	"How is this impacting you (and/or others) at this time?"
"You need to talk to a counselor, not to me."	Statement may seem judgmental, which results in shutting down the connection.	"What do you think needs to happen to make things better?"

Responding to Conflict Online

Pre-pandemic, we did most of our conflict coaching in-person (or for faculty, by phone); although, we would arrange the occasional video call upon request. This was mostly with students who were doing research in remote locations or international students who were home for family reasons. From my experiences, I felt it would be easier for the peer advisors to quickly build rapport with and pick up on visual communication cues from their fellow students when meetings were face-to-face. At that time, it was challenging to facilitate co-coaching (i.e., two peer advisors would meet with each grad student complainant) over video.[57]

Unless communication in writing was required for accessibility reasons, we chose not to coach over email or text, other than to provide links to resources and policies or to answer basic questions. This was a useful practice because (1) we didn't keep written files, and (2) information in writing can sometimes be interpreted as instructions rather than options for careful consideration. We were always mindful in our coaching that individuals might be looking for us to tell them what to do to solve their conflict, and we managed expectations throughout our coaching conversations.

I would answer the question, "Should I try to resolve my grad school conflict online?" differently than a year ago. Times have changed; technology has improved in leaps and bounds since March 2020 when we moved the Grad CRC services online and started doing coaching by video chat or phone. Now my response is "yes," with the caveat that I heavily favor online visual/vocal means of communicating over those that rely exclusively

on the written word. For reasons such as accessibility, poor internet, or audio connections (this was a concern for many international graduate students who returned home during COVID-19, or for those who were doing research abroad) email may be the best option or play a much larger role in resolving a conflict. With those caveats, I recommend having video or voice interactions over written correspondence (email, chat) for the complex storytelling and active listening that precedes problem-solving and conflict resolution.

While this recommendation is unlikely to resonate with people who "find it easier to deal with work conflicts through words on a screen than face-to-face conversation,"[58] here is why it is worth the work (and the risk of discomfort) to use video or voice interactions for graduate conflict resolution:

- Everyone thinks they are better at communicating over email than they actually are; this includes communicating as intended and interpreting as intended.[59]
- Even when hours are spent composing an email (and grad students told us they often did), taking the time to turn on your audio or your video and being present online will be perceived as a greater investment in the graduate relationship.
- It may be easier to tell if a conflict has been resolved than over email (i.e., are they okay, or are they crying or shouting at the computer screen as they write?).
- It sets expectations for how conflict should be addressed (directly) and builds skills (discussion) for the next time an issue arises.

As one example of the first point, we talked with a new graduate student who was upset about emails from their supervisor: when we were shown one example, the faculty member's email was precise, direct, and to the point, but it had been perceived by the student as terse and "cold" due to the absence of "feel good" words.

Texts tend to be (overly) informal, and may not be easy to follow, retain, or reflect upon if a matter is not resolved and is escalated within the university. A carefully crafted email can be useful for summarizing discussions, documenting steps taken, and outlining next steps for resolving a conflict. Texting is a good "supporting" mode of communication, making scheduling easier ("Can we start our call at 3:15 p.m. instead of 3 p.m.?") and highlighting issues for quick response ("Before our call tomorrow, can you please send me your latest timeline?").

Using email to resolve conflict may include writing about personal/identifying details, so it is important to check your institution's guidelines and best practices for emails, online security (especially for work from home), privacy, and document retention.[60] For example, email messages may be classified as university records and accessible under freedom of information legislation such as the Ontario Freedom of Information and Protection of Privacy Act (FIPPA). In addition, there may be policies or resources related to unacceptable or unwanted online behavior (cyber-bullying/cyber-aggression) such as angry, rude, or threatening emails or texts, or those that reveal personal information. Note that it is likely that your institution has policies or resources related to unacceptable or unwanted online behavior, and familiarizing yourself with such policies can help you to understand how to prevent and navigate conflict online.[61]

WHAT YOU CAN DO

! Take your time. As one of the peer advisors noted, "There's an assumption that because you are online (or supposed to be online) you have to respond immediately." You don't have to respond in the heat of the moment. An intentional pause can show that you care and give you an opportunity to explain that the issue is important to you: *"I'm going to have to get back to you on this – I want to think about what we have been discussing and make sure that I can give you a thoughtful response."*

! Remember you can shift gears. Just because you've started a text exchange, doesn't mean the discussion can't be shifted to video: *"I think we should continue this on video chat – can we arrange a time to talk later today or tomorrow?"*

! Have an honest talk with your grad students about preferred methods of communication. Scheduling time for video/voice chats can be time consuming: *"Does it make sense for us to share calendars so you can find workable appointment times for us?"*

! If you want your student to take action as a result of you sending an email, be clear about that expectation. Email can become "a bit of a de facto 'to do' list – but one that never ends." The student (or you) may have read the email and then closed it without answering it, saying to themselves: "I'll deal with this one later, when I have time."[62]

Q1. What are some of the advantages/disadvantages of communicating concerns over email? (e.g., intention, tone)

Q2. Are there ways to address potential disadvantages?

TIP SHEET: EMAIL BEST PRACTICES (FOR EMAILS YOU SEND)

BE BRIEF

- Put important information at the top or in **bold**.
- Limit content to a single topic or 2–3 main points.
- Keep it short ... no one likes to scroll!

BE ACCURATE

- Have a clearly worded short subject line so someone doing a quick scan of their inbox can find the email – e.g., Nov. 2020 Thesis check-in (1).
- Double check information and links. Using voice to ~~test~~ text? Even more reason to check!
- Read aloud before sending (2).

BE KIND

- Imagine you are the one receiving the email (2). In uncertain or stressful times, people may default to "fight or flight" responses: intended tone/purpose behind an email may not align with the received tone/purpose.
- PAUSE before sending. If you have time, save the email in draft and revisit.
- Experiencing a sense of regret after hitting "send"? Make time for a follow-up phone call or a video chat.
- Consider how you sign off at the end. Offer gratitude (3). Thank you!

SOURCES

(1) Ricardo Twumasi, Cary Cooper, and Lina Siegal, "Ten Rules of Email that Will Reduce Your Stress Levels," The Conversation, 28 March 2019, http://theconversation.com/ten-rules-of-email-that-will-reduce-your-stress-levels-113670.

(2) Derek Loosvelt, "3 Rules for Writing Important Work Emails," *Firsthand* (blog), 16 April 2019, https://firsthand.co/blogs/workplace-issues/3-rules-for-writing-important-work-emails.

(3) Smith Brain Trust, "Regards? Sincerely? Cheers? The Best Email Closings Now," Robert H. Smith School of Business, 12 June 2018, https://www.rhsmith.umd.edu/research/best-and-worst-ways-sign-email.

Resolving Conflict Informally

As an advocate for early resolution, I see enormous benefit to students and faculty in having flexibility and discretion at initial stages in a dispute to engage in informal conversations.

Informality gives everyone an opportunity to share perspectives, ask questions, and determine interests perhaps more freely than in a formal process (especially at universities where formal processes tend to be adversarial in nature). The good news is that references to informal resolution are relatively common in post-secondary policies, guidelines, and processes. For example, an academic policy might include a statement such as:

> If an issue or problem arises, first try to resolve the issue through informal discussion with the individuals directly involved.

Faculty may also have the discretion (subject to any conditions set out in the policy) to decide whether an informal discussion is the end of the matter or if it needs to be escalated.

Even though "informal" suggests "relaxed and friendly; not following strict rules of how to behave or do something,"[63] it doesn't mean that the topic of conversation isn't serious or important, or that the discussion must lack structure or elements to ensure fairness. Advance preparation can help make the most of an informal discussion. In advance of a meeting, consider:

- Is this just the first step in a formal decision-making process, and if so, have you provided this information to the student?
- Are there reasons to hold a more formal meeting instead of an informal meeting?
- Will a decision be made at/after the informal discussion, and if so, who will make the decision and on what basis?

For the last point, the student needs to be given notice in writing of whether the discussion is for decision-making purposes and reminded of this at the outset of the discussion. There should be no uncertainty about whether and how decisions are being made.[64]

WHAT YOU CAN DO

! Informality may mean that personal stressors or unrelated issues are disclosed. Try a gentle redirect back to the purpose of the meeting or a referral.

! Be conscious of impressions left by your past interactions with a student. If you regularly have casual check-ins and then you ask a student to come to your office for an "informal meeting" without providing any additional detail, they may expect another friendly chat. An informal meeting should not feel like an ambush.

Consider the "Guest List." Before arranging an informal meeting, read this cautionary tale from Wilfrid Laurier University, in Ontario, Canada, about a professor who invited a graduate teaching assistant (TA) to an "informal meeting" to discuss concerns that had been raised by a student in the TA's tutorial group. Objectively, the meeting was anything but informal. In an open letter, the instructor explained how an "informal meeting" between an instructor and his TA turned into a panel of three faculty members plus the TA, noting, "In the process of arranging this [meeting], others indicated they should attend as well. This is one of the facets of working at a university – meetings can often become de facto committees due to relevant stakeholders being pulled in." The instructor acknowledged that, "I should have seen how meeting with a panel of three people would be an intimidating situation and not invite a productive discussion." [65]

In our coaching, students often mentioned being afraid or nervous about an upcoming meeting, and they would ask whether they could have us (no!), or a friend, or an advocate (perhaps) attend the meeting with them. We would talk about the role and purpose of support people, and how involving other people in an informal meeting can change the character or tone of a meeting. We would ask:

- "Have you considered how it might look from the perspective of the person who called the meeting if you show up with a friend/parent/advocate?"
- "Does your support person need to be in the room or could they talk with you beforehand, walk with you to the meeting and sit outside, or meet you afterward?"
- "If you intend to bring a support person, have you given the other person notice?"

Considering the guest list also includes anyone who might not attend an informal discussion, but will be involved in making the decision or be advised of the decision. This would include a situation where a faculty member, after talking with a student informally about a concern, determines that it would be helpful to consult with the graduate chair (or someone in an equivalent administrative position) about what has happened in the past with other students in similar circumstances. In such cases, they should let the student know this is what they intend to do (who, why, and when), and then follow up with the student after doing so.

WHAT YOU CAN DO

! If you think that it makes sense to have someone else attend the informal discussion, give the student notice. For example, a short "heads-up" email might look like this:

To: STUDENT
From: SUPERVISOR

I would like to invite the Grad Coordinator to join us at the meeting because they are familiar with how the department has handled requests for leaves of absences in the past. Please let me know right away if you have any issues with them joining us. For your reference, here is the link to the policy and the department handbook which mentions leaves of absences at page 16.

Build or Re-establish Trust. Simple "housekeeping" remarks can help students to feel welcome and ensure that you are setting the stage for an open discussion:

- "Thank you for connecting with me." (Welcome)
- "How much time do we have to chat today?" or "As you know, we have forty-five minutes to chat today." (Logistics)
- "Let's make sure we are in agreement about what we are going to talk about today" or "Do you have anything to add to the email agenda you/I sent earlier?" (Purpose)

In an informal discussion everyone should have an opportunity to speak and share their perspective on the issues being discussed. They should also have an opportunity to respond to any information presented by others before any final decisions are made. In this way, informal discussions mirror what is expected of formal meetings and processes.

- "Have you got a copy of the _____ policy, so we can look at it now together?
- "I want to make sure that we have a chance to clarify _____. I'd like to get more information from you about _____."

A senior staff member whose responsibilities included supporting faculty around escalated and high-risk graduate student issues told me to share with faculty the following advice: "In situations like this it's often not what you do to address issues, but how you do it that matters. Don't offer a discussion and then provide a lecture!"

I note that there may be opportunities to incorporate restorative approaches into informal meetings where there have been violations of expectations and/r trust – "at the center of the restorative justice concept lies the idea that crimes or wrongdoings are violations of people and relationships." Recall the restorative discussion starting at page 63.

WHAT YOU CAN DO

! Have an agenda or relevant policy (or other something "on paper") that everyone can refer to before, during, or after a conversation. In conflict resolution language, having the ability to follow and focus on agenda items is one way to "separate the person from the problem."[66] During the meeting, an agenda can help everyone to stay on topic and remain within one's role as well as keep track of topics that may require follow up discussion.

! While the student is speaking, make note of questions that you have and things you want to say rather than responding immediately – there will be a time during the meeting to circle back to ask those questions and clarify.

! Listening can be a good starting place for building or re-establishing trust. Learn about how listening circles (a form of restorative practice distinct from problem-solving circles) are currently being used online: "IIRP Graduate School: The Power of Listening Circles."[67]

Remember to Document, Informally. Informality doesn't mean you can't refer to documents or document the discussion itself. For example, a pre-meeting email or short agenda that includes a list of discussion items can help everyone understand the purpose of the meeting and manage expectations (and stress levels!) by setting an appropriate tone for the conversation.

- "When we meet, I'd like us to talk about your progress against the research timeline that we talked about when we met on DATE (see timeline attached). This is an issue that needs to be talked about sooner rather than later."

A pre-meeting email can also outline logistics (how long the meeting will be, location, offers of accommodation, etc.) and attendees. While normally an informal discussion will involve just you and the student, if appropriate, include an invitation for the student to bring an advocate or support person:

- "If anyone will be joining you, please provide us with their email so we can send them the details of the meeting."

It is also important at the outset of the meeting to clarify how the discussion will be documented:

- "Could you take notes while we chat so you can send me a follow up email after the meeting?" or "Would it make sense if I took notes during the meeting?"

End the Informal Discussion Fairly. At the end of an informal discussion, everyone should be on the same page about whether the issue has been resolved as a result of the discussion or if it will be forthcoming. If not, next steps need to be outlined, including whether there will be further opportunity for informal discussion or if the matter will be redirected into a formal process. Summarize and then explain how the decision-making process will unfold:[68]

- "Before we conclude and I give you my answer on [THE ISSUE], I just want to double check that we haven't missed anything. We talked about [SUMMARIZE RELEVANT DETAILS], and you provided me with information about [RELEVANT VIEWPOINT]. Is there anything that you would like to add?"

- "As we talked about earlier, I didn't think that I'd have an answer for you today, and that is still the case. I am going to review [POLICY] and the other documents you provided as well as everything we talked about today, and then give you my decision and reasons by email by the end of next week. If you don't agree with my decision, there is an appeal process which I will outline with my decision. Do you have any questions at this point about the process?"

If the issue has been resolved, there is an opportunity to potentially manage future conflict by asking for input (and coming to a joint agreement) on how to deal with future issues:

- "This was a helpful discussion. I'd like us to have more opportunities like this to [discuss whatever it is you are hoping to discuss]. Do you have any suggestions or thoughts for how best to do that?"

TIP SHEET: PITFALLS AND BETTER PRACTICES FOR INFORMAL MEETINGS

> *Given the risks and rewards of having informal discussions to resolve conflict in grad school, here are a few best practices for avoiding five common pitfalls of informal meetings. These tips came from a faculty workshop I ran in collaboration with the campus ombuds office.[69]*

1.	**AMBUSH.** Inviting someone to attend a meeting without giving them any information about what will be discussed. An informal meeting is a chance for all directly involved to talk about an issue or concern, to clarify possible misunderstandings, and to get/share enough information to determine what the next steps should be.
✓	Describe the purpose of the meeting briefly, specifically, and accurately (or provide an agenda), so that the person you are meeting with can prepare.
2.	**UNINVITED GUESTS.** Arriving to find a room full of people when the meeting had been arranged with only one person. Informality is not a license to invite anyone you want to a meeting without checking with the other invitee(s).
✓	If it is appropriate or necessary to include others in an informal discussion, provide that information (who and why) to the original invitee. Sometimes there is a policy or guideline that speaks to who should be at a meeting – provide a link/reference if applicable.
3.	**FAIT ACCOMPLI.** Having a meeting with someone who seems to have already made up their mind before you walk in the door. An informal meeting is supposed to be a preliminary stage in a process that may (or may not) result in a final decision, with all participants having minds open to new information and other perspectives.
✓	Keep an open mind during informal discussions, even if you have "seen this a hundred times."
4.	**POWER PLAYS.** Being in a meeting where one person dominates the conversation, and feeling like you weren't given the chance to participate as you would have liked. Graduate students told us they don't feel like they are (nor are they seen as) powerful in most contexts. Formal processes give both "sides" the opportunity to present their views, so should informal processes.
✓	At an informal meeting, everyone should have an opportunity to speak and share their perspective on the issues being discussed. They should also have an opportunity to respond to any information presented by others before any final decisions are made.
5.	**EVERYBODY KNOWS.** Feeling that what you assumed was a private discussion is widely known. There may or may not be a need to share information about an issue that is being dealt with informally beyond the individuals involved; however, informality is not permission to gossip.
✓	Be discreet. Is there a "need" to share the fact that an informal meeting has been scheduled to discuss a concern? Is there a way to prepare for the meeting without "naming names" or revealing identifying details about who is involved?

If It's Not My Conflict, How Can I Help?

As compassionate people, we may instinctively move into "problem-solving" mode as someone describes their problem to us. This is particularly true if we (with our outsider perspective on the conflict) can see an easy resolution to the problem. We want to jump in and resolve the conflict for the other person. I'm recalling faculty who told me things like:

- "I have tried everything to resolve the student's concern!"
- "I just don't know how to help this particular student."

Telling someone how to solve their problem ("You should just do X") may seem like the quickest way to get that person out of your office/that problem off your desk. Going one step further and intervening to solve a conflict on behalf of another person takes more time and effort on your part. However, since you are now the point person for problem-solving, you may be able to control how quickly and efficiently the problem is resolved ("Let me do X for you").

In most cases, I recommend an alternative approach to keep the individual who has shared their problem with you at the center of the problem-solving. The key question is, How can you try to resolve the conflict with (rather than for) the other person? By allowing the other person to determine what they want to do (or not do) to resolve an issue, you are respecting their individual autonomy and experiences, and their role and responsibilities in a particular situation as well as your own.

When people come to their own solutions or can participate deeply in decision-making processes, they can have a profound sense of "buy-in," even if outcomes are not entirely in one's favor.[1] Coming to their own resolution to a conflict (one that meets their needs/circumstances) is empowering, and can help them develop skills for resolving the next problem.

Whose problem is it? | Is this something I need to *report* or which requires my *intervention* to help the student resolve?

Is this something the student can/should deal with on their own with guidance and support?

Figure 5. Grad CRC slide from "Faculty Conflict Coaching" workshop, 2019

WHAT YOU CAN DO

! If someone comes to you for advice, instead of thinking, *"How can I resolve this person's conflict?,"* ask yourself, *"How can we have the best possible interaction?"*

! I found it helpful to remember that (most) grad students are adults. As adults they can make their own decisions (and mistakes) and understand the consequences of action and inaction. In our coaching conversations, unless we felt that there were safety concerns (for the individual we were talking to or others), we had no reason to intervene or report the conflict. In our work, we respected and prioritized the student's problem-solving autonomy:

- "Thank you for sharing with me [your conflict]. It sounds stressful. Have you thought about what you might like to happen?"
- "How do you think I can support you to try and resolve this conflict?"

MINI-CASE STUDY: CAVALIER COMMITTEE COLLEAGUE

Imagine that a student has come to you for help about a committee member. As you read the following, think about how your approach might change depending on how closely you work and how friendly you are with the faculty committee member in question.

Kris is one of the five PhD students I supervise. Kris came to me for help about one of their committee members, Dr. Q. At the last full committee meeting, Dr. Q asked Kris tough questions and seemed pleased when Kris struggled to respond. I know from talking to Dr. T (Kris's third committee member) that students have complained about Dr. Q's feedback and lack of response to students' questions. Kris seems extremely frustrated and upset about what happened at the committee meeting, and believes Dr. Q's questions were proof that they hadn't read the latest draft and that they are "out to get" Kris.

Q. If you were Kris's supervisor, how could you respond to their concern while keeping them at the center of the problem-solving?

Listen to Words and Clarify Meaning

Consider the following example where the words chosen by the student to describe the concern may be significant: *"I am afraid to talk to my supervisor/instructor."*

As university staff members providing advice/conflict coaching to students, we had a responsibility under the Grad CRC's terms of reference, to maintain confidentiality except if there were concerns about risk of harm to self (the person we were talking to) or to others during a conversation.

Here are some examples of the questions we might have asked to clarify the words used, and what actions (if any) the person had already taken to address their concern:

- "You used the word *afraid* which is very concerning. I need to check – do you feel that you are at risk of harm right now or that you are unsafe in any way?"
- "You mentioned you are *afraid to talk to your supervisor* – can you give me some more information about that?"

- "I'd like to make sure I have all the information you want me to know about your concerns, so I know how best to proceed/what supports to connect you with. What is making you *afraid to talk to your supervisor?*"

If *afraid = interacting with my supervisor makes me afraid for my safety*, I would have let the person know I was stopping the conversation in order to connect them immediately with university supports. If *afraid = talking to my supervisor makes me nervous/uncomfortable*, we could have continued our conversation and explored how they might approach the issue from a conflict management perspective.

In my experience, it was more often the latter, and showing genuine concern and seeking clarification was appreciated and understood in the context of our conversation.

WHAT YOU CAN DO

! In our conflict coaching we encouraged individuals to consider:

Priorities

- "What issue is most pressing/important for you?"
- "What are pros/cons of pursuing one issue first/later?"
- "Can X issue wait until after Y is resolved?"

Information and Resources

- "What information do you need to bring this forward under policy A or to advocate to change policy B?"
- "What kinds of support do you think might help? I know a number of university supports that other students have told me they have accessed."

! In the past I've used and recommended the phrase "Help me understand what you mean by X" as an open-ended way to gain information. I recently read a description of an employment investigation,[2] where apparently the investigator repeatedly used the phrases "I am just trying to understand" and "help me understand," and as a result, the interviewees felt that they were being told that they were not clear or understandable, which was upsetting. Being mindful about power and perception, and the objective of clarity and gaining information, I would now recommend using these types of questions judiciously. "Tell me more about X" is another question to include in the mix.

! Emails don't always convey the writer's intentions or desired tone. For more emailing tips, see page 72.

Q1. How often do you assume meaning versus clarifying meaning in emails?

Q2. What are some of the challenges of clarifying words/ meaning over email?

MINI-CASE STUDY: WHAT DO YOU MEAN?

Using the strategies outlined above, how might you respond and what questions might you ask if someone said to you:

"A member of my group is harassing me."

"My supervisor is a bully."

"I can't take the abuse from my student anymore."

Expect Emotions and Be Trauma-Informed

If you have ever been caught off guard by unexpected behaviors or escalating situations and were unsure about whether what you were experiencing was within the realm of acceptable or needed to be flagged for someone, somewhere, at the university, you are not alone. Human interactions produce a range of human reactions, even conversations about what might seem to be mundane academic issues.

Based on observations and comments made by the individuals we talked to between 2016 and 2020, we found that over 50 percent of the time the student we were speaking with seemed upset, somewhat upset, or was upset at times during the conversation, and faculty and staff were upset about 25 percent of the time. Interestingly, conversations involving supervisory issues were more emotionally intense than the average: 68 percent of the time people were upset, upset "at times," or "somewhat" upset during the conversation.

This data isn't necessarily the full picture of how many people were impacted emotionally by the situation that brought them to our office – some people could have been very upset, yet did not reveal that to us either through actions or words. We found that expressions of what appeared to be anger, frustration, or tears were quite normal, but for our data, we didn't distinguish or label particular emotions.

Even for trained counselors, it can be complex to determine which emotions someone is feeling unless they expressly say, "I am angry/sad/frustrated."

More than one faculty member admitted to me that they felt ill-equipped to respond to the intense emotional reactions of some of their grad students. Others found it challenging to determine the best way to respond when there was no emotional reaction. A faculty attendee at a supervision workshop commented: "My grad student doesn't seem to appreciate the seriousness of the situation." Furthermore, the reality is that there may not be a university policy or guideline that applies to a particular situation, or there may be many! A faculty member might be expected to seek information from a variety of sources:

- human resources (e.g., workplace conduct, civility guidelines, or harassment policies)
- community safety office or campus security/police (e.g., cyberbullying, stalking)
- support team for high-risk students or university legal counsel (e.g., unusual, challenging, or distressing behavior)
- graduate school or departmental (supervision) guidelines

Given the difficulty of predicting if or when people will become upset by a comment or have a deep, perhaps unanticipated, emotional reaction to a certain topic of discussion, it can be helpful to infuse interactions with trauma-informed principles, discussed earlier at page 61, including:

- Be present and in the moment with the individual who is sharing their story with you.

- Listen with respect for their perspective and interpretation of a situation. They should remain at the center of the conversation.

- Don't over promise – what can or can't you do in your role; what do or don't you know; and if you don't know, how can the student get that information.

- Maintain boundaries.

Peer advisor Rebecca (MEd Ontario Institute Studies in Education) noted that after a discussion with a visibly upset student these types of conversations can "challenge the limitations of your role and professionalism." She suggested to the team that they prepare in advance their own individual response to a student's "expression of emotions so you're not caught off guard." The prepared response of one peer advisor to any student who begins to cry was to offer to get the individual a glass of water. This approach gave both the student and the peer advisor a moment to collect their thoughts before the peer advisor returned to the room with water and tissues. There was a wide range of comfort levels on the team to deal with various emotions, and the peer advisors were encouraged to define their own approaches within the limits of our mandate and their own boundaries.

Like our peer advisors, I encourage you to trust your instincts and individual gut reactions. Do you need to pause a conversation and reschedule to ensure safety, bravery (see page **15**), or self-care? Is there a requirement to report? Do you need to debrief with others if the conversation has been emotional? A commitment to protect personal information doesn't mean you can't practice self-care and share your own feelings with a trusted friend, family member, or colleague. (For example, "I just had a conversation that was very upsetting ... I can't share details, but I really need to vent a bit.") Reflecting on the importance of debriefing after conflict coaching conversations, peer advisor Mariam (SJD Law) noted, "Debriefing sometimes validates my thought process or challenges me to think about a situation differently."

WHAT YOU CAN DO

! Watch a short video about what it means to listen and support people experiencing crisis or conflict from Libby Mahaffy at MIT. *SPOILER!* Focus on the person, not the hurricane: "A Person with a Conflict Is Like a Hurricane."[3]

! Find out who you contact with questions about student crisis situations. If you prefer not to provide your name or other identifying details about a student or situation, perhaps because the situation is still new or uncertain, ask the service if an anonymous consultation is possible. I note that at our institution many student-facing offices were open to supporting faculty on an informal and/or anonymous basis. Under our mandate, if the peer advisors had any concerns about safety (their own, the student's, or others') or discomfort about how an interaction with a student had gone, they had to discuss their concerns to me as their manager so we could detemine the best options for helping this student and supporting the peer advisor.

! Do a self-assessment. *In what ways might you be (or have become) part of the conflict?*

! An awareness of the impact of our conscious and unconscious behaviors is important, including words and actions that might be unintended microaggressions (i.e., "Everyday comments or actions that subtly express a stereotype of, or prejudice towards, a marginalized group. Even if the intention was not to cause harm, microaggressions have a huge impact an individual's well-being").[4]

MINI-CASE STUDY: MY PHD NIGHTMARES MAKE ME CRY

A student has just confided in you about their experience with a prior supervisor:

"I still have nightmares about my first two years as a doctoral student. I've got a new supervisor now, but I worked for and was supervised by a professor who had extremely abusive tendencies. The supervisor's behavior was unpredictable and hurtful. It became clear that I was not the only student being mistreated which makes me really upset. Sometimes when I think about how I was treated I start to cry."

Q. *How do you respond to tears?*

Make Effective Referrals

Some campuses have a "many or any doors" approach to student support. Such intentional overlap of resources can enhance conflict management approaches provided that the role and purpose of the services are understood and that any nuances between options can be articulated to students as referrals are made.

Graduate students who are trying to access services may, as one of the peer advisors noted, be asking themselves, "Does my issue fit with this service?," and if it is not immediately clear, this may be a barrier to students seeking help. Allowing graduate students to unexpectedly open a door to support by way of a conversation with a faculty member can be hugely beneficial; especially, given that we found grad students tended to wait until academic and personal situations were quite complex before actively and specifically reaching out for help. We made referrals in almost two-thirds of our conversations.

Faculty told me that referrals helped them feel less alone in dealing with difficult situations and gave them confidence to set firmer boundaries and engage with students, knowing that they could reach out to other support services if their own efforts at resolving a conflict were unsuccessful. Our top referrals (in order of frequency) were to:

1. Graduate school (vice-deans, policies, awards/financial aid)
2. Graduate students' union/Student advocates
3. Department/Supervisors
4. On-campus resources (library, accessibility/disability services, website, career supports, housing supports, writing center, etc.)

5. Off-campus resources (student help phone line)
6. Health and wellness services (workshops, counseling)
7. International student services
8. Campus police/Community safety office/High-risk student support/Human Resources
9. University ombudsman
10. Equity and diversity offices[5] (accessibility, anti-racism and cultural diversity, family care, Indigenous initiatives, sexual and gender diversity)

While there are a few strategies we used to help our referrals to "land" as intended, making referrals was not always easy. Faculty were sometimes concerned that in providing a referral they might come across as judgmental or cause offense by making a referral to certain supports; for example, to campus counseling services, the writing center, or financial advising. An additional consideration is that a referral from a supervisor to their student may be heard not as an option but as a demand, given the power differential. An important note is that referrals to certain supports – such as campus security/campus police – may not be viewed as a viable option to a Black or Indigenous student.[6]

Here are four strategies we used in making referrals:

1. Is the person open to receiving a referral?

We might ask: "Would it be helpful if I gave you some options for where you might get more information about X on campus?" Or "Would you like me to give you some referrals?" Try to recall what the student said that made you think about making a referral (if you can't think of why you thought to make a referral, perhaps you shouldn't be making one).

2. Can we frame the referral as simply one possible option for consideration?

For example, we might offer what I called a "buffet" of options:

- "Here is information about a resource that I understand other grad students have found useful."
- "Here are a few resources for you to consider – if you want more information about any of them you can connect with the services directly – I'll send you links to all of them."

- "Are you familiar with A resource?" "Have you read B policy?" "Are you aware that the university has C support for grads?"

3. *How do we provide enough details about the role of the service or person we are recommending and about their normal processes for engaging with members of the graduate community, without promising specific outcomes?*

We knew (students told us!) that in some cases, the student may have already dealt with that particular service and been disappointed, or been told by another student, "That service isn't great if you are a grad."

4. *Time permitting, can we generate referral options with the student?*

Participating in problem-solving processes can create more durable solutions:

- "Sometimes taking a bit of time to review what your options are for support on campus can be helpful. Let's try and think about this from a number of different angles and brainstorm some supports you might be interested in approaching for more information."

No matter how you make a referral, it should be clear that it is the other person's choice whether or not to connect with the service or the support you are referring them to. For example, if the person says "No, I haven't gone there yet," or "No, I'm not interested in going there," respect that this is their decision, while leaving the door open for later reconsideration.[7] Remember this: if you are talking to the person subsequently – there was no requirement that they do what you offered to them as an option. An open-ended follow up question like, "How have things been going since we last talked?" reinforces this more than a closed-ended question like, "Did you go to counselling services like we talked about?" As noted in the U of T online (open access) mental health training module, "In following up, it's important to continue to respect their privacy, particularly regarding personal health information ... Although they may volunteer to share additional information, they shouldn't feel expected to."[8]

As a final point, referrals can be a two-way street – not only are they an opportunity to connect individuals with appropriate supports but also they provide you with an opportunity to connect with those supports yourself in order to:

- clarify where, how, or when to make a referral
- flag any surprising trends or issues (while always being mindful to not disclose personal information or identifying details if you don't t have permission to do so)

> **WHAT YOU CAN DO**
>
> ! It's possible to forget specific information that is shared during a stressful conversation, even as you recall how you felt at the time. As Maya Angelou observed, people may forget what you said or did, but not "how you made them feel."[9]
>
> ! Suggest students write down the names of the offices you mention, so they can find them easily with a Google search after the conversation. Or after having a conversation where you made a referral, email the student with links.
>
> ! Brainstorm with colleagues other phrases that have worked (or not!) for you when making referrals.
>
> ! Look for opportunities for collaboration. Making effective referrals is a problem that all faculty members and departments face. Try to find ways to involve graduate students in environmental scans to determine relevant resources (i.e., share the load and avoid duplication of efforts).
>
> Q1. Is there an opportunity to talk to these support services about how, when, and why you are making referrals?
>
> Q2. Do they have suggestions for making more effective referrals to graduate students?
>
> Q3. Do the graduate students in your department have thoughts on how faculty might make referrals (that will be more likely to be heard by students)?

QUIZ: WHERE DO I REFER THIS GRAD?

I used a version of this quiz to test the peer advisors about their knowledge of campus resources. Edit to reflect the supports available to grads on your campus and challenges that you know your students face.

Where would you refer these students?	
1. A PhD student who is concerned about completing their degree because of changes in family circumstances.	
2. A PhD student who is working closely with another graduate student on a project or paper and wants to understand the rights and responsibilities regarding intellectual property/authorship.	
3. A master's student who is dealing with a difficult roommate and thinking about moving out and concerned about breaking lease.	
4. A PhD student who is worried about the lack of communication and meetings they have with their thesis supervisor. They are wondering if is this normal.	
5. A master's student who is concerned about time management/completing coursework on time.	
6. A PhD student who wants help writing their thesis – they aren't feeling very productive working alone in their apartment.	
7. A master's student who is in a difficult financial situation because their basement apartment flooded last weekend during a storm.	
8. A graduate student who is involved in an appeal and wants someone to join them at an upcoming meeting at the graduate school.	
9. A PhD student who is unhappy because "grad students don't have the same opportunities to connect and have fun" as undergraduate students.	
10. An international master's student who feels homesick and alone in the city.	
11. A graduate student who had a debate with a colleague about personal pronouns and is now concerned that they inadvertently caused offense.	

12. A PhD student who wants to publish but is struggling to communicate with editors/reviewers and to understand the peer review process.	
13. A master's student who disagrees with their instructor about a final grade and thinks the appeal process was not done properly.	
14. A graduate student who received extensions for their chronic migraines at their previous university, but their current supervisor is unsympathetic to proposals for extended timelines.	
15. A PhD student who wants career advice because they are feeling anxious about graduating and finding a job.	
16. A master's student who says their supervisor is unresponsive to emails and wasn't at their office during regular office hours last week.	
17. A graduate student whose grandfather passed away, and they were not able to attend the funeral because of their TA responsibilities and because of the amount of time it would take to return home. They mention missing their local "community of worship" in difficult times.	
18. A master's student who doesn't want to work in a group anymore because one of the group members asked them out and has been a "stalker" on social media.	

What Are the Grad Conflict Hotspots?

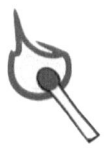

In conflict coaching sessions, the peer advisors mentioned being surprised to hear "eerily similar stories (often of power imbalances or miscommunications with supervisors or labmates) again and again" across various disciplines and departments (Jessica, PhD Drama, Theatre, and Performance Studies). I noted that the issues faculty and staff raised were often simply the "other side" of the student stories. Based on four and a half years of conversations, here are the Top Ten graduate hotspots:

#1 Supervision. Interpersonal relationships; communication and feedback (quality, quantity, tone, timeliness, progress); unexpected or unacceptable behavior or comments; roles/responsibilities (guidance, support and objectivity); finding a supervisor/forming committees; changing supervisors/committee members; setting up meetings

#2 Grad School Challenges (Miscellaneous). Whether to stay in grad school or leave; balancing competing priorities and interests (work/studies); research focus; coping with new challenges/workload/grad school in general (frustration, isolation; motivation/loss of interest); making friends and finding community

#3 Escalation & Appeals. Needing information/questions about university and department/faculty/program level policies and processes (grade appeals, conduct, plagiarism, comprehensive exams, defenses; extensions, late submission, leaves of absence, termination/withdrawal); how/when to escalate concerns

#4 Interpersonal (Not Supervisory). Relationships between grad students or between graduate students and their instructors, RAs, TAs, PIs, colleagues, post-docs, and administrators; group work; unexpected or unacceptable behaviors/comments

#5 Research & Thesis. Expectations (quality, quantity, scope); research (focus, changing topics, continuity); thesis writing process (stress, revisions, comments); intellectual property; publication (authorship, rejection)

#6 Academic Progress. Time to completion (delays, wanting to defend/graduate, timing of graduation); time management; extensions; comprehensive exams

#7 Family & Personal. Balancing responsibilities (personal, family, academic); roommate/housing; relationships with family and partners; time off for personal reasons (grief; pregnancy; return to home country; divorce); returning to studies; available supports

#8 Health & Wellness/Accessibility. Mental and physical health and well-being; feelings about grad school/conflict situation (anxious, overwhelmed, lack of confidence, scared, sad); tired or lack of sleep; medical issues; friends with concerning behavior; medical issues

#9 Laboratories. Interactions in lab (difficult interactions; lab dynamics, personalities, unexpected or unacceptable behavior, bullying, hostility); expectations; inappropriate relationships; setting boundaries; comments; toxic environment

#10 Career & Work. Workplace conflicts on and off campus (teaching, in role as TA/RA, off campus); feelings about work (overworked, underpaid); future and jobs after graduation (is PhD worth it? Postdocs? Long-term and short-term plans? Academic/non-academic options; résumé, references); academic placements (internship, practicums)

WHAT YOU CAN DO

! Not everyone will experience the conflicts from the Top Ten list in the same way or with the same intensity.

Q1. Do these hotspots and examples sound familiar?

Q2. Are there any others that would be on your list?

CONFLICT #1 – Supervision

Year over year, the number one topic raised in conversations with our office was supervision – supervision-related issues were raised in over one third of our conversations. This is not surprising given supervision's role as a graduate keystone for PhD and research master's students, and because student/supervisor conflicts are some of the most challenging to resolve in universities.[1] One peer advisor told me that in speaking with friends at other institutions, he realized that many of the conflicts and issues that he talked about with grad students in the peer advisor role were "ubiquitous." In his view, "The prevailing institutional culture continues to overwhelm students, especially when these individuals are at the beginning of their careers and lack the confidence and knowledge to navigate the supervisor-student relationship" (Nelson, MSc Institute for Medical Science).

We observed the following themes related to supervisory conflict:

- *Emotions run high*: 68 percent of supervisory conversations involved someone who was visibly upset, somewhat upset, or upset at times – higher than the average (52 percent) across all conversations.
- *Spring and summer are hot*: March, April, and July were the busiest months for conversations about supervisory issues.[2]
- *Conversations are long and complex*: Supervision conversations tended to be longer than the average – most taking more than thirty minutes with around one third of conversations extending over one hour.

A supervisory conflict was rarely a single or straightforward interpersonal "we just aren't getting along" issue. More often than not, we were presented with a ball of conflict string where there were several possible ends to pull out

 of the tangle. For example, although the heart of the issue might have been the supervisory relationship, individuals might have also been worried about making progress and meeting timelines (#6 Academic Progress), which might have also been tied to the impact of financial or personal circumstances (#7 Family & Personal). They also expressed concern about whether research priorities were aligned (#5 Research & Thesis) and wanted to talk about whether switching supervisors/committee members (#3 Escalation & Appeals) or dropping out of grad school might be the best option for them.

- "My supervisor won't let me defend. My timeline for completion was outlined months ago and my committee is supportive of me moving to the defense stage."
- "My first PhD supervisor died. My new supervisor is terrible and refuses to support any lines of research inquiry that aren't completely in line with their work."
- "I am co-supervised, but it looks like both of my supervisors will not be getting the funding they expected for the upcoming year. I'm really worried – I can't change supervisors now – I'm only a year away from defending!"
- "How do I tell my advisor (for my master's) that I'm looking for a different supervisor for my PhD?"

Feedback was also one of the common threads: getting too much or too little feedback about research or writing from supervisors or committee members, or where there were concerns about inaccuracies or the timeliness or tone of feedback. Other common and often related sources of supervisory conflict were poor communication and unclear or unmet supervisory expectations around roles and responsibilities (i.e., who does what):

- "My supervisor is a micromanager and very difficult to talk to. Are there campus supports to help me finish writing my thesis and just move on?"
- "I supervise a PhD student who feels some committee members are difficult to talk to and have unreasonable expectations. I know the student doesn't want me to intervene, but I want to figure out what I might be able to do to help this incredible student."

We heard from both faculty and students about rude, unacceptable, or unwelcome behavior during supervisory interactions, and a few individuals wanted to talk about how to change supervisors, to move students to other supervisors, or to replace committee members.

- "One of my committee members is poisoning the whole committee with their feedback and causing me extreme stress. Is there anything I can do as a student to get this person to stop or get them off my committee?"
- "I'm being bullied by my supervisor. The workload is overwhelming, yet all they do is constantly minimize my efforts."
- "I am talking with a female student in our department who is having difficulty communicating with her male supervisor. I think there are sexist undertones to the situation. What are my responsibilities as a faculty member if I believe her supervisor is the one at fault?"

As the examples above illustrate, supervisory issues were multidimensional with potential for ripple effects outside of the confines of the supervisory relationship when issues escalated. The individuals (both the grad and the supervisor) were impacted, with the most significant potential impact of an unresolved conflict landing on students, but also on departments and the wider organizational culture.

The importance of the supervisory relationship to the academic and post-graduation success of a graduate student means that effective management of conflict within the supervisory relationship is crucial. Finding the right academic "match" between a supervisor and a student is an important component of conflict prevention.[3] Many universities have developed guidelines, best practices, or regulations for graduate supervision (for students and/or for supervisors), including general recommendations for how to select a supervisor and for informal problem solving.

WHAT YOU CAN DO

! For an amusing exploration of common supervisory concerns, read *57 Ways to Screw Up in Grad School*,[4] written by Canadian professors Kevin Haggerty and Aaron Doyle. Enjoy the following ironically titled chapters:

- Screw-up #13: Do Not Clarify Your Supervisor's [or Your Own] Expectations
- Screw-up #14: Avoid Your Supervisor and Committee
- Screw-up #15: Stay in a Bad Relationship

Looking beyond Positive Graduate Survey Results

Although institutions will frame survey results in the most positive light when sharing data with the university community (e.g., "More than 91 percent of grad students are satisfied with their supervision!," see page 5), from a conflict management perspective, the negative spaces are much more interesting – each one is a student and a conflict prevention opportunity.[5]

Consider, for example, these possible interpretations of three results from a graduate-specific survey (Grad SERU) at the University of Toronto (U of T). The results suggest that advisors can actively manage or prevent conflict by:

- Having discussions regularly about what "help" the student is looking for and what "help" they (as supervisors) can provide at each stage in the graduate journey.

    SURVEY RESULTS: 11 percent of survey respondents disagreed or strongly disagreed with the statement, "My advisor is able to effectively help me."

- Being more proactive about initiating communication with students or pre-arranging regular check-ins, including different (student-centered) ways of communicating.

    SURVEY RESULT: 22 percent disagreed or strongly disagreed with the statement, "Students and faculty have open lines of communication."

- Critically examining where, when, and how they are interacting with students, and incorporating trauma-informed approaches.

    SURVEY RESULT: 13 percent of doctoral students and 9 percent of research master's students found "interactions with my supervisor" either "very stressful" or "extremely stressful."[6]

Although the Grad SERU survey doesn't publish comparative university data, these questions reflect common supervisory concerns (i.e., expectations, communication, and power – discussed further in the next chapter), so I would expect to see similar percentages across other research-intensive universities and similar room for improvement.

WHAT YOU CAN DO

! According to the U of T Grad SERU results, 19 percent of doctoral students and 12 percent of research master's students identified "inadequate advising" as a "large" or "very large" barrier to their academic progress.

Q1. How might you interpret these results if they were the same (and they probably are similar!) at your institution?

Q2. What opportunities are there to be proactive about this potential source of conflict?

Supervisors and Grad Students Flag Similar Sources of Conflict

A 2007 Canadian study examined how international graduate students and their supervisors identified sources of conflict in their academic relationship.[7] This study provides an excellent list of where to start in terms of preventing and managing conflict in the supervisory relationship. While various sources of conflict are dynamic and may shift over the course of a supervisory relationship, five points of overlap (agreement!) stand out between the sources of conflict that were identified by students and those identified by faculty:

- supervisor doesn't have enough time
- supervisor/student have different expectations about responsibilities
- supervisor/student have different values regarding important graduate skills
- supervisor/student demonstrates a lack of openness
- supervisor/student feel they have unclear conversations[8]

During coaching conversations and workshops, the following five common sources of conflict came up consistently:

- *No time to disagree*: A supervisor emailed their PhD student to ask them to review and summarize a large data set. The student sees this task as largely unrelated to their research, and it will take away from the time that the student has to write their thesis. The supervisor is a busy research "superstar" who is difficult to book time to speak to, and even more difficult to say "no" to.

- *Closed for discussion*: A PhD student had multiple academic setbacks that they attribute to their supervisor's unrealistic expectations about the research. When they tried to address their concerns directly, their supervisor made several "insensitive remarks" and shut down the conversation. The student is upset and wants to "report" their supervisor.

- *Of course, I'm responsible!*: A first year PhD student is wondering how to set up a committee and create a timeline to graduate in less than five years. They feel anxious and overwhelmed because they want to get everything finalized (and perfect!) before talking to their supervisor who seems like "someone who doesn't tolerate mistakes."

- *Scarce skills*: A PhD student is struggling to prepare for an upcoming advisory committee meeting. At their last meeting, to the student's surprise, their supervisor told the committee that the student's lack of progress was likely due to "underdeveloped research skills." The student is very uncomfortable about seeing their supervisor again and facing an unsupportive committee.

- *Fuzzy feedback*: An upper year PhD student is upset about the unclear conversation they had with their supervisor about the latest draft of their thesis. The student disagreed with the supervisor's feedback, but didn't want to risk the relationship (or the reference letter!) by speaking up.

In resolving conflict, it is important to think about the other person's perspective and interests in addition to our own and to try to identify where there might be common concerns or goals. Acknowledging that graduate students might share similar concerns or identify similar challenges to your own is a great way to start conversations and to identify where conflict may be lurking just beneath the surface.

WHAT YOU CAN DO

! Consider talking through the five examples of conflict sources outlined above at a faculty meeting or as part of in-service training. Brainstorm possible solutions. Share within your department the examples and any best practices for conflict resolution that emerge.

! On a regular basis, ask open-ended questions that highlight these common conflict sources as a way to manage expectations. For example:

- *Time*: "How can we make the most of our next meeting?"
- *Responsibilities*: "We are both responsible for keeping the research on track – what does your timeline look like for the next six months?"
- *Skills*: "Up to now, we've focused on the data – what do you see as some of the challenges moving into the writing phase?
- *Openness*: "I'd like to hear your perspective on A, B, and C."
- *Clarity*: "Please send me a follow up email – this will help to make sure we are on the same page."

Power, Pressure, and Personalities

Supervisory conflict is challenging to resolve because it involves a dynamic combination of power, pressure, and personalities (or supervisory styles).

Power

Grad students rely on their supervisor for academic advancement, connections within the department, contacts in industry, and references. The supervisor is (seen as) all powerful. Even graduate students with excellent professional and academic communication skills can become overwhelmed by what one of the peer advisors described as "the power dynamics embedded in supervisory relationships and the institutional layers of the University" (Manaal, PhD Social Work).

Whether or not you feel powerful as a supervisor (often faculty members shared with me that their actual power to make decisions or act independently was quite limited, either within the department or within the institutional hierarchy), perception of power is an important consideration. When we asked grad students in workshops about how powerful they felt within the university, they would locate themselves at the bottom of the power pyramid – just above undergraduate students – and often tied with postdocs.

Pressure

Graduate research is difficult work in a high-pressure environment. There is often no "down time" in grad school. Grad students told us that they are either working all the time or feel that they should be. A combination of self-imposed pressure with pressure from the institution, peers, family, and you (whether intentional or not!), results in an environment where grad students may not feel comfortable raising issues with faculty or department administrators because of fear of being judged or viewed as "less than."

> **WHAT YOU CAN DO**
>
> ! If a student seems overwhelmed dealing with a conflict on top of the many moving parts of grad school, try an approach used by one of the peer advisors. Tony (MA Public Health) would ask a student to imagine that all their graduate concerns were rocks that they were carrying in a backpack. He then asked them which one of those rocks they wanted to take out first to make their backpack a little bit lighter. He encouraged the student to focus on the heaviest issue for them in the moment, so that they could prioritize what to talk about with him (rather than be weighed down by many possible "what-ifs …?"). Empowering students to take out even a tiny rock from their "issue backpack" can start to make the graduate load feel lighter and more manageable in the present.
>
> ! If your graduate students always answer "I'm fine," when you ask, "How are you doing?" consider asking alternative questions:

- "How are you treating yourself?"[9]
- "We are all feeling under a lot of pressure these days (I know I am) – what is most pressing for you at the moment?"
- "What about your research is hardest when you can't come to campus?"[10]
- "If you could show me how you are feeling about grad school today with your hand – with a full high five being great, and one finger being not so great – how many fingers would you hold up right now?"

Q1. When you were a grad student, did your supervisor do anything that helped you to deal with the pressure?

Q2. If not, is there anything they could have done?

MINI-CASE STUDY: NOW WHO'S IN CHARGE?

"I feel way more pressure than I did as an undergraduate student. As an undergrad, I reported to a senior graduate student in the lab who planned out my research program and managed most of my schedule. Now I'm 'in charge' of the undergrads and I feel overwhelmed by my many responsibilities. I'm doubting whether I'm cut out for grad school, and I'm starting to dread going into the lab."

Q. What types of support might the student be looking for? What do you think their interests might be?

MINI-CASE STUDY: PUBLISH OR PERISH

"When I compare how many publications I have to other grad students in my department, I feel like I'm falling way behind. I want to write, but there is too much pressure! My supervisor keeps emailing and asking me how I'm doing, and I don't want them to find out I'm not doing anything."

Q. What are two to three questions you could ask this student?

Personalities and Supervisory Style

People have unique backgrounds, experiences, identities, and distinctive personalities all of which bring richness and complexity to academic relationships.

When we talked to grad students in workshops about why they selected their supervisor, many times they mentioned being impressed with someone's academic research and reputation (i.e., what they do), rather than basing their choice on having worked with the individual before and liking their academic approach (i.e., how they do what they do). The how is really about "personality" (i.e., ways of thinking, feeling, and behaving),[11] and more specific to graduate studies, it will include supervisory approach or style of supervision. While engaging in a discussion about your personality traits and those of your student might be enlightening, it could also be quite uncomfortable – striking us at the core of "who we are."

In our workshops, we encouraged faculty to locate their own supervisory style on the model of doctoral supervision that was developed by Terry Gatfield. Gatfield identifies four styles (pastoral, contractual, laissez-faire, and directional) located along two axes: high/low support and high/low self-direction.[12] Gatfield provides a good jumping off point for discussion about the ways in which supervision styles may differ from, or align with, personality styles. We recommend using Gatfield's matrix as a way to frame discussions with students around their expectations for support, and with your expectations for self-direction, as they move through their graduate degree.

While in the early days you may feel that students simply need to get to know you (and you them!), in order to set expectations clearly, however, as a way to prevent some types of conflict, don't leave your graduate students guessing about your style of supervision.

> **WHAT YOU CAN DO**
>
> ! Your personality isn't set in stone, and neither is your supervisory style. Both can evolve. For more about personality and various supervisory styles, read "What Determines Supervision Style?" (Lund University in Sweden)[13] and watch "How Personality Traits Change Over Time" (American Psychological Association).[14]

! Supervision priorities (e.g., punctuality, clarity, ownership, career development) may change over the course of a graduate relationship – for a graphic representation of this, see page 26 of the "To Lead the Way," a guide based on interviews with supervisors and PhD students in six faculties at the University of Copenhagen.[15]

! Be amused by graduate student personalities such as "cocky/bombastic," "lifelong learner," and "here for Mom/Dad" identified in this Inside Higher Ed blog post: "Grad School Personalities."[16]

Q1. What are some of your personality traits that might play into a supervisory relationship?

Q2. Where might you position yourself in the Gatfield supervisory model?

MINI-CASE STUDY: OVERSUPERVISION

"I feel like my supervisor is always looking over my shoulder and interrupting me with questions and comments! The work is at a crucial point and I can't concentrate. I'm a grad student, so why am I being treated like a child?!"

Q. Is this personality or a supervisory approach (or both) and why?

MINI-CASE STUDY: AMAZING (EXTROVERT) OPPORTUNITY

"My supervisor wants me to present a paper at an industry conference next year – they told me that they know 'everyone' who will be attending and that it will be 'an amazing opportunity to network and to get to know the key people in our field.' Trouble is, I find meeting new people really stressful– actually I'm terrible at small talk and I don't think that I'd make a great impression since I would be so nervous about presenting!"

Q1. How could you try to uncover common interests?

Q2. Are there other opportunities to collaborate across differences in personality and supervisory style?

CONFLICT #2 – Grad School Challenges (Miscellaneous)

When I examined the data from our conversations, this topic was essentially a "catchall" category of various "grad school is challenging" type concerns that we heard from students at all points on their graduate journey. Students expressed the following concerns:

- *"How should I spend my time as a grad student?"* Frustrations with the grad school experience, including the transition from master's to PhD or managing first term/new challenges.

- *"I'm not sure I'm cut out for grad school."* Difficulty with grad school workload/pressures; feeling overwhelmed, like an imposter, or that they didn't belong in such an impossibly competitive and intellectually difficult environment; trouble managing full-time work and studies.

- *"I went home to visit family a few months ago, and for a lot of reasons I don't know if I can return."* Not feeling welcome or supported; trouble making friends/connections or finding community; feeling alone or isolated as a grad student.

- *"I want to talk to my professor about my research but I don't know where to start." "I'm tired of grad school." "I have a love/hate relationship with my research topic."* Lack of motivation or fulfillment/loss of interest in research; questioning the decision to go to or to stay in graduate school.

For the most part, these were internal and deeply personal intellectual, emotional, and value-driven conflicts (aka intrapersonal conflicts), not conflicts with others (aka interpersonal conflicts). I observed that it was the little things – the small "c" conflicts – that had a profoundly negative impact on the student's graduate experience.

Occasionally we spoke with students who had already decided to change their research focus, their department, or leave graduate school altogether. In these instances, the students were looking for a kind, non-judgmental listening ear – they wanted an opportunity to say aloud what they had been figuring out in their heads for a long time.

We heard from several grads over the years that when they started graduate school, they had envisioned having candid conversations with their supervisor and or other faculty mentors. They understood (even as they complained about it!) that grad school isn't supposed to be easy and had hoped for some appreciation from faculty about how hard they had worked to get into grad school and for acknowledgment that they deserve an opportunity to be successful in their graduate studies.

By verbalizing concerns that are swirling around in our heads, we are better able to identify which issues are potential conflicts, to appreciate where a situation might simply be difficult in the moment, and to get a better sense of "what next" (resources, supports), if things change and matters escalate.

Our conflict management service with a peer advisor team at its heart was ideal because many students simply wanted to talk with a fellow student who understood the day-to-day challenges of graduate school. However, as faculty, you can provide this type of sounding-board support yourself. Alternatively, you can create or support opportunities for students to connect and chat with fellow students (ideally with a knowledgeable facilitator present), and perhaps realize that what they are experiencing is a shared experience.

WHAT YOU CAN DO

! Share some stories of your early research successes and failures. Leave room during the conversation for students to ask questions or share some of their hopes/concerns for their research.

- *Normalize*: "Most people will feel like an imposter at some point in time (I know I do) and the path through grad school isn't always going to be straight, smooth, or easy to navigate."

- *Listen without problem-solving*: "I can hear from what you are describing how [frustrated/overwhelmed] you are."

- *Help students celebrate the small stuff*: "Very interesting article you found – tell me more." "I see that you've put together a timeline for the next few months – this is an awesome start." Just don't follow up these sentences with a "but…." because all someone will hear is what is said after the but!

- *Encourage students to map a support network*: "Tell me about who you have as your champions for your work as a grad student (at the university and outside of the institution)."

- *Ask your student what success would look like for them*: "I'm just thinking about how far you've come since you've started as a graduate student – what do you think has been the biggest shift for you?" Encourage comparisons with their own progress, rather than comparisons with other grad students in the department.

CONFLICT #3 – Escalation and Appeals

The third most common category of issues that brought individuals to our conflict management service related to escalation and appeals.

Graduate students, staff, and faculty came to us because they were struggling with a particular situation and looking for information about which policies and processes might apply and for advice on how and when to take matters forward. Examples of the types of queries we would get included:

- How do I, and when should I, escalate an academic concern (including grade appeals, misconduct, or plagiarism)? *"I don't have any options for escalating my concern because my supervisor is the graduate chair!"*

- Where do I find, and can you help me to understand, the university or departmental policies and appeals processes (regarding comprehensive exams, thesis defenses, extensions, or late submissions; leaves of absences, withdrawals, program terminations, etc.)? *"I have an online meeting soon with my instructor and the graduate chair about a plagiarism issue, and I need help to prepare."*

- Where can I go if I think a decision or process is unfair? What if I want to report inappropriate behavior of faculty, or staff, or other students? *"I've been told that I have to defend this semester or pay for another year of grad school – this is so unfair – it is my supervisor who caused all the delays!"*

In some cases, students had been told by a faculty member or administrator that a "formal process" was being initiated related to their grad studies. Often, students weren't sure about what that meant nor about what other options they had.

We were often referring students (or faculty who were supporting students) to the graduate student advocate (an employee of the graduate students' union) or the on-campus legal clinic for advocacy and support with the appeals processes. When these services were at capacity (no longer accepting student cases), we would help (without advocating) students locate the relevant policies online, read through the policies with them, and help them find the answers to their questions in often complex and lengthy documents. If a student described a process or a decision as unfair, we would also make referrals to the university ombuds; if there were concerns about inappropriate behavior or relationships, we would refer to the campus equity offices or to human resources.

Faculty would also raise concerns about whether students might escalate a particular complaint, including threatening legal action. We would talk about how to support students who might be distraught and would outline various informal and formal resolution options.

Most institutions don't consider the state of mind a reader may be in when they are putting together a FAQ and information about appeals, complaints, and conflict resolution processes. Typically, they are writing as if the reader is in a similar mental state as they might be in – perhaps comfortably seated, well-caffeinated, and far removed from the chaos of any actual appeal, complaint, or conflict.

In my view, this misses the point. A process should be easy to understand on your worst day, not your average day. Most of the individuals who connected with us were worried, upset, confused, angry, etc., and had either tried to figure out the right processes on their own and had given up in frustration, or more likely, had been avoiding doing anything to try and resolve their issue through any formal process.

WHAT YOU CAN DO

Q1. What do conflict resolution pathways look like in your department/at your institution?

Q2. Is there a process (like taking a leave from graduate studies) that is particularly complex, lengthy, or that graduate students tend to need help with or submit incorrectly?

! Hire grad students to map processes and create FAQ. Encourage them to use their vernacular and get them to test out answers with fellow grad students. Have them review

> their work when they are tired or feeling grumpy (e.g., early in the morning *before* they have had their morning coffee, when they are at their worst, or are not their best editing selves).

Taking a Leave from Grad School

One summer, we had a quite a few conversations with grad students about how to and whether to take a leave of absence (temporary), and questions and concerns about terminations (permanent action done by a department to a student – student may appeal) and withdrawals (permanent action taken by the student – no appeal) from graduate studies.

I flagged the issue for the graduate leadership team, and I showed them a tip sheet (unbelievably eleven pages long) that I had put together for the peer advisors who used it to help explain to students the various policies and processes related to leaves, withdrawals, and terminations. The leadership team was surprised – they had not realized the complexity and potential for conflict related to these issues.

MINI-CASE STUDY: TOUGH BREAK FOR A PHD

Consider the implications of a leave in relation to the following case study.

"I was in a serious car accident, and I need surgery and extensive therapy over the next six to eight months. I don't know if I should 'tough it out' by trying to do research remotely in between medical appointments or request a formal leave of absence. I'm worried that the other members of the lab will be very upset and angry, since my research is part of a much larger project."

Q1. How would this type of concern be handled at your institution?

Q2. How would you want the student to approach you if you were their supervisor?

Processes for Escalating Conflict within Universities

	Informal Conflict Resolution
Step 1	Raise the issue with the individual(s) involved or those at the lowest possible level. Initiate a discussion to try to come to a resolution that is acceptable to everyone involved. Summarize the discussion, outcomes, and next steps in writing.
	If no resolution ...
	Informal with Assistance
Step 2	Request assistance from an appropriate office/individual to see if the issue can be resolved informally by way of a facilitated discussion or shuttle diplomacy. Everyone should be clear about whether the person/office who is assisting will later be a decision-maker or an investigator. Have a written summary of discussion, outcomes, and next steps.
	Mediation/Restorative Process
Step 3	Consider a structured alternative dispute resolution (ADR) process like mediation or a restorative conference. These voluntary and normally confidential processes are led by an external third party who will not be a decision-maker or an investigator. Outline the resolution/next steps in writing at the end of the process.
	If no resolution ...
	Formal Process (including investigation or appeal)
Step 4	Follow the formal processes set out in policy/guidelines. Students may want to seek representation or advocacy, but they must follow the principles of administrative fairness. Before the conclusion of a formal process, individuals may choose to abandon the appeal or investigation. Provide outcomes in writing, with reasons provided, and any possible next steps.
	If unsatisfied ...
	Appeal or Formal Review of Process
Step 5	If allowed, appeal the decision. If individuals are concerned about the process or outcome, there may be recourse from a designated person or office. If an appeal is not allowed, other possible options are to request a fairness review from the university/external ombudsperson or to remedy through the courts (judicial review/civil action) or a tribunal (e.g., human rights tribunal).

CHECKLIST: TAKING A LEAVE FROM GRAD SCHOOL

Here is a checklist that might be useful to customize and provide to students on a department website, or in a grad handbook, or if they come to you to talk about what is involved in taking a leave.

What to Do before Requesting a Leave

- ☐ Read the university's leave policy and review the leave application process. *[Include links to policies and supports]*
- ☐ Gather all the required documents.
- ☐ Prepare a list of questions related to the impact of a leave on funding, fees, finances, deadlines, progress/time to completion. Consider: How many terms do I think I need at a minimum/maximum? How do I extend a leave?
- ☐ Contact your department and the school of graduate studies for clarification.
- ☐ Develop a personal plan to deal with the issues/the reasons for the leave – what supports will you need?

How to Request a Leave

- ☐ Fill in forms and practice what you will say to your supervisor.
- ☐ Communicate your need for leave to your supervisor(s) and committee members. Clarify expectations, timeline (tasks, milestones, graduation), funding (if tied to supervisor).
- ☐ Submit leave materials. If applicable, make requests for access to student services (library, health/dental coverage) during your leave.

What to Do during a Leave

- ☐ Follow your personal plan.
- ☐ Do self-check-ins regularly – is your anticipated return date reasonable? Do you need to extend?

What to Do as You Complete a Leave

- ☐ Create a re-entry plan – keep an open mind about possible changes in the environment (people, places, and processes).
- ☐ Practice your "I'm back" conversation and responding to questions about your absence.
- ☐ Re-establish communication. Share your re-entry plan with your supervisor(s) and committee members. Make sure everyone is on the same page, and clarify details (timeline, funding, etc.).
- ☐ Seek ongoing support and follow up on any issues or concerns.

CONFLICT #4 – Interpersonal Conflict (Not Supervisory)

This category includes all non-supervisory, non-lab-related, and non-housing (roommates or landlords) conflicts that arise between and among students, faculty, and staff. It includes interpersonal conflicts arising from or relating to:

- Group work: "*The politics in my group are intense and I can't find my voice to contribute to the project.*"
- Co-authorship: "*I think I should be first author on the paper I'm writing – I've done way more work.*"
- Collegial relationships: academic or romantic. "*I have a shared office with other grads who gossip constantly – it is really distracting.*"
- Unacceptable behavior: racism, sexism, sexual harassment/violence, cyber aggression, and online bullying. "*I wish that there were more opportunities for women in my PhD program – it is such an old boys' club.*"

I note that there were fewer than ten conversations each year that raised the latter concerns,[1] which may be because grad students found their way to one of the dedicated offices on campus to get support or formally report their concerns (instead of coming to our office), or because they did not bring these concerns forward anywhere on campus.

This stands in contrast to what I call "romantic" interpersonal conflict (e.g., where two students dated, broke up, and still needed to work in proximity to each other, or where one student's romantic interest in another student was respected but not reciprocated). For the latter, there weren't really any campus supports to refer students to, so grad students appreciated having a peer advisor to talk to, simply as a sounding-board.

Here are examples of interpersonal conflicts that were common to both faculty and graduate students:

- "I'm having a conflict with a co-instructor for a course I teach, and it is making it difficult to see how we will be able to finish the semester together!"
- "I am worried about how my vocal support for some grad students who are advocating for changes in the department might impact my relationships with other faculty."
- "I found out that one of the instructors for a graduate class in my department has been behaving unpredictably and making last minute changes to the course content, but the students don't want to talk to the instructor directly in case it makes things worse."
- "I've been asked to get in the middle and 'mediate' a conflict between several students, which I'm not comfortable doing. What other options are there?"

MINI-CASE STUDY: COLLEAGUE OR COMPETITION?

"I'm trying to balance a job, parenting, and my research. I'm having a conflict with one of my colleagues – we used to be very close friends (our research is complementary) but things have changed. This person canceled several pre-arranged meetings that were very difficult for me to organize. They have been unfairly critical of my work in front of others and have taken credit for some of the ideas we had talked about that were mine! Maybe they think making me look bad will make them look better? I don't know whether to confront them – what would I say? When it is just us two chatting, this person is nice and supportive. My family tells me to just keep my head low because there is too much at risk if things go wrong."

Q. What are two or three questions you could ask?

ROLE PLAY: DUMPED AND IGNORED

Time Required. 30 minutes = 5 preparation / 15 role play / 10 debrief

Instructions. In pairs, one person plays the role of a PhD/master's student and the other plays the role of a graduate coordinator/chair (i.e., the graduate support faculty member within your department). Each person has confidential background information, and the student has additional information that they can share throughout the role play. You will have five minutes to prepare (get into character). Feel free to ad lib and add additional details to make this role play more realistic (i.e., you can go off script). After five minutes, we will call Ready? Action! and read the role play introduction aloud to set the stage. You will have fifteen minutes to act out the scene. At the end we will have a debrief discussion with the larger group.

Debrief Questions for Group Discussion:
- What did the coordinator do well?
- Were there any great questions?
- Was there anything that the coordinator could have done differently?

READY? ACTION! *Read aloud:* The student has arrived for their appointment with the graduate coordinator (virtual or in person). The coordinator welcomes them and invites them to share why they've booked the meeting/why they wanted to talk. The student begins to share their story.

SHARE WITH COORDINATOR ONLY *Confidential Background.* You have been in this administrative role for several years and have heard many stories (excuses) from students in that time. Master's students rarely live up to your expectations – they are all too happy to blame faculty for their own problems. You understand your coordinator role to include listening, asking questions, and supporting grad students so that they can resolve their own issues.

SHARE WITH STUDENT ONLY *Confidential Background. Think about how you normally act when you are upset as you role play this scenario; however, remember that in this role play it is difficult for you to talk about the personal issues because they are so upsetting to you.*

You are a second-year master's student. You just had your first appointment with the campus wellness counselor. They recommended that you book an appointment with your graduate coordinator. You want help talking to one of your professors about an academic extension in their course because you are dealing with a personal issue (you were just dumped by your partner of two years).

STUDENT Details to Share Immediately. My professor has been ignoring my emails. About a month ago, I had to deal with a personal situation that required my immediate attention, and I emailed my prof to let them know that I wouldn't be in class and that I needed an extension for my paper outline. I didn't get a response and it is due this week. So, I emailed them again over the weekend, and again, no response. I really don't know what to do now. I can't fail this class – what do you think I should do?

STUDENT Details to Share if Asked about Emotions/Feelings. I'm worried about contacting my professor again. I mean, I've emailed twice and was ignored both times. A few weeks ago, I chatted with them after class; they seemed nice and told me to email with any follow up questions, so why aren't they responding? What should I do? I tried to work all weekend so I wouldn't actually need an extension but that didn't work. I'm not sleeping. With all this drama, it isn't going all that well. My partner just broke up with me – and that is all I can think about. I'm just so gutted – it was a total surprise – it came out of the blue. I'm overwhelmed.

STUDENT Details to Share if Asked about Trying to Resolve the Conflict. Well, I asked one of the other students in the class whether they had any issues with email and they said "no, they are usually really quick at responding over email." Why would they have responded to the other students and not to me? They suggested dropping by during office hours, but I'm afraid I'll get emotional and start to cry if I have to explain things face to face. That would be really unprofessional. My email didn't provide any details of why I needed an extension.

STUDENT Question to Ask if Given Silence to Fill. Do you think you can talk to or email my professor for me?

END OF ROLE PLAY Move to Debrief.

When Storms Hit Grad Group Work

Year over year, we were increasingly hearing about conflict in group work. Each year, one proactive graduate program manager invited us early in the term to run workshops on navigating conflict in group work – she felt that bringing our team to do training early in the group work process helped to prevent as many issues as possible from escalating to her office.

In our group conflict management sessions, as well as sharing basic conflict prevention strategies (interests and positions, active listening), we also focused on normalizing conflict or "storming" (as Bruce Tuckman referred to this phase in his 1960s work on team development) in group work. As others since have argued, conflict isn't a defined stage of group work, but a possibility at any point while groups are engaged with one another, as members try to establish independence or vie for leadership positions, or when disagreements arise over group values, individual ideas, group tasks, or goals.[2] In order to develop effective conflict management skills in group work, it helps to focus on three key "P's":

- *Perspective*: Group members see each other as individuals with strengths and weaknesses, and as part of a collective "us." (= EMPATHY)

- *Process*: Group members work together to create and agree upon processes (setting timelines, developing agendas, agreeing on goals and how decisions will be made; determining what will happen when there is a conflict, etc.), which can create "buy-in" in a way that simply providing the group with these tools will not. (= CLARITY)

- *Problem-solving*: Group members are aware, open, and realistic about the reality of storming in group work, and build into group processes opportunities to practice problem-solving and conflict resolution strategies (i.e., "small stakes" mini debates/disputes).
(= OPENNESS)

WHAT YOU CAN DO

! When forming groups, invite them to consider the inevitability of conflict by discussing the following:

- What are our interests/goals (vs. positions)? What if group goals need to be revisited?

- How will we handle differences of opinion, opposing positions, or strongly held views? What is "constructive" feedback? How can we focus on group goals rather than confronting/calling out individuals?

- Should we have a "group contract"? What happens if the contract is broken?

Q1. From your experience supervising groups, what are some characteristics of highly functional groups?

Q2. How do they manage conflict/differences?

! Read more about supervising conflict in groups in articles by William A. Cunningham et al., "Conflict in Your Research Group? Here Are Four Strategies for Finding a Resolution"[3] and N. Sharon Hill and Kathryn M. Bartol, "Five Ways to Improve Communication in Virtual Teams,"[4] and in Kathryn Woodcock's blog, "Group Work."[5]

In each of the following four "storm" case studies,[6] and in addition to the questions included below each of them, consider how attention to perspective, process, and problem-solving might have prevented or prepared the group for the conflict. Hints are provided for the first two mini-case studies.

MINI-CASE STUDY: GRAD GROUP SHARED STRUGGLE

You supervise a group project. Beta, a group member, has come to talk to you "on behalf of the group." According to Beta, Delta is always completely revising other group members' work after they upload it to the shared online doc, without asking their permission. The other group members are angry and a few of them have commented privately to Beta that they can't really see the point of working hard on the project if Delta is just going to change everything. Resentment and apathy are building, and when Beta tried to talk to Delta (e.g., "we didn't appoint you as our group editor"), Delta laughed off the comment as "bruised group egos."

Q. *What would you do as the group's supervisor?*

Mini-Case Study HINTS:

> Ask questions: "How has the group dealt with other issues with other group members?"
>
> Separate the person (Delta) from the problem (editing without permission): – can the group have a meeting to talk about "How can we ensure that our work is reflective of all of our efforts and is the best quality before it is finalized?"
>
> Refer to the group contract and the course requirements.

MINI-CASE STUDY: GRAD GROUP PLANNING

You supervise a group who has a major project due in six weeks. One of the group members, Epsilon, has emailed you to complain about a group member, Lambda. Lambda has proposed a revised timeline to the group which "everyone is just going along with," but many of Lambda's new deadlines conflict with Epsilon's personal schedule, which is "totally unacceptable!" The group is scheduled to have a video chat tomorrow.

Q. Considering interests, questions, and perspectives, how would you approach this?

Mini-Case Study HINTS:

> Ask questions: "How are group members communicating and coordinating schedules?"; "What is the process?"; "What is the group trying to achieve?" (Big picture interests.)
> Separate the person (Lambda) from the problem (deadlines that Epsilon can't work with and Epsilon wanting to contribute to the group work): "How might you focus a conversation around goals/interests?"; "How might you frame an agenda to focus on the problem rather than the person?"

MINI-CASE STUDY: GRAD GROUP TARGET

You assigned your master's students into groups at the beginning of term to complete a major group project. Alpha, a student in your course, showed up to your office hours earlier this week. Alpha is confused and upset because at the group's last meeting, Omega yelled at Alpha and said some very unkind things for no reason. Alpha insists that "I've been a good group member!" and emphasized perfect attendance and good quality work. You talk separately with Omega to get more information. Omega tells you that Alpha is consistently late for meetings and submits work to the group late. Other group members seemed content to "just let it slide," but Omega couldn't take it anymore! Omega called Alpha out for being "lazy and inconsiderate" and has asked you to remove Alpha from the group.

Q. How might you approach this?

MINI-CASE STUDY: GRAD GROUP CREATIVE DIFFERENCES

You assigned your master's students into groups at the beginning of term to complete a major group project, and you've just checked in online to see how one of the groups (Group C) is doing. As you read, you note that Zeta, one of the members of Group C, has written some very creative (perhaps too creative) ideas about how to present the project. You also note some online comments toward Zeta that seem quite rude and aggressive. Another team member, Kappa, seems to have tried (once) to steer the chat back to group tasks ("Let's talk about what's next on our group timeline"), but since no one else in the group has commented or intervened, you are worried things are going to get worse for Zeta and the group.

Q. How would you approach this?

TIP SHEET: NINE STEPS TO APPROACHING CAMPUS CONFLICT

For interpersonal conflict, while who was involved may differ (teaching assistant, postdoc, instructor, co-author, group member, fellow faculty member, etc.), the advice that we would give about how to prepare and respond to a conflict generally would follow these nine steps.

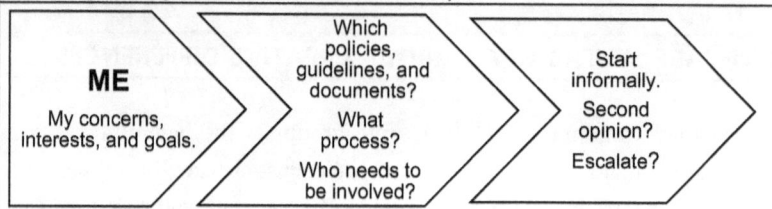

1. Frame your concern(s) and consider your interests or goals (aka your conflict resolution "elevator pitch").

    I am really bothered about ...
    In order for this to be "better," I need ...

2. Reflect on what you've done. It's okay if you've done nothing or tried something – what you are trying to do is figure out the starting place for resolving the conflict.

    I've already tried ...
    I was thinking about trying ...

3. Find and read any relevant university policies or guidelines.

    List the sections that seem to apply to the situation.
    Take note of how the informal/formal processes start for resolution.

4. Organize your documentation (if any). Were there any emails exchanged? Do you regularly keep notes in an agenda?

5. Determine who needs to be involved to resolve the conflict.

    The people directly involved are ...
    Are there other people who might have an interest in the outcome?
    What are other possible campus supports?

6. Consider the other person's perspective.

    I think they might think the issue is about ...
    I think their interests and goals might include ...

7. Start informally. General good practice is to try to talk with the other person first (after preparing!).

    I've drafted an email about getting together to talk about [see question 1 above].
    I've drafted an agenda or talking points for the meeting including ...

8. Consider seeking a trusted second opinion. Check in with campus supports, or a committee member or trusted faculty members, or fellow student or graduate administrators. Refer to question 5 above.

9. Escalate appropriately. If the issue isn't resolved (i.e., if you can't get to agreement) through informal discussion, consider next steps (e.g., bring the issue to the attention of the department's graduate coordinator/graduate chair; go to the appropriate faculty dean/vice-dean). Refer to question 3 above.

CONFLICT #5 – Research and Thesis

Grad students told us they were struggling to determine the scope and to refine the focus for their graduate research. ("How big is too big for a PhD?" "How close am I to being able to submit a final draft?" "Is it too late to change topics?" "I'm having trouble understanding what my advisor expects from this part of my research.")

As well as the nuts and bolts of the thesis writing process ("How much should I be writing each week?" "How quickly should I/my supervisor turn around revisions?"), we also heard about:

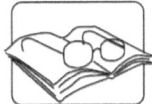

- publication and (co-)authorship issues (credit, rejection)
- intellectual property (IP) issues related to data and research
- writing stress/anxiety; managing revisions, comments; English not a first language
- stresses related to switching research topics, or around research continuity during leaves of absence
- concerns and expectations about preparing and defending a final thesis

From faculty, we heard things like: "I don't think my grad student is taking the research seriously enough," and "What can I do if a student has taken my feedback comments personally and now seems to be avoiding me?"

As grad students, the peer advisors related to many of the general concerns and stresses related to research and thesis work that their fellow students were sharing. They would work with them to come up with a set of priorities (i.e., what was most important at the moment), and with a plan for how they might talk to their supervisor about their concerns. The peers would also make sure that the student was aware of key campus supports (library, graduate center for academic communication, academic success consultations, and writing centers).

Conversations around authorship and IP involved a review of policies or processes to help the student understand what might be required to resolve a concern. IP and authorship issues were common because completing a graduate degree necessarily involves the creation and sharing of ideas and knowledge. The challenge for an institution is how to develop "a shared vision of graduate students as independent researchers who can solve problems and progress by themselves" (Hiro, PhD Higher Education). Here are three amplifiers of IP- and authorship-related conflicts that we heard about in our conversations:

- *Power*: When there is nothing agreed in writing, decisions may come down to a student's word (recollection) versus a supervisor's word (recollection).

- *People*: Many people can be involved in trying to resolve an issue in particular where there might be cross-departmental research, multiple authors, or a team of contributors to a body of research.

- *High stakes*: There are high stakes for both students and faculty (funding, future opportunities, reputations, etc.).

Prevention is a key element of effective IP and authorship conflict management. Having early discussions around IP matters can establish clear lines of communication, foster comfortable working relations, reduce misunderstandings, and hopefully prevent conflict. Once a dispute has arisen with respect to IP or authorship, things generally get more complicated and legalistic, so clarity around escalation for resolving disagreements is also critical.[1] Everyone should be on the same page about which policies or guidelines apply, including guiding documents from the department, the graduate school, the institution or the funding bodies, and so on.

WHAT YOU CAN DO

! *Prevention through awareness.* What information is easily available to help students (and faculty) better understand IP and authorship issues? For example, an online FAQ (frequently asked questions), IP agreement templates, or checklists? Where do IP and authorship "live" at your institution and with whom (office, library, or department)? Check out this guide from the Canadian Association of Graduate Students: "A Guide to Intellectual Property for Graduate Students and Postdoctoral Scholars."[2]

Q. *If you have identified an awareness gap, what would you include in an FAQ to help grad students understand potential intellectual property and authorship conflicts and take steps (early on!) to prevent them?*

! *Start discussions early.* Do you review IP policies with your students? When you are co-authoring, are you explicit about who is first author, and so on? Make sure that understandings and agreements are put in writing in plain language.

! *Understand what to do if things go wrong.* If a conflict over intellectual property arises, what is the process for resolution? Many times, the first step recommended in policies or guidelines is an attempt to resolve the issue through informal discussion or negotiation[3] – consider what this means in practice for a graduate student if the issue is with their supervisor (and how might that be different from an issue between students or between faculty members).

MINI-CASE STUDY: RESEARCH REALIGNMENT

Imagine your student has just told you:

"Our research interests aren't aligned any longer. You are doing ABC and I want to focus on XYZ."

Q. How would you respond? Do you check in with your students about their research interests and priorities regularly?

MINI-CASE STUDY: WHOSE NAME IS ON FIRST?

As you read the following, consider how this conflict might have been avoided.

"Last year, I came up with a great idea for an article and told my supervisor about it and we wrote the article together. After that, he came up with another idea for a publication and I wrote most of it. So, now we are submitting two papers and my supervisor just told me that he wants me to be second author on both papers. I don't think that's fair because I really did most of the writing for the first one. Maybe the second one, I can see it's his idea, but … I should be first author."

Q1. Is there an office or individual on your campus that can provide information and advice about authorship issues?

Q2. If yes, do they provide conflict resolution (e.g., facilitation/mediation) for disputes?

FAQ: INTELLECTUAL PROPERTY AND AUTHORSHIP

Here are some common IP/authorship questions from grad students that you can use to create a customized FAQ (hire a grad to develop the answers and reference university policies/IP offices). Original developed in collaboration with peer advisor Sam (MA Public Health).	
Question	**Answer**
When should I be having discussions about authorship/IP?	Before the research begins, so that everyone is on the same page about author contribution and order from the start.
Should I be listed as a co-author? Who gets first and second author?	
How do I make sure that I get full credit for the work that I have done/contributed?	
Who can claim authorship of creative works that I make as a grad student?	
If I make a discovery while working with my supervisor, committee, or others, who gets credit?	
What happens if I collaborate with someone who is not at the university?	
If I change labs, can I bring my research data with me?	
Where can I find the policies and guidelines on IP/authorship?	
What happens if the work I created occurred during the course of my employment with the institution (as teaching assistant or research assistant)?	
How do I make sure that I get full credit for the work that I have done/my contribution to the project or research?	

ROLE PLAY: PUBLISHING LETDOWN

Time Required. 30 minutes = 5 preparation / 15 role play / 10 debrief

Instructions. In pairs, one person plays the role of a PhD/master's student and the other plays the role of a graduate coordinator/chair (i.e., the graduate support faculty member within your department). Each person has confidential background information, and the student has additional information that they can share throughout the role play. You will have five minutes to prepare (get into character). Feel free to ad lib and add additional details to make this role play more realistic (i.e., you can go off script). After five minutes, we will call Ready? Action! and read the role play introduction aloud to set the stage. You will have fifteen minutes to act out the scene. At the end we will have a debrief discussion with the larger group.

Debrief Questions for Group Discussion:
- What did the coordinator do well?
- Were there any great questions?
- Was there anything that the coordinator could have done differently?

READY? ACTION! Read aloud: The student has arrived for their appointment with the graduate coordinator (virtual or in person). The coordinator welcomes them and invites them to share why they've booked the meeting/ why they wanted to talk. The student begins to share their story.

SHARE WITH COORDINATOR ONLY Confidential Background. You have been in this administrative role for about a year and have supervised PhD students for many years. You understand your coordinator role to include listening, asking open-ended questions, and supporting grad students so that they can resolve their own issues.

SHARE WITH STUDENT ONLY Confidential Background. You are a third-year PhD student. You are really upset about a situation with your supervisor and need to vent to someone. Your department is too competitive to share your story with another grad student, so you booked an appointment with your graduate coordinator. You express your anger, sadness, and frustration in waves as you recount various parts of your story. PAUSE often while you share your story and wait for the coordinator to ask questions or say something. You don't have to share everything at once.

STUDENT Details to Share Immediately. For the past few months, I have been practically begging my supervisor to co-author a paper with me, and I'm constantly getting the brush off. I have presented multiple solid ideas for papers we could write together, but my supervisor is always, "too busy at the moment" or "sorry, this isn't a great time." Maybe my proposals aren't good enough – I can't understand why my supervisor is avoiding me! We used to be close – having coffee together a few times a week and I could text day or night and get a response. Last year we had some amazing intense conversations about my research, and my supervisor promised that we would work together on some articles. I'm the first PhD that my supervisor has ever supervised; however, they just got three new graduate students, so it is getting harder and harder to get any attention, no matter how many times I text or email.

STUDENT Details to Share if Asked about Emotions/Feelings. The pressure is relentless because in my department we have to have at least one published research article in order to graduate. I'm stressed out about how to deal with this situation without impacting my relationship with my supervisor. I'm really angry at my supervisor for putting me in a position where I'm almost begging for approval. I really miss how close we used to be. I feel a bit duped by my program to be honest – they brag in all their materials about how collaborative the department is – and about how "the PhD curriculum is carefully designed to support students as publishing scholars as early as possible in their doctoral studies," but I don't feel supported at all!

STUDENT Details to Share if Asked about Trying to Resolve the Conflict. I spoke to one of my other committee members and they offered to talk to my supervisor, which I appreciated, but I asked them not to do so because I don't know if that would make things any better. I really want to get published so I can stay on track to graduate in two years. I think that if my supervisor was a co-author, I'd have a much better chance of my paper being accepted. I tried submitting one article on my own and it was rejected. I just want things back to the way they were.

END OF ROLE PLAY Move to Debrief.

CONFLICT #6 – Academic Progress

Ask a graduate administrator what keeps them up at night, and they will likely include "PhD time to completion" on a, no doubt, lengthy list. Ironically, this is one of the issues that contributes to sleepless nights for graduate students as well. As a result of the pandemic and its long-term impacts, more students may seek program extensions,[1] and feel pressures to complete quickly for financial or personal reasons. As noted by the Wellbeing Lab at the University of British Columbia, "Good student–supervisor relationships are ... associated with higher completion rates and faster times to completion."[2]

In our conversations with students, academic progress issues often overlapped with other issues such as supervision, health and wellness, research/thesis, family and finances, and grad school challenges. These included:

- questions and concerns about time to completion, graduation timing, wanting to defend/graduate but being slowed by either their supervisor, committee,/or personal circumstances; or wanting a different pace of progress ("I think it makes sense to go part-time for a while, and I need help talking to my department about this option")
- concerns about comprehensive or qualifying exams
- extensions, time management, delays receiving feedback or data issues that impact progress

In our conversations with faculty, they primarily wanted to find out about academic supports for grad students on campus and to talk about options for challenging situations, such as "The student I'm supervising isn't making any significant progress – they are clearly struggling academically. What can I do to support them?"

We participated in an initiative for faculty, from the Faculty of Medicine, that was designed to address concerns around extended graduate student times to completion. Over several months, supervisors were invited to participate in a series of professional development workshops.[3] Our session focused on tools for conflict prevention, management, and resolution in graduate school – all important considerations for academic progress.

WHAT YOU CAN DO

! Students were often surprised when their supervisor told them they weren't making academic progress. Like you, students are juggling many responsibilities and priorities.

Q1. Are you telling students early on and regularly about concerns?

Q2. If there are several areas for improvement and multiple places to seek guidance or support (e.g., librarians, student services staff, departmental or online resources), have you provided enough direction so the student can determine where they need to focus their time?

Q3. Are there ways to be more specific about which graduate skills need improvement and in what ways?

! Do a quick supervisor feedback self-assessment using Hugh Kearns's tool "My Feedback Style,"[4] or watch his video about feedback, "What to Do with Writing Feedback."[5]

! Change "buts" to "ands" as recommended in this *Inc.* article by Ken Sterling, "Eliminate 'but' from Your Vocabulary When Giving Feedback."[6]

Family/Financial + Academic Progress

"I'm having trouble balancing my family responsibilities, a part-time job (my degree isn't funded!), and my grad course work. I don't know if I can graduate as planned. It's all too much to juggle."

> **WHAT YOU CAN DO**
>
> ! Listen. Acknowledge the other person's perspective and feelings about a situation: *"Balancing family, job, and course work responsibilities must be stressful."* If you get it wrong (i.e., if they don't think it is "stressful"), they will usually correct you (i.e., "it is way more than stressful, it's making me wonder if I should stay in grad school").

MINI-CASE STUDY: ENOUGH IS ENOUGH

Consider how you might use conflict coaching tips to help continue the conversation if a student came to you (because you are known as a friendly faculty member to discuss this concern:

"I am ready to start writing so I can get back to my life and my family (and make some money!), but my supervisor told me I have to get 'a bit more' data. I tried to ask how much more data I need, and she said, 'You'll know when it's enough.'"

Q1. What is the student's position?

Q2. What questions could you ask to get the student thinking about their interests?

Q3. What about the supervisor's position and interests?

Grad School Challenges + Academic Progress

"I'm struggling to meet deadlines and to keep on top of all of my graduate responsibilities."

"It is so hard to stay motivated, but then I feel guilty that I'm not working all the time."

WHAT YOU CAN DO

! Be curious. Ask students about what they are doing to manage tasks at present and what might have worked for them in the past. Help students to generate their own time management plan going forward, and see how you can help them stay on track/be held accountable.

MINI-CASE STUDY: JUST ONE MORE!

"I am ready to defend my thesis, but my supervisor wants me to produce 'one more' publication. I know all about 'publish or perish,' but I'm starting to resent the fact that I'm working so hard and still not getting any closer to finishing."

Q. If you were on the student's committee, what would you do?

Health/Wellness + Academic Progress

"I am having trouble completing tasks and assignments due to serious health issues. I have a meeting with my supervisor and chair, and I have to outline a full plan for the upcoming year including research and writing."

> **WHAT YOU CAN DO**
>
> ! Suggest to the student that they take notes to prepare for a difficult meeting. If they are worried that someone will think negatively about them referring to notes, suggest that they acknowledge at the outset of the meeting that the discussion is important to them, so they will be referring to their notes to make sure they address all the points they want to cover.

MINI-CASE STUDY: LOST IN PHD TIME

"I discussed a timeline with my supervisor several years ago, but I'm anxious about how to have a conversation about revising it with my current mental health being so poor."

Q. How would you coach this student about their concern?

Supervision + Academic Progress

"I want to finish my degree quickly, but my supervisor isn't giving me any project direction – how do I get him to tell me whether I'm on track to graduate?"

"AGHHH! My supervisor is terrible at turning around drafts, and then when I get my draft back, their comments are contradictory. Now I'm being told that I need several more drafts than we had agreed earlier!"

> **WHAT YOU CAN DO**
>
> ! Separate the issues. Get more information. Help students to identify what is within their power and control and what they actually need (interests) from their supervisor.

MINI-CASE STUDY: AN UNSATISFACTORY GRAD SURPRISE

"I've had a difficult relationship with my PhD supervisor for a few years now. I recently submitted the final draft of my thesis, and instead of getting feedback, I was invited to meet with my supervisor. To my surprise, my supervisor told me that I had failed to make satisfactory academic progress and that I will be terminated unless I withdraw voluntarily from the program!"

Q. *What information could you provide to this student about the policies, appeals processes, or campus supports that may apply?*

Research/Thesis + Academic Progress

"I can't believe I just failed my comprehensive exam. What should I do next? My committee members were clearly trying to demonstrate that they know more about the research than me – would it hurt me if I challenge the result?"

WHAT YOU CAN DO

! Review applicable policies and processes with the student. Encourage them to pause to separate the people (committee members) from the problem (failed comprehensive exam) before problem-solving.

MINI-CASE STUDY: DATA DISASTER

"My data has been compromised, and I'm worried this will set me back another year."

Q. *As this student's supervisor, what would you do?*

TIP SHEET: FIVE WAYS TO DEAL WITH NEGATIVE FEEDBACK

Original written by Grad CRC peer advisors, Manaal (PhD Social Work) and Terence (PhD, Molecular Neuroscience).

Feedback includes what you say, how you say it, and how often you say it. Feedback (even negative feedback!) should motivate us to improve the quality of our work and focus positively on areas of growth. However, students often interpret thesis feedback from their supervisors in ways that may not have been intended. Consider this example about written feedback from author and professor Hugh Kearns:[7]

SUPERVISOR: "Unclear."
STUDENT reads: "I can't write clearly. I thought it was clear but obviously I have no idea."

What difference might it have made to the student's interpretation of the feedback if the supervisor had instead written:

SUPERVISOR: "This paragraph is unclear – what is the main point and how does it relate to this section?"

Here is some advice that the peer advisors gave to students who were concerned about negative feedback from their supervisor:

1. **Negative feedback is not necessarily a personal attack.**

Try to separate your immediate emotional response from the comments, so you can evaluate them on their own merits. Try to see feedback as an opportunity for growth and learning.

2. **Listen to understand the feedback given.**

You can absorb more information when you aren't defensive and focused on how to counter the comments. Open-ended questions can help you to understand the feedback you received and to clarify unclear comments. (Ask yourself: who, what, when, where, why, and how?)

3. **Reflect and decide what to do.**

After listening to the comments, identify which to prioritize, which to deal with later, or even which to overlook (along with justifying your decisions). It is your call.

4. **Consider feedback styles.**

Does your supervisor provide clear, direct feedback (blunt) or indirect suggestions that require more work to decipher and implement? Is feedback provided "in the moment" (e.g., quick phone call or text), or do they set up formal meetings to discuss written work? What is your preferred style?

5. **Follow up.**

After making revisions based on the suggestions given to you, it may be a nice idea to schedule another meeting to further discuss the revised work. Make sure that if a lack of written feedback had caused confusion, ask for future feedback to be summarized in writing. This can help provide a joint plan to work from (or toward), and it may be easier to clarify any misunderstandings.

Sources/Resources
For STUDENTS

Atif, "Dealing with Negative Feedback," *Gradifying* (blog), Queen's University, 7 October 2013, https://www.queensu.ca/connect/grad/about/.

Alison Crump, "Managing Conflicting Feedback on Your Thesis," *The Thesis Whisperer* (blog), 30 September 2015, https://thesiswhisperer.com/2015/09/30/do-you-really-own-your-thesis/.

FOR FACULTY

Daniel Coyle, "The Simple Phrase that Increases Effort 40%," 13 December 2013, https://danielcoyle.com/2013/12/13/the-simple-phrase-that-increases-effort-40/.

"Receiving and Giving Effective Feedback," Centre for Teaching Excellence - University of Waterloo, accessed 8 November 2021, https://uwaterloo.ca/centre-for-teaching-excellence/resources/teaching-tips.

Daveena Tauber, "Using Oral Feedback to Complement Written Feedback," *The Thesis Whisperer* (blog), 11 July 2018, https://thesiswhisperer.com/2018/07/11/using-oral-feedback-to-compliment-written-feedback/.

Susan Carter, "Doctoral Writing and Supervisor Feedback: What's the Game Plan?" *Doctoral Writing SIG* (blog), 5 July 2017, https://doctoralwriting.wordpress.com/2017/07/05/doctoral-writing-and-supervisor-feedback-whats-the-game-plan/.

TIP SHEET: FIVE WAYS TO MOVE FROM REJECTION TO RESILIENCE

Original written by Grad CRC peer advisors, Manaal (PhD Social Work) and Terence (PhD Molecular Neuroscience). This advice is intended to help students move forward after a publication has been rejected.

1. Take some time out.

Receiving a rejection for a manuscript is very common in academia. Step away from the computer and take some time and space to focus on activities that rejuvenate and motivate you.

> "Yes, rejection hurts. It is okay to react to it and acknowledge your emotions. Use the rejection as fuel to engage in problem-solving and encourage yourself." – PhD student

2. Don't fire off a response to the journal.

While you may want to pour out your feelings as soon as you read the rejection email, let your emotions and thoughts settle.

3. Separate the rejection from "you."

There are likely several reasons (some related to the work and some not) for a rejection. A rejection is not a personal attack or a reflection of you as a person or as a grad student.

> "A committee member once shared that a rejection does not always reflect the quality of your work and potential. Sometimes, a paper could be rejected simply because it did not fit within the journal's scope. Identifying another journal and resubmitting promptly can be a quick and effective strategy to keep moving forward." – PhD student

4. Review the reviewers' comments thoroughly.

As you review, determine areas that you could improve. Candid feedback may help you to address issues you had not previously considered.

5. Determine next steps.

Take time to revisit the journal and the review process. Come up with a game plan that keeps you moving forward whether you resubmit or submit elsewhere.

> "Use rejection to your benefit. The reviewers' feedback and the research needed to revise the manuscript can help you expand your knowledge of the topic and the field." – PhD student

Sources/Resources

Eszter Hargittai, "From Review to Publication," *Inside Higher Ed*, 26 September 2011, https://www.insidehighered.com/advice/2011/09/26/review-publication.

"Feeling Rejected? Graduate Students and the Journal Review Process," American Psychological Association (APA) Student Council, September 2007, www.apa.org/science/about/psa/2007/09/science-council.aspx.

sauvik, "A Letter to My Younger Self about Dealing with Rejection in Academia," *MakeWriteLearn*, 21 November 2015, http://makewritelearn.com/rejection-letter.

CONFLICT #7 – Family and Personal

 For graduate students, figuring out how to balance academic, family, personal and responsibilities is a constant challenge. Importantly, we observed that a conflict doesn't necessarily have to happen on campus to have on-campus implications; for example, grad students talked with us about conflicts with family members who were scrutinizing their academic choices and activities.

Grad students came to us looking for help with a wide variety of family and personal issues, including:

- navigating relationships with family members or partners (lack of support for academic pursuits)
- approaching a supervisor or committee member about taking time to deal with a family or personal issue, including pregnancy, homesickness, divorce, loss/bereavement, and returning to academia after being on a leave for personal reasons
- looking for supports and resources for graduate students with children, dependents, and other responsibilities (re: family members)
- navigating relationships with roommates or landlords and managing housing concerns
- dealing with the financial and academic impact that their family responsibilities (academic progress, time to completion, questions related to taking leaves of absences, difficulties coping with workload)

Faculty would sometimes identify a family- or personal-related concern such as: "One of the faculty members in the department is concerned about a student's personal life interfering with their research."

Many of the individuals who connected with us were either unaware that the university had a dedicated equity office for students, faculty, and staff with family responsibilities (including children, dependents, and aging parents), or they had been referred to our office because the issue likely would require negotiation with a supervisor or department. One of the peers observed, "While graduate students might have friends, partners and/or family members to support them during their graduate experience, some may not understand what it's like to be a graduate student, and it takes too much time or effort to understand all the terms and steps involved" (Amika PhD Health Informatics). We would help students with strategies on how to talk with their advisor and how to set boundaries in these types of situations.

> **WHAT YOU CAN DO**
>
> ! As faculty and administrators, you have likely already had conversations with grad students that wandered uncomfortably into territory that was more personal than academic. Find an authentic way to balance compassion with clarity about the type of support that you can and cannot provide. For example, in coaching we might say (and perhaps repeat):
>
> - "I am happy to talk to you about [academic issue], however, since you mentioned [XYZ issue] and I'm not a [counselor/social worker/familiar with that issue], it will be more helpful for you to connect with [appropriate XYZ service on/off campus]."

MINI-CASE STUDY: PARTNER-LESS PHD

"I don't feel like my partner supports me doing a PhD. I feel so isolated – I haven't been able to make any friends outside of my department. I don't want to talk with my colleagues or my supervisor about my personal situation."

Q. *Whether or not you talk with your graduate students about personal issues, how do you ensure that they feel supported as a PhD student?*

MINI-CASE STUDY: PHD PLUS ONE

"I'm pregnant and concerned about my ability to complete my PhD; plus, I'm worried about childcare options and about how to tell my supervisor that I won't be able to do as many hours in the lab as I did before. I'm also concerned about t the financial impact of my pregnancy. Will there be anyone/anything to support me when I return after my maternity leave?"

Q. Does your institution have an office or any specific initiatives (e.g., bursaries, loans, peer groups) to support graduate students who are parents?

SKIT: FAMILY PRIORITIES

Original written by peer advisor Melissa (PhD Developmental Psychology and Education).

Audience. Faculty, students, or both. Small or large groups.

Time Required. 20 minutes = 5 min prep / 5 min skit / 10 min debrief

Instructions. The facilitator invites two workshop participants to play the roles of a PhD student and their supervisor. They have three minutes to read the script and get into character. After three minutes, the facilitator reads the background aloud and then calls "Ready? Action!" When the skit ends, the facilitator leads a discussion with the larger group around the debrief questions. There are debrief prompts that the facilitator can use to help guide the discussion.

Background (Read Aloud by Facilitator). The student, [insert real name of actor], is a first-year international PhD student who recently learned that a family member is terminally ill. [Student's name] is overwhelmed by this news and wants to go back home to be with their family, so they are considering a leave of absence.

Debrief Questions for Group Discussion:

- What are the student's interests? The supervisor's?
- Did you hear any great questions? Are there any other questions you might have asked?
- Was there anything that the supervisor or the student could have done differently?

Debrief Prompts (for Facilitator):

- Point out any documents, resources, or campus supports that are available.
- Highlight where the supervisor made effective use of pauses and silence.
- Review trauma-informed approaches.

READY? ACTION! (Script for Actors)

STUDENT: Thank you for meeting with me. I have a personal situation, and I'm not sure what to do, or where to go for help.

SUPERVISOR: Okay ... thank you for coming to talk to me. [*Pause*]

STUDENT: Sure ... two weeks ago I found out that member of my family is really sick. Doctors say they don't have long. [*Student gets emotional*]

SUPERVISOR: [*Offers tissue. Gives student a moment.*] I'm so sorry to hear that.

STUDENT: Sorry to be so emotional – it's just that I'm an international student, and I don't want my family going through this while I'm in another country. My mom really needs me.

SUPERVISOR: [*Nods empathically. Says nothing*]

STUDENT: But I just started my PhD. I haven't even completed a full year yet. Is it even possible for me to leave now? I'm pretty sure the withdrawal deadline has passed, if I leave now would I receive a failing grade for all my courses? What about my funding? My study permit? Would I lose this opportunity and everything I've worked so hard for and everything my family has sacrificed? I just don't know what to do. [*Again student gets emotional*]

SUPERVISOR: This sounds like a very difficult situation, especially because your family is so far away. Just to make sure I understand, you are wondering about taking a leave of absence from your PhD to return home to see your ailing family member and support your mother? [*Pause for student to correct/acknowledge*] You are concerned about how this could impact your program, funding, and study permit, and you want more information about the process for taking a leave?

STUDENT: Yes, that sounds right.

SUPERVISOR: Okay. I've never had to deal with a leave with one of my students, but I know there is some paperwork. I'm going to suggest that we connect with the grad coordinator – I think they might have a better idea of the process. There are also some campus resources for grad students in similar circumstances, such as the family support office. If you'd like, I can point some out and you can make notes, or I can send links after our meeting.

STUDENT: Thank you, it would be helpful if you sent me links.

SUPERVISOR: I'm glad that you reached out and shared this difficult situation with me. We can talk again if that would be helpful. I'll reach out to you once I have information from the grad coordinator.

***END OF SKIT** Move to Debrief.*

Roommates and Housing

Roommate and housing conflicts were a small subset of the Personal/Family category, a topic raised in less than 5 percent of all of our conversations. November was a busy month for this topic – housing-related issues tended to be the sole issue raised in a conversation – as compared to the more wide-ranging, multiple issue conversations that we had on other topics. Students were primarily concerned about:

- escalated conflicts between roommates or with landlords (and occasionally tenants) about chores, noise, study/social balance, etc.
- challenges finding appropriate and affordable housing, in particular for grad students with families or who were unfamiliar with the costs of living in a large expensive city.

We talked with grad students about strategies for effective communication and ways to approach interpersonal conflict, and many times, students were open to role playing potential conversations with the peer advisors. We directed students to the university's housing service, and where appropriate, recommended mediation as a process for potentially resolving an ongoing conflict and restoring positive relations. Luckily students were able to access several off-campus free mediation services;[1] although, we always included the "reality check" that both the student and their roommate (or landlord) would have to agree to participate. In other cases, after sharing their story and exploring options, the student would determine that the best course of action was to look for a new roommate!

> **WHAT YOU CAN DO**
>
> ! Since the pandemic, most people have a greater appreciation of the challenges of integrated work/life spaces. For many grad students, this has always been the case – where they "live is also where they work." As a result, housing conflicts, disruptions, or uncertainties (roomates or landlord) can be particularly unsettling. When supporting a student with housing issues be kind as well as strategic.

Q. Ask yourself in the moment – is it more helpful for me to offer a moment of calm listening or for us to engage in a joint problem-solving session?

MINI-CASE STUDY: MY MESSY PHD ROOMMATE

One of your graduate students is distracted by a housing issue.

"I've had a difficult relationship with my roommate for a long time, and I want to know how to be more 'assertive' about my concerns about cleanliness and shared household chores. I find the whole situation really distracting, but I'm 'stuck' until the end of the lease."

Q1. Do you think they would tell you?

Q2. How could you support them?

MINI-CASE STUDY: FAMILY, FINANCES, AND FRUSTRATION

"I'm an international PhD student. I have to go home for family reasons which will mean I have to break a lease which involves a financial penalty which I can't afford. Not to mention I don't know how to tell my supervisor."

Q1. If a graduate student in your department came to you about the issue presented above, how would you respond?

Q2. Do you know if your graduate students have secure housing and if your university has any emergency funding for housing?

Grief and Loss

The reality of being an informal and confidential service that promoted "no issue is too small (or big) to discuss" meant that over the course of our conversations about whatever conflict brought them to us, individuals might share that a death or an injury of a loved one, a divorce, a breakup, or another family or personal issue was having an impact on their academic experience. As a frontline student-facing service, we also had to be prepared to speak with students who may have been directly or indirectly impacted by a death on campus or by a tragic event off-campus that involved students.

It can be difficult to know what to say when someone is grieving, suffering, or has experienced loss. We may be tempted to say nothing. Be courageous – say something to the other person, so they know that you understand the impact that the situation is having on them.

- "Thank you for sharing this with me."
- "That really sounds like a difficult/bad situation."
- "I'm so sorry that this happened – how can I help?"

> **WHAT YOU CAN DO**
>
> ! While engaging in compassionate listening, be aware of your own state of mind. Listening to someone describe a situation of loss or grief can leave an impression on us.
>
> ! Here are some tips that I adapted from the Canadian Association for Suicide Prevention[2] to share with the peer advisors to help them provide support to their fellow grad students who might be experiencing loss:
>
> - Be mindful that people experience grief and sadness in different ways; grief can be expressed through behavior and actions. In addition to referrals to campus counseling and grief support groups, include non-specific resources/supports like exercising (walking, gym), journaling, or open letters (not to send, but to express).

- Reassure the student that feelings of sadness or grief are normal and understandable. Grief is not always a linear or continuous experience – it can emerge in spurts or be experienced in cycles that last just a few minutes.

- Help the student focus on what they can control. What are some of the ways they can support themselves and friends or community members during a difficult time?

- Acknowledge that lack of information about a campus crisis can be frustrating. Highlight the many factors that play into the release of information by the university or police including: respect and dignity for the student and their family and friends, for the family's wishes, for privacy, legal, or safety considerations; and for cooperation with police, or coroner, etc.

MINI-CASE STUDY: FAMILY LOSS IN GRAD SCHOOL

"I recently lost a close family member in a tragic accident. I'm angry and grieving, and I think my department is being hostile and unempathetic about performance and deadline expectations. I'm considering a leave to deal with family estate matters, but maybe I need legal advice to help me with the accident."

Q1. If a student came to you with this concern, would you be comfortable talking to them using the grief and loss tips above?

Q2. Are there any grief counseling services or support groups on campus that you could refer them to?

CONFLICT #8 – Health and Wellness/Accessibility

These conversations tended to be long (approximately 60 percent were over 30 minutes) and more emotional (over 70 percent of the time the individual was either upset, upset at times, or somewhat upset during the conversation) compared with other hotspot topics. At the end of these conversations, many students shared that talking with a peer helped them to gain new perspectives, to alleviate stress, and over a quarter of them mentioned that they would reconnect with the peer advisors if they required further assistance.

Health and Wellness

In our conversations, health and wellness issues were identified as both a cause of and an effect of conflict. For example, a student might describe how their strained relationship with a supervisor or fellow student was negatively impacting their health or wellness, or they might say that their poor health or mental wellness was making it difficult for them to communicate with their supervisor or other students.

As we were not counselors or trained health professionals, we were careful not to explore cause and effect or to diagnose students. In most cases we were simply listening (peer-to-peer) and responding to requests for referrals to various healthcare resources and supports both on and off campuses. Students described feeling:

- "anxious" and "stressed" about requesting a personal leave because of their supervisor's expectations for working hours and pressure to make academic progress
- "sad" and "hopeless" because they couldn't meet various thesis defense deadlines due to chronic health-related issues

- "tired" and "unable to perform well" from lack of sleep
- "lonely" and "isolated" because they aren't connected with many other students in their department
- "distressed" about grad school or their department culture
- "overwhelmed" or "worn out" because of their workload on top of physical and mental health conditions, or because they felt unsure about how to ask for more time and direction for their research, or whether they should take a leave from grad school because of their issues

A few students we talked with were anticipating difficult conversations with their supervisor and department administrators after returning from a leave. Other times, the individual was worried about the health and wellness of their students or friends, "What can I do if a student I'm supervising is experiencing a mental health crisis?"

I note that our service had been created partly in response to recommendations set out in the university's 2014 Mental Health Framework:[1] to create graduate programming that would "enhance support for graduate students in their interactions with their supervisors" and that "has a focus on personal skill development, including individual resilience, coping skills, problem solving, and self-advocacy."[2] Recent surveys and studies continue to flag mental health and wellness as a significant concern for graduate students, especially post–COVID-19.[3] Canadian researchers from the University of Toronto and McGill University concluded that there is a need to "prioritize developing early intervention and prevention programming for students for whom the pandemic may be particularly challenging, such as students who are beginning to show declining mental health in response to increasing social isolation."[4] An American study, of over 15,000 graduate and professional students at nine public research universities, concluded that the pandemic has "looming negative impacts on mental health of undergraduate and graduate students at research universities," with particular impact on students who have not adapted well to remote instruction.[5]

Improving the mental health and wellness of PhD researchers requires universities to focus on key areas of concern including supervision and leadership, work-life balance and demands of work, supports (financial, administrative), development (career) as well as the social environment (making connections).[6] Health and wellness are deeply intertwined with graduate conflict, and more attention to these areas, which align with our identified Top Ten conflict hotspots, will be needed in the post–COVID-19 era for effective conflict management.

WHAT YOU CAN DO

! Here are some considerations for institutional conflict prevention related to health and wellness that is aligned with post-pandemic research:

- Communication with graduate students is vitally important – whether from staff, faculty, or peer support group.
- Focus on prevention, including support for remote learning.
- In what ways is your institution engaging front-line faculty and academic advising staff in supporting student mental health and wellness?
- Meaningful contributions from diverse student voices is essential as new strategies are developed to improve students' mental health and reduce anxiety and stress.

! Supporting effective conflict management may help grad students to thrive, rather than just survive, grad school. Find advice for grad students on procrastination, parenting, stress, and anxiety (among other topics) from various mental health professionals in this book edited by Arielle Shanok and Nicole Benedicto Elden, *Thriving in Graduate School: The Expert's Guide to Success and Wellness*.[7]

Accessibility/Accommodation (Disability)

Graduate students living with disabilities (mental, physical, permanent, long-term, intermittent/dynamic, or temporary such as an injury like a broken bone) may require unique academic accommodations in order to meet the academic standards of their research program and participate as a member of the graduate community.  While some students will know to or opt to register with the accessibility/disability office on campus, other grad students may be trying to manage their disability and academic responsibilities without university assistance. Concerns brought to our office related to accessibility included:

- disabilities or health conditions that were not being properly accommodated which impacted graduate experience and progress
- lack of understanding of accessibility needs by supervisors or departments
- questions about how to get support at the university (referrals to the accessibility office)

Given the somewhat amorphous nature of a PhD and of the related accommodations that might change multiple times over the course of the PhD (course work, research, writing, defense stages), often a grad students' dialogue with supervisors about alternative arrangements/accommodations would be complex and ongoing. There was a belief, expressed by both students and faculty, that conversations about PhD academic accommodations were among the most difficult of supervisory conversations.

We spoke to grad students who described strained or difficult supervisory relationships ("My supervisor ignores me") and who felt like the lack of accommodation for their mental or physical disability from a supervisor or the department was having a direct impact on their academic progress/their ability to complete their degree.

More specifically, these grad students had the impression that their supervisor or department decision-makers:

- compared their (slow) progress or (reduced) workload to other graduate students in the department
- didn't think they actually were in need of an accommodation
- didn't want to accommodate requests for additional time to progress through the program or course, and if asked, would either insist upon completion of work at the pace set out in progress guidelines or the "same as everyone else in the department" or recommend that the student withdraw from the program
- failed to understand that there was a legal obligation to accommodate

Some students were looking for advice on how to self-advocate for alternative arrangements without disclosing their disability, while others were interested in learning more about how to advocate for accommodation plans that had been developed in collaboration with the university accessibility/disability office.

For their part, faculty wanted clarification on specific student requests for accommodation (is this reasonable? how do I respond?) and on their responsibilities as supervisors. I would refer them to a guide developed by campus accessibility services for faculty about "demystifying academic accommodations" or to the graduate and professional program student accessibility services handbook.[8]

> **WHAT YOU CAN DO**
>
> ! When responding to accessibility and accommodation issues, consider:
>
> - Advanced preparation, information gathering, and sharing, so that everyone will feel better prepared for a productive and open discussion focused on shared information (information power!). Can the university's accessibility/disability office or advisor provide support or advice for the discussion? Is there a handbook or guide to help faculty or students navigate accommodations in the graduate context?
>
> - Ways to frame conversations around interests and joint goals rather than the disability (e.g., "It seems like you and I agree that starting your writing in the spring is a reasonable goal – let's start from there to put together a workable timeline and check-in points. How does that sound?")
>
> - Brainstorming options for how things can be done to achieve common interests, rather than focusing on deficiencies (in what ways things can't be done): "As we review all of the things that usually fall within the pre-writing stage, let me know what might work best from your perspective."
>
> - What happens next (step by step) if a discussion doesn't go as planned and a resolution on the accommodation issue can't be reached? Can the disability office/advisor provide advice or facilitate a conversation? How are accessibility concerns escalated (to whom and how are decisions made?)

MINI-CASE STUDY: MEDICAL REVEAL

"I just emailed my two co-supervisors (Dr. Y and Dr. Z) to let them know that I won't be able to attend an upcoming presentation. I didn't mention why, because it relates to a flare up of an ongoing and very personal medical condition. Dr. Z responded by saying, 'I am extremely disappointed in you. This is not the behavior of a dedicated graduate student,' while Dr. Y countered by saying, 'I know the situation is not ideal, however, it is reasonable given the student suffers from [diagnosis].' I can't believe that Dr. Y shared details about my personal health condition with Dr. Z. When I talked with Dr. Y about my condition at a previous meeting, I assumed it was a confidential conversation. I don't know what to do – I am not registered with or supported by any campus services."

Q1. What are some options for the student? Does your campus have specific accessibility supports for graduate students?

Q2. What could have supervisors Dr. Y and Dr. Z done differently?

MINI-CASE STUDY: LAB AGITATOR

"The postdoc in my lab gets angry when we don't finish testing all their ideas. They slam doors and shout a lot. However, what they want isn't possible – the stress is starting to affect my health. I'm so worried about the situation sometimes I feel like I can't breathe – my chest is so tight when I think about going into the lab."

Q1. Is this a mental health issue or a physical health issue?

Q2. Does it matter in terms of supporting the individual? Why or why not?

MINI-CASE STUDY: ACCOMMODATING DISCRETION

"I don't think I am being properly accommodated. I'm connected with the disability office, but I haven't wanted them to intervene on my behalf because it might look like I'm less capable than the other PhD students. The department culture is very competitive, and I don't want to share any details of my disability with my supervisor (or anyone else!)."

Q. Are there ways for the student to advocate for what they need in order to be properly accommodated without sharing too many details?

MINI-CASE STUDY: BROKEN GRAD

"I seriously broke my leg three weeks ago and I had to have surgery to set the bones in several places. My committee meeting is next week, and I don't think I should go ahead with it since I'm still on some serious medication. I've emailed and called a few times and I can't reach my supervisor. Even if I do get a hold of them, I'm worried because the last time I asked if we could delay a committee meeting my supervisor said 'no, these meetings are set in stone.'"

Q. What are some options for the student?

MINI-CASE STUDY: MY PHD MENTAL HEALTH VACATION?!

"I have just returned from a leave of absence that I took to manage a mental health issue. I'm angry because my supervisor is calling the leave a 'vacation.' Before I left, my supervisor seemed supportive, but now that I've returned, they've suggested that perhaps I'm 'not a good candidate for a PhD,' and that I should consider simply completing a master's degree!"

Q. If the student asked you for help, would you intervene? Why or why not? What would you talk about?

CONFLICT #9 – Laboratories

Laboratory environments are petri dishes for conflict – especially interpersonal conflict. Labs are a part of and yet, apart from the wider university; every lab has its own unique makeup, and as a result, a diverse range of lab-specific issues. Between 2016 and 2020, the Grad CRC saw an increasing number of lab issues and identified this as an emerging concern for the school of graduate studies. Lab conflicts were multi-party: involving grad students (junior/senior, PhDs/master's), undergrads, postdocs, RAs (research assistants), staff, and principal investigators (PIs). Issues were sometimes complicated if the lab was located off-site or operated in collaboration with nearby hospitals and institutions.

We heard from students in the sciences that they were actively avoiding conflict and, in fact, any situations that might potentially lead to disagreement, discomfort, or dispute. They did not feel they had "permission" to leave the lab to attend training to learn the skills that would ultimately benefit them and the lab. Our conversations were wide-ranging and touched upon multiple issues at once; for example, a lab issue might be raised as well as a supervision or health/wellness issue. We also heard questions and comments like:

- "How can I move past a lab conflict and set new lab expectations?"
- "My PI expects me to run experiments that are outside of the scope of my research."
- "I supervise a lab and I'm concerned about a PhD student who has been behaving inappropriately. What can I do?"

As one peer advisor noted after a challenging conversation: "Labs! Issues between individuals can potentially 'infect' the whole lab." Overall, student and faculty lab concerns seemed to run parallel as illustrated in the chart on the following page:

Grad Student Concerns	Faculty Concerns
Personality differences	Lab dynamics – personalities
"Unpleasant" conversations	None of the members of lab are getting along – strong personalities and poor communication
Power dynamics between senior and junior PhD students in the lab	
	Complex dynamics between staff, grad students, and faculty supervisors
Lack of trust in lab supervisor due to increasingly aggressive and disrespectful behavior toward lab members – should the student stay or leave the lab?	Hostile environment in the lab – concerns about proprietary data and sharing of equipment
	Student behavior is unprofessional
Uncomfortable working with one lab member, how to change labmates when principal investigator (PI) does not support a change	Impact of one student's behavior on rest of the lab
	Student is often absent, and when is in the lab is disruptive
"Toxic" lab environment	Students feels intimidated and bullied by a colleague who shares the lab – they changed schedules so they don't have to work at the same time
Avoiding the lab	
Finding one's place in the lab – no idea what to do but everyone expects them to already know everything	Student's performance slipping (poor attention to detail, not following through on commitments, rejecting feedback)
Lab manager won't help with training and PI doesn't deal with day-to-day running of lab	

In 2005, journalist and professor Irene S. Levine observed, "Resources, responsibilities, intellectual ownership, and personality conflicts are a few common sources of laboratory tension."[1] When we consider how long sources of lab conflict have been studied, is it possible that many labs have become resolution resistant? This would explain why so many conventional conflict resolution treatments ("listen more and talk less"; "focus on the problem not the personality") have not had the intended or desired impact in terms of curing conflict in university labs. They may work for isolated conflicts, but not for the lab environment as a whole.

It may be time to challenge the narrative that this is "just the way our lab is." Consider what might happen if a lab was actively preventing and managing conflict – how much less time and energy might be consumed, and how many more productive research hours might become available with lab members truly engaged across differences?

Overcoming lab conflict resistance requires a 360-degree approach for the entire lab community – shifting from a focus on resolving individual conflicts to managing conflict more generally within the lab environment in a holistic and restorative manner. In other words, we shouldn't be looking for a cure as much as for opportunities to better manage common sources of laboratory tension and, as a result, the impact that conflict has on students and faculty members who work in labs.

A holistic approach might emphasize the following themes (derived from the lab issues outlined above):

- building trust and setting boundaries (lab dynamics)
- day-to-day lab interactions and life outside the lab
- how to escalate concerns (lab supervision, protocols)

Forming a "lab contract" or a "lab social contract"[2] or co-creating a set of shared expectations is an important part of effective conflict management. Skills like self-reflection and looking at the big picture can be learned by students and brought into the lab.[3] Lab members can benefit from having opportunities to think creatively and collaboratively outside of the four corners of the research. The relationships and strategies that they develop outside of the lab can help them to find ways of working with each other within the lab, especially when there are differences of opinion or experience.

WHAT YOU CAN DO

! The Lewis Lab at the University of Alberta[4] has developed an EDI (equity, diversity, and inclusion) statement, which states in part: "Movement towards equitable, diverse, and inclusive environments requires reflection and action at the level of institutions, departments, and research groups. This statement reflects that process for the Lewis Research Group and our collective plan and expectations for reflection, self-education, action, and accountability."

Q1. Does your lab have a similar EDI statement or perhaps an unwritten commitment to EDI?

Q2. If not, how might you involve the students in your lab in the development (and ongoing engagement with) of such a statement?

Q3. What else could you do to demonstrate your lab's commitment to an inclusive and equitable learning and research environment?

TIP SHEET: BRAINSTORMING HOW TO PREVENT LAB CONFLICT

Use this to help brainstorm strategies to prevent conflict in your lab.
1. Build a better lab from within.
PhDs, master's, and postdocs will bring with them into the lab past understandings of lab culture and etiquette (e.g., lab space, equipment use/time, funding). Certain protocols may be clear to those who have worked in the lab for years, and less clear to newcomers. **BRAINSTORM:** *How do we welcome and integrate new lab members? (training/onboarding)*
When people participate (*and feel heard) in a fair process, they are more likely to acknowledge the legitimacy of the process and accept the outcome. Invite lab members to participate in discussions about lab guidelines/problem-solving processes early on. Consider an essential list of lab values that lab members can interpret in plain language and adapt to their current environment. Revisit regularly to ensure buy-in. **BRAINSTORM:** *How can we create an environment where assumptions can be made explicit and be discussed openly?*
In the lab, proper process is very important. The same goes for interpersonal problem-solving. Does everyone in the lab know what to do if they have an issue and how and to whom to escalate an issue within and outside of the lab? **BRAINSTORM:** *How can we encourage early communication about concerns and ensure appropriate escalation?*
2. Link to communities outside the lab.
Lab space can become personal space – encourage students to find their "other" spaces on campus. For example, do students feel like they can visit alternative spaces to the lab (for coffee/lunch) or participate in non-lab activities (meditation; music; exercise). In addition to the people in the lab that students can go to for support/advice, map out others outside of the lab. **BRAINSTORM:** *How can we encourage lab members to build connections and seek support both within and outside of the lab?*

3. Talk early and put things in writing.
Smaller problems can be magnified by the lab lens – early action and communication is key. Certain situations call for more clarity of understanding and formality than casual discussions. For example, the nature of the research being done in the lab – who owns what, who gets credit and when (for research papers/publications) – can be sources of confusion and disagreement. **BRAINSTORM:** *How can we develop frameworks that encourage early discussion and promote advance planning to prevent common conflicts?*
Sources/Resources
Reinhart Reithmeier and Sarah Williams, "Promoting a Health Lab Culture at the University of Toronto," School of Graduate Studies, University of Toronto, 2020, www.sgs.utoronto.ca/wp-content/uploads/sites/253/2020/12/Healthy-Lab-Initiative-Final-Report-2020.pdf. Sandy Ong, "Conflict Control in the Lab," Asian Scientist, 13 July 2018, www.asianscientist.com/2018/07/columns/conflict-control-in-the-lab/. Lauren Tebay, "Dealing with Tension and Conflict in the Lab," BiteSizeBio, 9 July 2016, https://bitesizebio.com/27373/dealing-tension-conflict-lab/. Joan C. Waters, "Conflict in the Lab: Concepts and Tools for Managing Interpersonal Conflict," Columbia University Ombuds Office, September 2013, https://womeninscienceatcolumbia.files.wordpress.com/2013/09/conflict-in-lab.pdf.

MINI-CASE STUDY: DR. DETAIL AND MR. LAISSEZ

Consider this emerging lab conflict:

Dr. Detail is known in her lab as a micromanaging principal investigator – she checks in with most of her students at least once a day. Laissez is a second-year PhD student who is struggling to get his experiments up and running. He is overwhelmed by the constant check-ins, and he freezes up every time Dr. Detail drops by.

Q. What are Dr. Detail's and Laissez's positions and interests?

MINI-CASE STUDY: LAB DISTRACTION

You supervise a lab group, and one member, Sigma, has come to you for advice. Sigma tells you that when he started working in the lab, he assumed that everyone would be really focused and committed, but apparently the situation is the opposite! Every lab meeting, someone mentions a trending news item and the group gets distracted. Sigma tells you: "We are having great debates but what we really need is to finalize our research timetable and get down to work! It's not that I'm not interested, but everyone's political views are irrelevant to our work."

Q1. How might you respond?

Q2. What are two to three questions you might ask to get at interests?

MINI-CASE STUDY: OPTIONS FOR ESCALATION?

Pick the best response and reflect on why the other responses might be less effective:

Grumble is a third-year PhD student who has recently changed labs. Today, Grumble and a senior postdoc in the lab had a disagreement about lab protocols. *Which is the best first step for Grumble?*

(a) Send a long email to the PI supervisor describing the situation from their point of view and asking the supervisor to intervene on their behalf.
(b) Go talk to graduate chair about the "unacceptable lab working conditions."
(c) Contact the lab manager to inquire about whether there are any lab manuals/guidelines.
(d) Talk to the other students in the lab about how difficult it is to work with the postdoc.

MINI-CASE STUDY: UNDER AND OVER IN THE LAB

"I'm feeling really undervalued and overworked. My lab has totally unrealistic expectations."

Q1. Do you think your students would be comfortable bringing this type of concern to your attention?

Q2. If you found out that this was what students in your lab were thinking, how could you use the Brainstorming How to Prevent Lab Conflict Tip Sheet?

SKIT: LAB WORKLOAD OVERLOAD

Original written by peer advisors Kim (PhD Social Justice Education) and Margeaux (PhD English/Gender Diversity Studies)

Audience. Faculty, students, or both. Small or large groups.

Time Required. 20 minutes = 5 min prep / 5 min skit / 10 min debrief

Instructions. The facilitator invites two workshop participants to play the roles of a PhD student and their supervisor. Tell them they have three minutes to read the script and get into character. After three minutes, the facilitator reads the Background aloud and then calls "Ready? Action!" When the skit ends, the facilitator leads a discussion with the larger group around the debrief questions. There are debrief prompts that the facilitator can use to help guide the discussion.

Background (Read Aloud by Facilitator). Lee is a few months into the third year of a PhD and has two years until (anticipated) graduation. This year things have changed. Lee's supervisor, Professor Omni, has been expecting everyone to work longer days and Lee has spent the last month working twelve hours a day in the lab; and is expected to email Professor Omni with an update at the end of each day. Lee is incredibly stressed out and is realizing that this is no longer doable. Lee needs to talk to Professor Omni about reducing the workload or possibly dropping out. Lee visits Dr. Omni's office during office hours and knocks on the door.

Debrief Questions for Group Discussion:

- What issues does this raise?
- Expectations – how are they set? Interests/positions?
- What resources on campus might help the student?

Debrief Prompts (for Facilitator Only):

- Stress/culture of the lab
- Permission to take time away from lab for non-academic related priorities
- Efficiency – time management
- Productivity and "taking a break"
- Plan for week/day/month – what needs to get done and when
- Individual development plans[5] to help open up the dialogue for career and project – related project management

Supervising Conflict

- Health and safety (supervisor's responsibility)
- Work as a student or as an employee (TA, RA)?

READY? ACTION! (Script for Actors)

SUPERVISOR: Oh, hi Lee, Did we have a meeting scheduled for today?

STUDENT: Hi, Professor Omni. Sorry. No. I was just wondering if perhaps you had time to talk about the lab?

SUPERVISOR: Well, I suppose.

STUDENT: Thanks so much! I really appreciate it. [*Pause*] Well, um, I was wondering if it would be possible for me to leave the lab a little bit earlier each day? The last month I've been putting in twelve-hour days and I'm finding it hard to carve out time to work on my thesis.

SUPERVISOR: Why have you been spending so many hours at the lab? It really shouldn't take you twelve hours to complete the tasks I've assigned. Clearly there are some efficiency issues. Do you not know how to perform the tests?

STUDENT: No, of course I do, Professor Omni.

SUPERVISOR: Then what's the problem? Everyone else seems to finish their work in less time. Perhaps I need to reassign your duties to a more senior student.

STUDENT: [*Starting to become visibly upset*] No, no. I can do the work. But I guess ... what I'm trying to say ... is that it's just taking more time than you've allotted. Everyone's putting in twelve-hour days – not just me. And I can tell that we're all exhausted.

SUPERVISOR: Well, no one else has come to me to complain.

STUDENT: I understand. Maybe I shouldn't speak for everyone. But as you can see by the lab records, everyone's days are much longer than last year.

SUPERVISOR: You know that the project is ramping up and working a little extra is par for the course. When I was doing my PhD, we'd work fourteen hours or more in the lab each day. Sometimes we'd even sleep there so that we could get up the next morning and be right back to work. That's what commitment looks like. I'm starting to wonder if you're just not cut out for the demands of graduate studies.

END OF SKIT Move to Debrief.

CONFLICT #10 – Career and Work

The career and work issues category included far more conversations with students than with faculty and staff. Faculty had concerns about workplace/teaching mechanics – "How can I support another faculty member who has a concern about how a graduate course has been structured (attendance, engagement, expectations)?" – and about content – "What are my options if another faculty member seems to be copying my course?" Student concerns, on the other hand, ranged from the philosophical to the practical:

- "Is a PhD worth it?" "What about a postdoc?" (self-doubt, financial/personal/intellectual considerations)
- "How do I make the right long-term or short-term plan? What is the role of a PhD in my life?" "What else can I do with a PhD if I don't want to be an academic?"
- "How will I ever find a job after graduation?" "How do I put together a résumé and cover letter?"
- "How do I tell my supervisor I don't want to stay in academia?" (Pressure, strategic communication)
- "What if my supervisor won't give me a (good) reference?"
- "How do I find a part-time job during grad school?' "What do I do now – I was rejected for a part-time job on campus?"
- "I'm tired of working as a teaching or research assistant/feeling overworked and underpaid."
- "What is the process to transfer from a PhD to a master's? I think a master's is good enough."
- "How do I find a postdoc?" "How do I approach a faculty member who I might want to work with for a future postdoc?"

Other topics touched upon in our conflict coaching conversations included employment-related and work-related issues, challenges or conflicts in academic placements, practicums, and internships.

In our conversations with students, we often talked about strategies for effective and respectful communication and tried to determine who else supported their research. This was particularly so for students who may have had a difficult or conflict-ridden relationship with their supervisor and were now trying to figure out how to transition out of their graduate studies into a career, and realizing they would likely need a reference, contacts, or referrals from their supervisor.

Due to the short and long-term impact of the COVID-19 pandemic on the job market for students who have recently completed or will be completing their graduate studies, it is reasonable to expect career issues will be a growing graduate hotspot. Students are likely to be even more anxious about what life will look like for them after they finish their graduate degrees.[1]

WHAT YOU CAN DO

! Whether or not grad students mention these aloud, they will have concerns about their future and their careers. You can:

- Help students to understand the *value of a PhD* from your perspective (beyond allowing you to become a supervisor). Share how a PhD changed the way you think, engage with others, or benefited you as an intellectual.

- *"Choose your words wisely."* This advice is from *PhD to Life* blogger Jen Polk who wrote a post about faculty who may "express sadness about careers not launched (research not published, impact not made)."[2] Your career path to academia may not be the one that your grad student(s) want to follow, so be mindful that their journey may not follow the same course as your own, and that your words carry weight.

- Fill in gaps. Use your industry knowledge to help students appreciate the range of career options that might be available in the field and how to get from A (PhD) to Z (career). Are there industry-specific books or supports you recommend?[3] Professional development skills that you feel may open doors? Take a moment to note any that have come to mind.

- Remind students about campus career centers (they aren't just for undergrads) and online career resources. Students can ask if there are specific advisors who work with grads or workshops specifically for grads.

! Why start a recommendation letter from scratch? Here are a few resources for faculty: Wendy Hall, "Writing Strong Letters of Recommendation,"[4] Michael Ernst, "How to Write a Letter of Recommendation,"[5] and the Commission on the Status of Women (Arizona), "Avoiding Gender Bias in Letter of Reference Writing."[6]

! Dr. Nana Lee (University of Toronto) recommends talking with students about identifying and tracking their "growth insights." Dr. Lee has created a series of graduate professional development videos, including one on growth insights and the importance of reframing failure as a step toward success: "Graduate Professional Development GPD 19 – Reframing Failure."[7]

MINI-CASE STUDY: NOT IN IT FOR THE LONG HAUL

Consider how you might respond if this student came to you for advice:

"I originally applied to grad school to complete a master's degree, as entry-level occupations in my field generally only require an MSc. My supervisor, Dr. Academe, is frequently making jokes about 'the long haul' and is encouraging me to collaborate on long-term, well-funded, interdisciplinary projects that could lead to a PhD. I'm not sure how to tell them I'm not in it for the long haul."

Q. Is there an opportunity to talk about interests? How?

MINI-CASE STUDY: PRESENTING ... NOTHING?

"I was working closely with Professor A as a research assistant, and I considered them a mentor. Last year, I decided to switch the direction of my research and work with another professor, which I think upset Professor A. Before the change, we had an abstract accepted for a conference and I expected to present my research there with Professor A, but they withdrew the abstract without discussing it with me, and I had already paid for my flight and accommodation! So, I went to the conference without presenting. I am so upset, but I really want to reconcile our relationship because a strong reference from Professor A could help my career."

Q1. *Where would you start in talking with this student?*

Q2. *If you could turn back time, how might this conflict have been prevented?*

Work Placements and Internships

We had relatively few conversations about issues arising in practicum settings (or placements, internships). Instead, faculty members who supervised these types of professional learning experiences invited us to run pre-departure workshops for conflict prevention year over year. Our workshops were intended to provide students with some strategies for conflict prevention in the workplace (interests and positions, managing expectations where there is a power imbalance, asking the right questions), and to help students know when and how to escalate concerns to the employer and when to involve their faculty supervisors.

What did the master's students in our workshops tell us they expected might result in conflict with their employer? Here are some potential sources of placement conflict:

- complexity/boredom
- workload/hours/environment

- lack of time/distraction
- defining role and managing expectations
- power imbalances
- assumptions/past experiences
- personalities

WHAT YOU CAN DO

Q. If you supervise or are a faculty liaison for placements – are there any other areas of potential conflict that you would add to the list?

MINI-CASE STUDY: EXPECTATIONS OF REALITY[8]

"When I was given my first assignment, it was totally different than I had expected. I had assumed the work I would be doing would be like my course experiences. These pre-set ideas about what my responsibilities would be really hampered my experience. The reality was much less research oriented than I presumed, which caused me to question how I could spin my final project."

Q. How might you coach the student in approaching this situation?

MINI-CASE STUDY: DUTY DILEMMA

"I have been in my placement role at a large institution for around a month. At today's staff meeting I was told that I had been assigned to a 'special project.' I have some concerns that I'm being given the work because none of the other staff want to do it, and I'm worried that this project could ruin my placement."

Q. If you were the student, would you speak up?

SKIT: CAREER COLLISION

Original written by peer advisors Margeaux (PhD English/Gender Diversity Studies) and Sam (MA Public Health).

Audience. Faculty, students, or both. Small or large groups.

Time Required. 20 minutes = 5 min prep / 5 min skit / 10 min debrief

Instructions. The facilitator invites two workshop participants to play the roles of a PhD student and their supervisor. Tell them they have three minutes to read the script and get into character. After three minutes, the facilitator reads the background aloud and then calls "Ready? Action!" When the skit ends, the facilitator leads a discussion with the larger group around the debrief questions. There are debrief prompts that the facilitator can use to help guide the discussion.

Background (Read Aloud by Facilitator). Jaye is an upper-year PhD student getting ready to submit a final draft thesis. Jaye hasn't yet told Dr. X (supervisor) that pursuing academia is no longer something of interest. Jaye had an interview for an exciting new job, and just received two emails, one from Dr. X and the other from the prospective employer.

Debrief Questions for Group Discussion:

- What issues does this raise?
- What is the student/supervisor looking for?
- How might you manage this conflict?

Debrief Prompts (for Facilitator):

- Setting expectations earlier/time to completion
- Definitions of success
- Open communication re: changes in career goals
- Considerations: location, power, confidence, transparency
- References (future) and relationship (moving forward)
- Reputation/power/retribution

READY? ACTION! (Script for Actors)

Jaye Reads Emails Aloud:

> To: STUDENT
> From: PROFESSOR X
> Hi Jaye – I thought we should set up a meeting to talk about next steps now that you're getting closer to submitting your dissertation. Let's meet on Thursday of this week to discuss. Regards, Professor X.

> To: STUDENT
> From: GENXTECH
> Dear Jaye – Thank you for coming in on Monday for the interview. We're pleased to let you know that we'd like to offer you the position here at GenXTech Industries. Please let us know when you've submitted your thesis so that we can schedule your start date by first of July. We're sure that will give you enough time. Best, A. Stark

Facilitator Narrates:

Flash forward to student meeting with supervisor.

DR. X: I know you're thinking of closing off this experiment as you wrap up this chapter of your thesis and get ready to finalize your revisions, but I think that the work you've been doing here could really be expanded into a postdoc project in my lab.

JAYE: Oh, well, um thank you so much for thinking of me ...

DR. X: It's no problem! I've already contacted Mega Lab about a potential collaboration and they're keen to work with you as well. We're all getting ready for the long haul [*Knowing laugh*]

JAYE: Thanks Dr. X, that would be an incredible opportunity. But I have some exciting news. GenXTech Industries asked me to come in for an interview. And I got the job!

DR. X: What?!?!??! Who contacted you???? I had NO idea!!! I thought you were serious about pursuing a postdoc.

JAYE: Well, at our last committee meeting, I mentioned that I was maybe considering work opportunities outside of academia.

DR. X: Oh, I didn't think you were serious. I remember mentioning to you at that meeting that I was going to contact Mega Lab about collaborating. I just don't understand your lack of interest.

JAYE: You know I've really enjoyed the work we've been doing but GenXTech is embarking on some very exciting ground-breaking research, and I'd love to be a part of this new frontier.

DR. X: [*Butting in over top of Jaye*] What? Are you saying you don't find this postdoc research exciting??? This is my life's work!

JAYE: [*Quietly*] And they've told me that I can start once I've submitted a final draft of my thesis to you for approval.

DR. X: Well, this is disappointing, Jaye. I really thought you had what it took to follow in my footsteps. I'll have to let Mega Lab know that this project is a no-go. [*Pause*] And as for our next deadline, I'm just not sure if your thesis will be approved by then …

END OF SKIT *Move to Debrief.*

What Can Supervisors Do to Prevent Conflict?

Disputes between students and faculty can be difficult to resolve once they have emerged and solidified. Based on their own lived grad school experiences and conversations with other grads, the 2019/20 peer advisor team came up with a list of things that supervisors can do to help prevent conflict (that I imagine they might have wanted to share with their own supervisors!):

1. *Be approachable.* "Foster an environment where there can be open communication. Make time to talk with me casually (outside of formal meetings)."

2. *Be curious.* "I often need a kind word or a sincere: 'How are you doing?' to check in about how I am doing both academically and personally."

3. *Listen.* "When you actively listen for the (whole) response to your question, it goes a long way toward showing that you care and have my best interests at heart."

4. *Talk about what you expect from me as a grad student.* "I benefit from explicit and proactive communication about expectations. Your words and opinions are weighty."

5. *Consider how, as well as what, you are saying.* "The way you give feedback– direct, constructive, vague – can make a difference to my academic experience (and to my entire life!)."

6. *Lead by example.* "Be the type of academic mentor that I will look to when I feel lost, confused, or downtrodden."

7. *Engage in interpersonal/intercultural skills development.* "I am unique (like you!), and your experiences or communication style may not resonate with me."

8. *Seek support when you need it.* "Managing people isn't always easy and may not be what you signed up for as an academic! I get that – I'm trying to practice self-care too."

Start Thinking about Conflict on Day One

Conflict prevention means starting the supervisory relationship off right. While there are many things to talk about with grad students in the early days of a supervisory relationship, try to balance discussions about the "big picture" and practicalities. Cultivating a big-picture mindset is valuable for graduate students in terms of analysis, problem-solving, and creativity, and to prepare them for "a future with diverse teams addressing interesting topics from different angles."[1] Talking about practicalities helps to minimize everyday stresses.

In principled negotiation, negotiators are encouraged to "separate the person from the problem" to reach a mutually agreeable outcome.[2] In graduate supervision, it can be helpful to "separate the person from the research." Since both interpersonal and scholarly elements of the supervisory relationship are critically important considerations, taking an interest-based approach allows you to begin thinking about your own needs or motivations as a supervisor (as a person and as a researcher) and the needs/motivations of your student (as a person and as a researcher).

> **WHAT YOU CAN DO**
>
> ! When talking to new grad students, suggest that they summarize key points from the discussion and send it to you, so together you can revisit regularly and make sure you are on the same page.
>
> - "Since we are just getting to know each other, I'd like to talk about our roles and responsibilities – have you had a chance to look at the supervision checklist that I sent you? Let's start with page three and review together based on what is most important for your first year as a PhD. We'll have these types of check-in conversations at least once a year."

TIP SHEET: SUPERVISION EARLY DAYS

This tip sheet can be used as a template for a joint discussion between a supervisor and their new graduate student.
Be curious and try to get to know each other as people and as researchers. This information will not only ensure the relationship starts out positively, it will help you to manage conflict down the road.
Get to know the PERSON
Reflect on your/their needs and interests
<ul><li>What am I looking for from a grad student/supervisor? What is on my wish list and what is a deal-breaker?</li><li>What style of supervision do I provide/am I looking for? Am I willing to/expected to provide mentorship/coaching?</li><li>What are some of my academic and work habits? E.g., How do I respond to criticism, to questions, or to change? Do I prefer being presented with full solutions or working out solutions together? What do I know about their academic/work habits?</li><li>What else?</li></ul>
Talk to each other (and then reflect again)
<ul><li>Are we able to talk openly about roles and responsibilities and to share in the process of setting expectations around supervision? (Collaborative processes can build buy-in.)</li><li>Does it seem like my expectations for this supervisory relationship are realistic and that our interests are compatible?</li><li>Does it seem like our academic and work styles will be similar/complementary? Are comments and questions welcome? (Lack of openness is a potential source of conflict!) How do they respond when I seek clarification or provide critique?</li><li>Does it seem like we understand and respect one another?</li><li>If I have an academic problem, am I expected to bring it to their attention immediately or should I try to problem-solve on my own?</li><li>What else?</li></ul>
Find out more about the person
<ul><li>What or who else is competing for this supervisor's/student's time?</li><li>Are they new to supervision, mid-career, or close to retirement? What are their experiences being supervised?</li><li>Talk with other supervisee(s)/previous supervisor(s) – what do they say?</li></ul>

Get to know the RESEARCHER
Reflect on "BIG picture" items (goals and priorities)
<ul><li>What are our research goals (at this point in time)? What is a priority for me or for them? Where do we align/differ?</li><li>In general, what graduate skills are important to develop now (at this point in time) and in the future?</li><li>What are the institutional (departmental) documents that guide the supervisory relationship and set out expectations? (e.g., supervision guide) Do we know where to locate them and have we reviewed other important graduate documents? What about department-specific *unwritten* rules?</li><li>What else?</li></ul>
Talk to each other (and then reflect again)
<ul><li>Do I understand their research strengths and interests? Do they appear to align or complement mine?</li><li>How can we share in the process of setting goals and priorities?</li><li>How and when should we "check in" about the "big picture"? What happens if we no longer agree, or our goals or priorities have changed?</li><li>Do I prefer to receive/provide minimal or extensive feedback?</li></ul>
Find out how things will work "day-to-day"
Discuss what has worked (or not worked) in the past and try to negotiate a joint framework for how things will work on a practical level. Remember that the day-to-day can change quite quickly, so what works in year one, may not be what works in upper years.
Communication/Meetings
<ul><li>How should we communicate (in person, email, text, etc.)?</li><li>How quickly can I expect a response?</li><li>How often (daily, weekly, monthly)?</li><li>How formal will our supervisory meetings be?</li><li>If there is an emergency, how should this be communicated?</li><li>Who will set and send agendas for meetings?</li><li>Will someone prepare a summary and follow up emails re: action items?</li><li>How far in advance will I book meetings?</li><li>How quick is turnaround usually on written feedback?</li></ul>
Schedules/Timelines
<ul><li>What do our schedules/calendars look like?</li><li>Vacations?</li><li>Office hours?</li><li>How will we set initial timelines and best ways to propose changes?</li><li>Is there overlap in supervision between academics and employment (i.e., TA/RA)? If yes, how is this managed?</li></ul>

Everything Else
• Am I clear about funding? What's the financial plan? • What are expectations on publishing? (Be specific!) Number/frequency of publications? • Have we talked about intellectual property issues? • What else?
Sources/Resources: Get to know the PERSON
H.H. Wagner, S. Temple, I. Dankert, and R. Napper, "How to Communicate Effectively in Graduate Advising," *Facets Journal*, 21 December 2016, www.facetsjournal.com/article/facets-2015-0014/. H.H. Wagner, C. Boyd, and R. Napper, "How to Share the Process of Graduate Advising," *Facets Journal*, 14 December 2016, www.facetsjournal.com/article/facets-2015-0013/. Erin Clow, "Choosing a Graduate Program Supervisor," Career Advice, *University Affairs*, 15 March 2016, https://www.universityaffairs.ca/career-advice/career-advice-article/choosing-a-graduate-program-supervisor/. James Hayton, "What I Wish I'd Known before Starting a PhD," *James Hayton, PhD* (blog), 14 March 2016, https://jameshaytonphd.com/quick-tips/what-i-wish-id-known-before-starting-a-phd. Tara Brabazon, "10 Truths a PhD Supervisor Will Never Tell You," *Times Higher Education*, 11 July 2013, www.timeshighereducation.com/features/10-truths-a-phd-supervisor-will-never-tell-you/2005513.article. Matthew Killeya, "The PhD Journey: How to Choose a Good Supervisor," *NewScientist*, 20 February 2008, www.newscientist.com/article/mg19726442-500-the-phd-journey-how-to-choose-a-good-supervisor/.
Sources/Resources: Get to know the RESEARCHER
Nana Lee, "Finding the Right Supervisor-Student Match," Graduate Matters, *University Affairs*, 7 February 2019, https://www.universityaffairs.ca/career-advice/graduate-matters/finding-the-right-supervisor-student-match/. Hugh Kearns and John Finn, "Ten Key Activities for #PhD Students during the First 100 Days of Their PhD," in *Supervising PhD Students: A Practical Guide and Toolkit* (Austin, TX: Thinkwell, 2017), https://buff.ly/2t3n1qd. Sian Townson, "I Was a Terrible PhD Supervisor. Don't Make the Same Mistakes I Did," *The Guardian*, 24 March 2016, https://www.theguardian.com/higher-education-network/2016/mar/24/i-was-a-terrible-phd-supervisor-dont-make-the-same-mistakes-i-did.

FACILITATED CASE STUDY: STORM ON THE HORIZON?

Time Required. 30 minutes = 10 minutes (individually) reading and reflection/10 minutes (in small groups or pairs) discussion/10 minutes debrief with larger group

Instructions: Divide the group into pairs or small groups. Instruct the groups that as they read the case study, they should try to identify conflicts, potential conflicts, and issues and jot down answers to the five discussion questions. At the end there will be a debrief discussion with the large group with a focus on questions 2 to, 3 and 4.

The People (aka Background).

Hanna is at the end of the first year of their PhD. Hanna is interested in researching the relationship between alcohol consumption and anxiety. Hanna commutes to campus two hours each day and would like to work in the not-for-profit sector after graduation.

Dr. T, Hanna's supervisor, is an expert in metabolic mood swings. Dr. T supervises three other PhD students and is an active public speaker. Dr. T stops by the lab almost every week and holds office hours on Wednesdays (8:30–10 a.m.); although, sometimes public speaking commitments take priority. In addition to the four PhD students in the lab, Dr. T supervises two master's students, two undergraduate students and one postdoc.

The Problem:
Hanna's Point of View
According to Hanna, the last few supervisory meetings with Dr. T were terrible. Now Hanna is feeling "uneasy" about the focus of the research. Hanna isn't feeling very motivated and is "unhappy" about the supervisory relationship. Hanna wonders about changing supervisors "before it's too late." At their last meeting, Hanna started to ask Dr. T whether it might be possible to take the research in a slightly different (and, for Hanna, much more interesting) direction, but Dr. T immediately cut them off. Dr. T said bluntly, "You're silly to think about changing gears so early in your PhD – this could jeopardize your future." Hanna ended the meeting early to avoid bursting into tears in front of Dr. T.

Although Hanna sees Dr. T in the lab regularly, after cursory "hellos," Hanna makes an excuse to leave the area to avoid getting into another uncomfortable discussion in front of the other lab members. Hanna feels "lost" and angry with Dr. T for being so "rude and condescending." Hanna hasn't talked about any of these issues with the other students in the lab because that would be "unprofessional."

Dr. T's Point of View
Dr. T believes that as a first-year PhD student Hanna should be thinking broadly about the research and about keeping as many doors open as possible. Dr. T was shocked at their last meeting when Hanna started to talk about "not feeling committed" to the research and asked about changing research directions.

Dr. T expects students to come forward with clear, logical plans and timelines (students should know that time is always in short supply). At the meeting, Dr. T asked Hanna for more information, but Hanna avoided answering the questions and made an excuse to leave the meeting early. Dr. T knows that there are plenty of supports on campus for graduate students and doesn't feel the supervisory role is to "hand hold" graduate students (that's what the lab postdoc does) or to indulge last-minute "fickle changes of heart."

Discussion Questions:

1. Have you ever encountered any similar issues with your graduate students (personal experience)?
2. What are some of the "big picture" issues? Are there any "day-to-day" practicality issues?
3. Where do you see potential for conflict? Would you identify any cross-cultural elements or gender issues?
4. How might you respond if you were Hanna or Dr. T?
5. What are some ways that Hanna and Dr. T could get to know each other better as people and as researchers? Jot down a few questions they could ask each other.

Share answers to Q. 2–4 with the large group.

Clarify What "Effective Supervision" Means

> "Find a supervisor who is prepared to fully support your research process." PhD student, U of T

When I read this quote, I wonder whether the PhD student views effective supervision as:

- support that is unquestioning or unwavering
- support that is motivating or propels the student to do more/better
- support that extends only to the process (how the research is being done) or the substance of the research

Without a conversation, how the student defines effective supervision and whether their supervisor might concur are unanswered questions. In our "Getting the Most from Your Supervisor" workshops, we used a negotiation activity called the "4-Word Build"[3] to help participants understand what might be most important to them in their supervisory relationship. Everyone was asked to write down four words (without consulting with each other) which to them meant "effective supervision." We then asked everyone (i.e., we created conflict!) to work in ever larger groups (2, then 4, then 8) to come up with a joint list of just four words that everyone in the group agreed meant "effective supervision." There were many different ideas of what effective supervision meant among the groups. We ran this activity dozens of times, and although particular words were common, no two groups ever came up with the same list.

At the end of the activity, I asked the participants questions about the process of moving from individual to collective decision-making, about how it felt to disagree (i.e., be in conflict with) their classmates/colleagues about their ideas (positions they had taken originally – e.g., "Effective supervision means respect" versus "Effective supervision means mentorship"), and about how they resolved any differences of opinion (interests and approaches to conflict).

The discussion that followed would start to uncover interests (i.e., why the person chose the specific words "mentorship" and "respect") as the pair (and ever larger groups) tried to reach agreement or compromise on a single set of

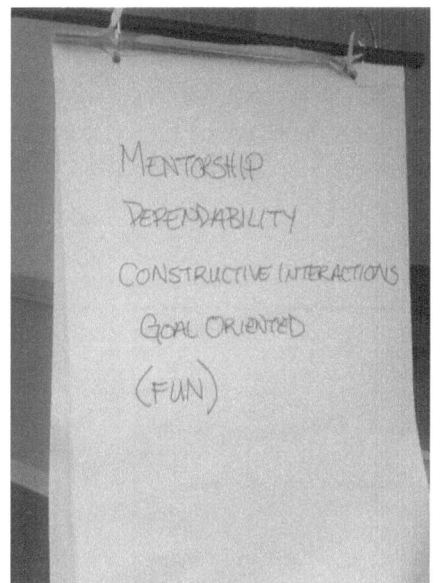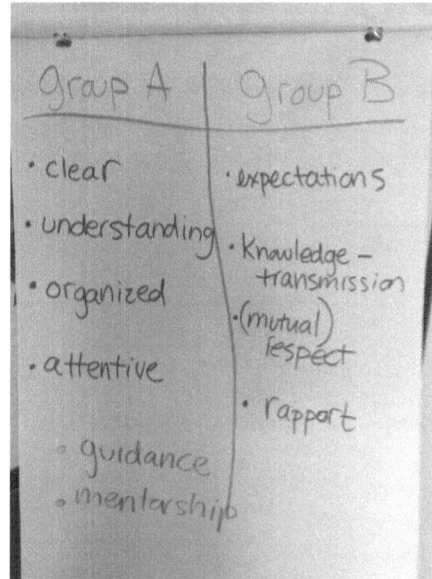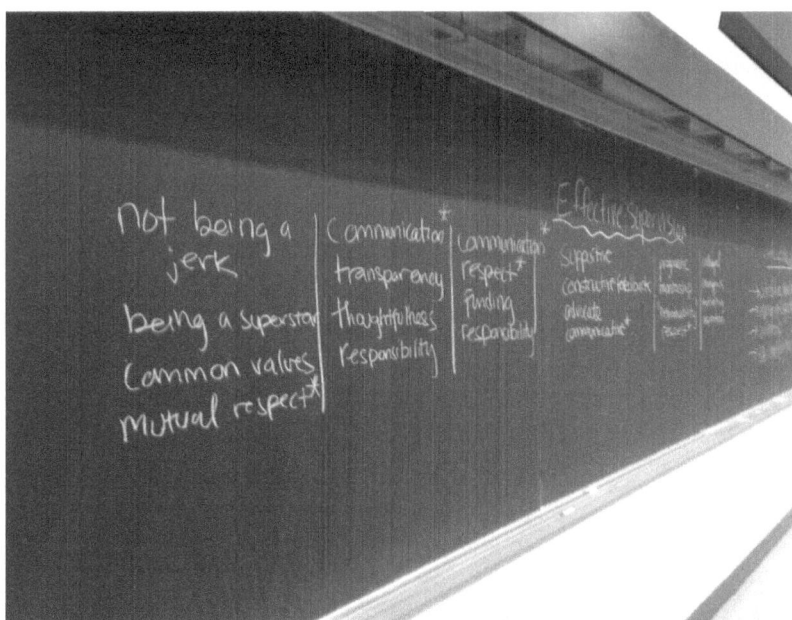

Figures 6, 7, and 8. Photos from Grad CRC workshop 4 Word-Build activity

four words. In the chart below, I categorized the words we heard from participants across various departments during this activity into the components of the "Tip Sheet: Supervision Early Days" (at page 175). Words in *italics* appeared on more than one group's list. I acknowledge that the choice of categories is based on my interpretation of what was meant by a particular word – the important take-away is how you and your graduate students define and clarify effective supervision.

Practicalities	"Big Picture"	Person	Researcher
Communication / Communicative	*Motivating*	*(Mutual) Respect*	Collaboration
(Constructive) Feedback	*Guidance*	*Supportive*	Knowledge transmission
Expectations	Champion	*Understanding*	Collegiality
Pragmatic	Openness	Inspiration	Networkability
Organized	Mentorship	Courageous	Being a superstar
Transparency	Advocate	Attentive	Funding
Clear	Common values	"Not being a jerk"	Access to resources
Adaptive	Responsibility	Thoughtfulness	
Available	Facilitative	Rapport	
	Helpful		

WHAT YOU CAN DO

! Consider what "effective supervision" means to you and whether how you define it is different than how you would have defined it when you were a graduate student.

! Try the "4-Word Build Activity" with a group of faculty colleagues, or an abridged version of the activity with your graduate student (e.g., come up with four words individually, then compare lists and try to come to a consensus.)

! If you work in a lab, consider if there is an opportunity to create a shared "Effective Lab Supervision" document that can be used by each graduate student to create a unique expectations plan with their supervisor. See also the discussion of lab contracts at page 159.

! How much influence might generation and culture have on perceptions of "effective supervision"? See, for example, Lauren Friese and Rumeet Billan, "How to Lead Millennials,"[4] Madeline St. Amour, "Gen Z Open to Nontraditional Education,"[5] "Executive Summary: The New Generation of Students,"[6] and Nanda Dimitrov, *Mentoring Graduate Students across Cultures*.[7]

Manage Expectations (Roles and Responsibilities)

We heard from a great many grad students who wanted to be more involved in the process of setting expectations with their supervisors. Even in difficult circumstances, a key priority for many students was figuring out how to engage fully and openly with their supervisor. As noted earlier, mismatched expectations about roles and responsibilities within the supervisory relationship is a potential source of conflict.

As one of the peer advisors noted, viewing conflict as a "misalignment" rather than as something that is "personally threatening" makes it an "opportunity to strengthen relationships and understand areas requiring clarification or explicit expectations" (Amika, PhD Health Informatics). Differences may be rooted in culturally informed expectations of who does what in a power-based relationship (e.g., supervisors talk, students listen), in habit (e.g., I've always done X, my supervisors have always done Y), in graduate folklore (e.g., I've heard that supervisors don't do A, B, C), or in a number of other factors.

Hundreds of articles have been written about the nuances of doctoral supervision, as well as guidelines, booklets,[8] diagrams, contracts, and letters of understanding. These latter tools should not be completed pro forma but should exist as living documents that are revisited multiple times throughout the course of a graduate degree. It can be very difficult to change expectations once they are set, and even more difficult to overcome a perceived violation of expectations. Managing expectations is an ongoing task.

An important distinction is made by the authors of *Crucial Accountability* between a single issue or concern (supervisor says to student: "You need to reference articles X, Y, and Z in your introduction") and a subsequent violation of expectations (supervisor says to student: "We talked about the need to reference X, Y, and Z articles to improve your introduction, and this draft doesn't do this. Have you reconsidered our discussion?").[9] This second discussion focuses on the pattern, not the underlying issue, which in this case might be a violation of the supervisor's expectations that the student will incorporate feedback (as discussed and agreed upon with the student) into their work.

We shared the following diagram in our "Getting the Most from Your Supervision" workshops, which were offered for both students and faculty audiences. We asked participants to talk in groups about what they thought were supervisor responsibilities, student responsibilities, and shared responsibilities using the blank diagram on our handout. We would debrief using a second diagram, which I had filled in based on the graduate school's supervision guidelines.

> **WHAT YOU CAN DO**
>
> ! Checking-in and making time for supervision discussions on a regular basis is a joint responsibility. Model your preferred approaches. An excellent example of a discussion sheet that you can fill in is one developed by the University of Copenhagen: "Alignment of Expectations between Supervisor and PhD Student."[10] Thinkwell (Australia) offers a set of free tools for supervisors and students based on psychological and educational research: "Tools for the Supervisor"[11] and "Tools to Give Your Student."[12]
>
> ! Be specific. Give your students a clear idea about your availability and preferences. Remember that if your availability or preferences change, let your students know. Compare these two invitations:
>
> - "I'm *always open* to questions"
>
> - "I'd like you to *email me when you have questions* – please don't save things until our next supervisory meeting. If you email me once a week, I can respond without multiple emails getting lost in my inbox. If something is

urgent, please call and leave a voicemail. How does that sound to you?" or perhaps you prefer, "Please email me separately for each question – with the topic and urgency in the subject line."

! Be clear about the amount of "hand-holding" provided and the skills development required. Do you talk about important graduate skills that should be being developed or refined at each stage/year in a graduate degree? For example,

- "Now that you are in YEAR X, I will be expecting you to take the lead on how much time we need to set aside each month to discuss your research. I will be less proactive about checking-in because I want to give you the freedom to set your own pace and priorities."

! Ask about past successful strategies that might be useful in the present:

- "Are there any other strategies you have used in the past to clarify expectations between you and a supervisor that you think might be useful for us to consider?"

! Remind graduate students that they can "do hard things." A research failure (what you have experienced) does not make you a research failure (who you are). In a video from Houston's UP Experience in 2011, Dr. Brené Brown notes that this is related to "hope" as a teachable, measurable cognitive approach, and hope is linked with moving through failure.[13]

186 Supervising Conflict

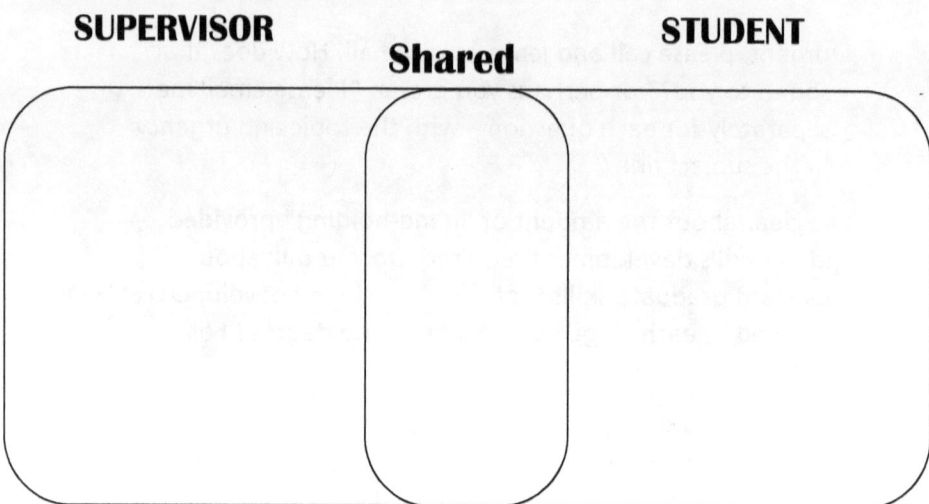

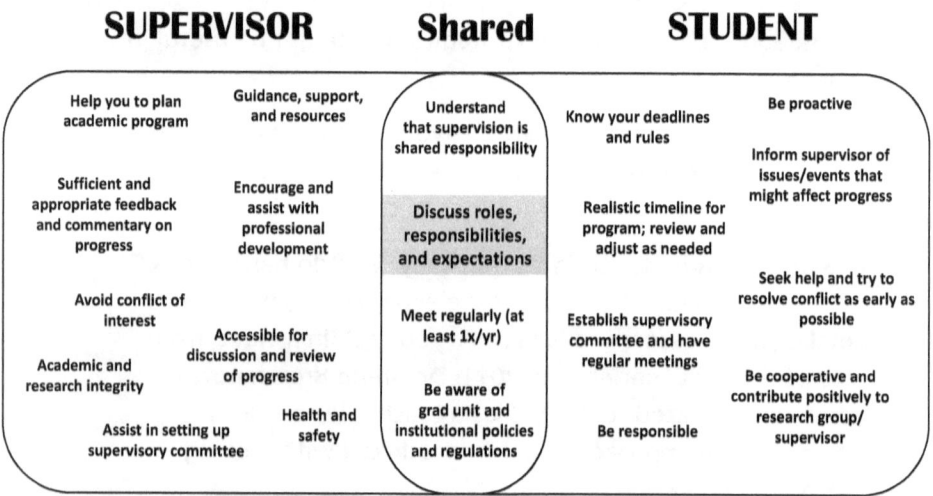

Figure 9. Supervisor/student/shared responsibilities chart from Grad CRC "Getting the Most from Your Supervision" workshop. Inspired by the Venn diagram created by Ashley Quan, Queen's University

MINI-CASE STUDY: MISMATCHED EXPECTATIONS

Consider these two perspectives on the same supervisory situation.

SUPERVISOR to FACULTY COLLEAGUE:
"My doctoral student was really unprepared for our last meeting. They didn't contribute anything of substance or value to the discussion. I think as a second-year PhD they should know that they can't just nod and smile – they have to be 100 percent in the game."

STUDENT to STUDENT COLLEAGUE:
"My supervisor has turned on me. We used to have great chats during our meetings but now they just look at me like I'm supposed to have all the answers! How am I supposed to know what to do next if I don't get any guidance? I don't want to cause problems, so I'm trying to just nod and smile like I know what is going on."

Q1. How do the supervisor and student's interests coincide?

Q2. How could a conversation about expectations begin in this situation?

Q3. How could meetings be structured differently or prepared for differently?

MINI-CASE STUDY: THERE'S NOT ENOUGH TIME!

"I am a third-year PhD student. My supervisor is extremely busy and supervises several other students. I really don't feel supported. I've been having some issues (personal and academic), and my supervisor hasn't responded to the three emails I sent last week!"

Q1. How do you determine the amount of time you spend with your graduate student(s)?

Q2. What are your (or your colleague's) most effective strategies for time management?

SKIT: TIME TO PRIORITIZE

Original written by peer advisors Kim (PhD Social Justice) and Megan (Master's Counselling Psychology).

Audience. Faculty, students, or both. Small or large groups.

Time Required. 20 minutes = 5 min prep / 5 min skit / 10 min debrief

Instructions. The facilitator invites two workshop participants to play the roles of a PhD student and their supervisor. Tell them they have three minutes to read the script and get into character. After three minutes, the facilitator reads the background aloud and then calls "Ready? Action!" When the skit ends, the facilitator leads a discussion with the larger group around the debrief questions. There are debrief prompts that the facilitator can use to help guide the discussion.

Background (Read Aloud by Facilitator or Actors). Riley is in the last year of their PhD. Riley's original plan was to finish up by August. For financial reasons, Riley wants to finish a few months earlier. Riley emailed the supervisor, Dr. Delay, to explain the change for time to completion and to provide the last round of revisions. Dr. Delay responded positively to this change, but a month has gone by and Riley hasn't heard anything about the revisions. Riley emails again and Dr. Delay suggests a video chat. Riley logs into the chat at the scheduled date and time, and five minutes later, Dr. Delay logs in looking very flustered.

Debrief Questions for Group Discussion:

- What are your responsibilities as the student/supervisor?
- What expectations may have been set and how? Were they reasonable? Why or why not?
- What are their interests/positions?
- What practical things could be discussed to manage this conflict?

Debrief Prompts (for Facilitator):

- Point out any documents/resources that are available to help determine supervisor/student expectations

- If this can't be resolved between the student/supervisor, what happens next?
- Ideas for practical conflict management, e.g.:
    - Create detailed schedule – work backwards from end goals
    - Share information – how and with who (supervisor or committee members)?
    - Keep track of action items – how?
    - How to manage changes (e.g., conferences, illness, expected/unexpected issues)

READY? ACTION! *(Script for Actors)*

RILEY: Hi Prof. Delay, how are you? Thanks for making the time to chat with me today.

DR. D: Good to see you, Riley. Unfortunately, it turns out I'm quite pressed for time at the moment.

RILEY: Oh okay, is now still a good time to talk?

DR. D: I only have ten minutes because I've just been pulled into a department meeting. I really don't like double bookings!

RILEY: [*Hesitantly*] Okay, uh, I guess we'll chat another day?

DR. D: Yes, yes that would be good. I'll email you to schedule something. I really must go. Sorry again.

Riley reads email to Dr. Delay aloud

> DATE: January 20th
> SUBJECT: Scheduling Meeting
> Dear Professor Delay,
> I haven't heard back from you yet. I'd really like to schedule a meeting as soon as possible. Please let me know when you're available.
> Best, Riley

Supervisor reads email to Riley aloud

> DATE: January 29th
> SUBJECT: Re: Scheduling Meeting
> Hi Riley, Next Wednesday at 1 p.m. – send me a video link. D.

Flash forward – Riley and Dr. Delay log in at 1 p.m. (moderator)

DR. D: Good to see you, Riley.

RILEY: I'm glad we could arrange this. As you know, I'm working towards a time to completion date of June. It's important for me to finish then as my funding will run out. I am simply not in a position to pay tuition fees and I need to return home to my family.

DR. D: Yes, I'm aware of that. However, this latest draft does need major improvements. It's really not as good as your other work.

RILEY: [*Shocked and dismayed*] Oh! Really?

DR. D: I think you need to do a complete overhaul of the end before our next committee meeting.

RILEY: Okay, I'll do my best. But I also have a conference presentation coming up, plus marking exams, and you know I've just received a revision for the publication you suggested I write.

DR. D: Riley, you really have to prioritize otherwise I don't see how your time to completion deadline could be possible. You might have to extend that date. And in fact, that reminds me: I'll need to push your committee meeting back. I'm attending a conference that day. Let's reschedule the meeting for May. Sorry, I really do have to go.

END OF SKIT Move to Debrief.

Considerations for Remote/Virtual Supervision

While being supervised off campus has always been a reality for many doctoral students, perhaps the result of geographic research location, challeng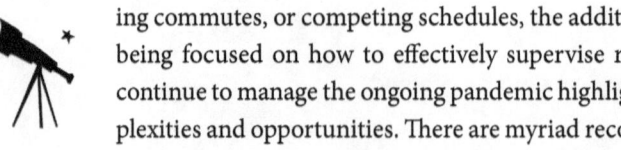ing commutes, or competing schedules, the additional attention being focused on how to effectively supervise remotely as we continue to manage the ongoing pandemic highlights both complexities and opportunities. There are myriad recommendations and strategies for remote supervision, many aligned with what we observed as common supervisory sources of conflict. For example, how would you:

- *Revisit expectations and manage (new) expectations?* For example, talk openly about requirements/guidance for graduate study at your institution and/or in a particular field – some shifts may be temporary, others permanent – and highlight elements that have stayed the same. Can you help students locate (new) guidelines/resources?
- *Demonstrate openness (flexibility)?* For example, look for ways to reframe: "How do I supervise in a pandemic?" becomes "How do we engage effectively in research in an ever-changing world?"
- *Communicate and connect with students in meaningful and effective ways?* For example, asynchronous and synchronous ways of sharing information and providing feedback, personalized plans, and check-ins that consider the research and the person.[14]

It may not be "business as usual" on campuses for some time, and some habits and practices may have changed permanently or will continue to evolve with technology and habit. Accepting a level of disruption and uncertainty is important in engaging respectfully across differences and dealing with new stresses related to academics, university life, and the after-grad-school world.

WHAT YOU CAN DO

! Here are four suggestions for preventing graduate conflict in an uncertain and evolving academic context:

1. Acknowledge that trust in the university or more broadly in higher education may have been shaken. As a faculty member, how can you demonstrate and cultivate trust on behalf of and independent of the institution?

2. Increase your tolerance for uncertainty. Students may not be comfortable talking about certain forms of accommodation that might be required (related to health issues, family matters, etc.) – where do you need to stand firm, and where can you exercise discretion?

3. Be patient. If remote supervision is a newer arrangement in your context, remember that feeling comfortable with new patterns and forming new habits can take time (for you and your students).

4. Be clear when things are not as they should be. Is it taking longer for you to respond to emails or to turn around drafts than it did previously? Are there limits to your availability to connect virtually? Let students know. Structure can be as important as flexibility.

MINI-CASE STUDY: SAME CONCERNS, NEW CONTEXT

As you read these three dramatic (but real!) supervisory concerns, consider how your understanding and response may be different now from five years ago because of the impact of current events.

A third-year PhD student emails you as their grad coordinator. They state that they can no longer work with their supervisor ("I don't agree with the direction the research has taken in the lab – it has become largely irrelevant to me") and they ask you to help them change supervisors.

A second-year PhD student leaves you a voicemail – you know the student quite well from faculty/student social events in the department over the years. They say that they haven't been able to reach their supervisor in several months, and they have heard a rumor that the supervisor has left for a position at another university in another part of the country.

A seventh-year PhD student sends you an email as their graduate chair. They are unhappy with the quality of their supervisor's feedback and are concerned about finishing their PhD (they have already taken longer than others in the department to complete their dissertation). They note their supervisor seems unwilling to provide any substantive feedback on their thesis – the comments are always about grammar and formatting.

Maintain Boundaries

Boundaries are as important in academia as they are in a workplace or in our personal lives. These "guidelines, rules, or limits" help us define what behaviors we personally will accept as "reasonable, safe, and permissible,"[15] and they build respect between you and your students. Boundaries can shift from situation to situation (who, where, and when) and can be linked to various cultural, individual, or social expectations.

We found that communication (swearing, yelling, or oversharing) and expectations (hours of work, lunch breaks, and keeping evenings/weekends free from academic work) are two common areas where boundaries often need to be clarified or asserted. Some other potential conflicts related to boundaries include:

- "My supervisor commonly sets arbitrary deadlines that have to be completed by working around-the-clock. Every time I get an email from my supervisor I panic!"
- "The postdoc in my department loses her temper regularly and raises her voice. I have had to adjust my schedule so I'm not in the office at the same time as she is."
- "I share a lab with another faculty member who is disrespectful – they never ask before using my equipment, and it is never put away correctly. It makes me furious!"

Conflict can arise when you or someone you work with is trying to (re)establish a boundary or where someone is avoiding speaking up about a boundary because they feel that doing so could have adverse consequences. Power  and authority (the person holding or not holding the power), expertise (the person with or without the answers) or personal connection (the friend or the mentor), may amplify boundary discomfort. While it can be particularly challenging to figure out boundaries moving between being an employee, a colleague, a supervisor, a mentor, or others, "it can be helpful to see boundaries as a tool that helps you work more effectively."[16]

WHAT YOU CAN DO

! Practice can help you to assert and recognize boundaries in your supervisory relationships.

! If you have ever used the phrase "Can you just ...?" then you might want to consider how it might be undermining boundaries:

> STUDENT: "I told my supervisor I'm out of town next week and they responded, "*Can you just* make sure that you get XYZ completed by then?"
>
> FACULTY: "I was saying goodnight to a postdoc who works in the lab, and they asked, "Before you go, *can you just* explain how to fix this (ridiculously complex and expensive) machine?"

! For a faculty training exercise, break into pairs and have one person share one of these "can you just" examples, and the other person respond to establish a boundary using the strategies discussed. Be persistent/persuasive. Repeat. Have pairs share their own personal experiences of "can you just" requests and discuss strategies for responding. Debrief as a large group.

Q1. When you begin a new supervisory relationship with a student do you talk about "ground-rules" for appropriate behavior and demands on your time?

Q2. If yes, have you revisited these boundaries recently? Why or why not?

! Practice saying "no" or "yes and..." in other contexts (not to be difficult but to become aware of your boundaries). Responses to a question like: "*Can you just* read my first chapter and give me feedback?" in a way that is both positive and clear might include:

- "Yes, are you okay with getting feedback verbally?"
- "Before I say yes, can you tell me what type of feedback you are hoping for?"

Q1. Can you think of other responses?

Q2. In the following examples, how might you reassert a boundary?

A. A colleague expects to hear back from you within a few hours – even in the evenings and on weekends.

B. You didn't stop your student from "venting" during your last meeting and now they want to share with you every detail of what is going on between grad students in the department.

! Learn more about boundaries that your grad students may be trying to assert (or should be) by watching these videos: "Setting Boundaries as a Graduate Student,"[17] and "The Basic Principles Every PhD Student Needs to Know."[18] Starting at the thirty-three-minute mark, Dr. Hayton talks about how he stopped checking email when things went wrong during his PhD.

MINI-CASE STUDY: COLLEGIAL COLLABORATION COLLISION

You receive a late-night email from a faculty colleague telling you that they need your help tomorrow on a project you've been collaborating on for several weeks. Their "to do" list is lengthy and will take you at least a full day to complete. This isn't the first time they've asked you for last minute help and while you usually just say "yes," this time it is clearly not your responsibility (you divided the tasks earlier!) – it is due to your colleague's disorganization. You had set aside the day to work on a presentation that you'll be giving the following week.

Q. How might you respond?

TIP SHEET: SETTING BOUNDARIES

Adapted from a workshop prepared by peer advisors Jessica (PhD Drama, Theatre and Performance Studies) and Megan (MEd Counselling Psychology)

1. Advance preparation can be useful for conversations that you anticipate are going to involve boundaries. Preparation involves figuring out your own boundary *interests* (the "why" behind your boundary) and considering if they might be different from the other person's interests.

2. Rehearse what you may want to say and some responses if the other person questions your boundary. Think about what information you want to share.

3. Be as specific about what you *can't do* as what you *can*. Make sure that whatever you agree to you are comfortable sticking to. Rephrase and repeat if necessary. "I prefer" or "I want" or "That doesn't work for me."

Do you recognize any of these (academic) boundaries? What types of boundaries are easiest/most challenging to assert in your department? For you personally?

INTELLECTUAL – e.g., *"I feel uncomfortable when a student or colleague asks me my opinion 'on the spot' or about something unrelated to my research."*

TIP: Acknowledge that this is an "interesting/important question that you've asked" and that (a) you will reflect or research it and get back to the person, or (b) ask a question – "what are your thoughts?"

EMOTIONAL – e.g., *"I'm not willing to argue/show my emotions in front of an audience or with people I've just met."*

TIP: Ask to book a meeting with them individually to discuss the matter further. If this is someone you will engage with in the future, consider sharing your boundary with them.

MATERIAL – e.g., *"I am not comfortable sharing my supplies/using equipment/work areas in close proximity to others."*

TIP: Be aware that others may feel the opposite way about supplies/space, offering context or assistance is one way to help others understand your boundary, i.e., "I've had bad experiences sharing supplies in the past – do you want help getting another set to use?" or "I am realizing I am not comfortable working in close quarters – could we talk about how we might coordinate our times in this space?"

TIME/TASK – e.g., *"I prefer time to plan and prepare for discussions – I have a lot on my mind."*

TIP: Rather than just saying you are "busy," be specific. When can you deal with the matter? "I'll be free to give you my full attention tomorrow at 10 a.m."

PHYSICAL – e.g., *"I feel more comfortable with video chats rather than with in-person meetings."*

TIP: Be clear and specific – is this an "I'm not going to meet in person until there is a cure" boundary or one that can shift under the right circumstances? "If you prefer to meet in person, I propose the lounge in the lobby – it's never crowded so we can socially distance."

Include "Light Touch" Interventions in Supervision

According to research out of the University of California, Davis, post-secondary students whose professors occasionally sent them emails offering support and "light touch, targeted feedback"[19] tended to have better perceptions of their instructors and their courses.

This could be characterized as a type of "nudge"– a small change in the regular course of normal interactions that makes it more likely that a person will make one choice over another or behave in one way over another.[20] However, as Kim Manturuk (Duke University) points out, some nudges don't work because they are actually a nag, and, "No one likes being nagged."[21] Within the context of a graduate relationship where helping students to develop research competency and independence is critical, nudges (i.e., not persistent reminders) may be helpful in "creat[ing] small, incremental changes in student choices" related to tasks in the normal course of graduate life.[22]

We know that perception, personalities, and prior experiences make supervisory conflicts more challenging, so improving your students' overall impression of you and your work could reduce conflict and make it easier to resolve conflicts when they do arise. As noted earlier, how feedback is provided is as important as what is said, and it can have a profound impact on a grad student's experience and feelings about graduate school. Perceiving that their supervisor/department cares about them is meaningful to a student.

An example of a "light touch" supervisory intervention might be sending grad students unsolicited emails at non-traditional times (i.e., not just before or after planned check-ins). These emails would have a positive and future orientation:

- sharing information about the underlying processes involved in completing future tasks, including links to relevant graduate policies/documents (i.e., what is on the horizon)

- providing feedback about performance to date and strategies for how to improve performance (i.e., where are we now and where are we headed)

Research out of the University of Virginia's (USA) Nudge4 Lab provides support for using nudges in higher education to help create resilient mindsets, facilitate goal setting, encourage the use of campus resources, and recognize and avoid pitfalls.[23] We were using some of the innovation recommendations in our program, including:

- Emphasizing the importance of early and effective conflict management through our individual coaching as well as workshops (Innovation 9: "Offer early, actionable information and guidance to help students avoid common pitfalls and stay on track ... e.g., offer workshops or other resources to help students develop strong academic practices that will help prevent problems before they arise").

- Highly trained peer advisor team who helped fellow graduate students to navigate a wide range of issues and concerns related to their graduate experience (Innovation 10 "Coaches can provide information and answers, help troubleshoot challenging situations, and guide students toward useful resources. Personalized coaching can enable students to persist in the face of challenges and to navigate both academic and 'real life' barriers to college completion").[24]

WHAT YOU CAN DO

! Instead of a "lunch and learn" or a formal two-to-three hour conflict resolution workshop, consider:

- Sharing a communication or conflict resolution "tip of the day" during a regular check-in with your grad students, setting aside three to five minutes to discuss.

- Sharing a mini-case study as a regular feature of faculty meetings, and then engaging in a quick brainstorming session. Here is a ten-minute brainstorm activity for an in-person meeting:

    Step 1. Set a timer. Each person, on their own, has three minutes to write down three questions or ways to approach the situation.
    Step 2. Pass papers to the left.
    Step 3. Each person has two minutes to choose one question or approach from the three written down and build upon it.

Step 4. Each person has three minutes to share those with the larger group.[25] For online brainstorming, a virtual whiteboard or sticky notes can allow multiple participants to add or comment on content.

! Consider short informal email check-ins – everything doesn't have to be "in-person." By this I mean we don't always have to connect by phone, video, or live in person, and consider pre-booked (standing) meetings ("The last Monday of the month at 2 p.m.") with an agreed process for cancellations? Read this Thesis Whisperer article, "How to Email Your Supervisor (or, the Tyranny of Tiny Tasks and What You Can Do About It)."[26]

Q. What other types of light touch interventions do you think might work to prevent the types of conflict that you experience most often with graduate students?

What Can Supervisors Do to Resolve Conflict?

While many supervisors replicate, consciously or unconsciously, their own experiences of being supervised as graduate students, it is possible to build upon personal know-how and expand the diverse set of skills and tools needed for effective supervision and management of conflict within the supervisory relationship.[1]

We all fall short of others' expectations at times: miscommunications occur and conflicts arise. In particular, the evaluative nature of academic supervision compounded by power differentials, "can raise anxieties, resistance, and avoidance in some supervisees" and impact trust and engagement.[2] Accepting the imperfection of supervisory relationships and the reality of conflict in the supervision process allows faculty to look for ways to mend and repair, rather than abandon or despair.

> "Conflict that reaches a resolution is more likely to result in a strengthened relationship, positive supervision outcomes, and professional growth for the supervisor and supervisee."[3]

Research reveals that student–supervisor conflict may be managed through "intelligent interaction," a catchall phrase which includes respect, support, guidance, and getting help from people outside of the department to avoid and manage conflict.[4] In addition, "individual preferences or conflict management styles are ... important determinants of how effectively conflicts are resolved," with the caveat that "ultimately, the combination of how both parties manage conflict within a particular context determines whether the outcome is desirable or undesirable."[5] Recall the discussion about conflict management approaches (styles) at page 33, and supervision styles at page 104.

In the Grad CRC, we would recommend various conflict management tools in customized combinations after extensive conversation. Since this is impossible in the context of a book of general advice for faculty dealing with a wide range of graduate conflicts, I have tried over the next few chapters to combine general conflict management advice for supervisors with specific examples of when the strategy might be useful.

Be "Open" to Resolving a Conflict …

As noted earlier, students and their supervisors both identify "lack of openness," "lack of time," and "unclear conversation" as common sources of conflict.[6] But when we asked workshop participants what they thought "open" and "openness" meant, there were no obvious answers.

In our conflict management work, we tried to demonstrate openness through curiosity, being receptive to hearing other (perhaps contrary) points of view and listening to hear rather than listening to respond. Over the years, I had valuable conversations with faculty about how the act of trying to resolve issues, perhaps as simple as trying again to address a concern using a different mode of communication (phone/letter/email), demonstrates openness.

We consistently received comments such as these after coaching sessions:

- "You are the first person who really listened."
- "Thank you for your time."

WHAT YOU CAN DO

! Finding time for active listening might seem like a deceptively simple way to prevent and manage graduate conflict, however, it also may be all you can do or need to do in order to help someone. A goal for an interaction may simply be to make sure everyone feels heard. Here are two videos that highlight the importance of listening: "Radical Listening,"[7] in which Chanel Lewis (senior diversity and inclusion program manager at Mozilla) confirms that "we are terrible at listening to people we disagree with"; and "The Power of Listening,"[8] in which William Ury (*Getting to Yes*) discusses "what makes it so hard to listen is that there is so much going on in our minds."

❗ I had the saying *"You don't have to attend every argument you are invited to"* (author unknown) on a sticky note on the wall of my office. The next time someone "invites" you to a conflict or a difficult conversation, before you RSVP yes, try an approach grounded in pre-performance anxiety research. Say aloud to yourself,

- "This interaction is going to be a positive experience. I'm excited that I have the opportunity to try to resolve this issue."

❗ According to Alison Wood Brooks (Harvard Business School), "The way we verbalize and think about our feelings helps to construct the way we actually feel. Saying 'I am excited' represents a simple, minimal intervention that can be used quickly and easily to prime an opportunity mind-set and improve performance."[9] For more information about managing unpleasant emotions, including Professor Brooks's research, listen to this great podcast by Katy Milkman, "A Bundle of Nerves."[10]

… And Be Okay if It Doesn't

Negotiation is commonly defined as, "discussion aimed at reaching an agreement."[11] Each person in a negotiation wants to communicate effectively and persuasively in order to be heard and to have their needs met. In the graduate context, the academic relationship and the willingness of students and faculty to engage in future discussions does not depend on agreement being reached in every negotiation, but instead on how each person feels they have been treated in the process. This is important because agreement is not always achievable or desirable.

At times faculty may feel pressure to "seek consensus at all costs" in order to resolve a conflict with a student; however, failing to come to an agreement or continuing to disagree doesn't equal failure.[12] This is particularly true where agreement may only be possible "on the basis of the position of the least flexible participant," as the Honorable Justice Winkler (former Chief Justice of Ontario) has stated, pointing out "there is value, even wisdom, in receiving, understanding, and tolerating other and competing perspectives."[13] Working together, despite our differences and notwithstanding a lack of agreement over a particular issue, demonstrates that the continuation of the relationship is a primary interest. Negotiation provides supervisors and students with an opportunity to better understand one another; by definition it is about "aiming" to reach agreement, it does not depend on agreement.

People may also have strategic reasons for not wanting to resolve a conflict. In other words, we can choose to avoid an issue, either for the moment or entirely, which is very different from avoiding as a default without considering other possible conflict approaches. As noted throughout this book, effective resolution requires time and energy, which are resources that someone may prefer to allocate to other tasks entirely or just for the moment (i.e., we might have time or energy to deal with this conflict at a later time). Consider timing – is this an issue that can be addressed at a later date, and if so, what are the possible impacts (both positive and negative) of any delay?

WHAT YOU CAN DO

! Take the pressure off. Be specific about what you can/can't do for the student and where they can find support outside of the supervisory relationship.

Acknowledge (Faculty) Power and Take the Lead

Graduate students are not tenured faculty members or full-time unionized university staff members, and they may never be or want to be. Power is the "elephant in the room" when a student is negotiating with faculty. Perceptions of a lack of power can undermine a student's confidence in their ability to resolve conflict with their supervisor, committee members, administration, and even more senior graduate students. Grad students told us that they worry that if they challenge the status quo or bring up concerns, it might have a negative impact on them (but it won't impact you!).

We found it helpful to bring the issue of power into our supervision workshops, acknowledging that "power is complex and situational"[14] and that one's power and perceived power can be impacted by various intersections of personal, group, and social identity. After a discussion about the challenges that grad students face in negotiating with faculty (see Figure 10), we would challenge participants to also consider "What are some challenges for faculty of negotiating with students?" Students could always point to a number of their own student challenges that might also be a faculty challenge; for example, reputation, competitive environment, or personalities.

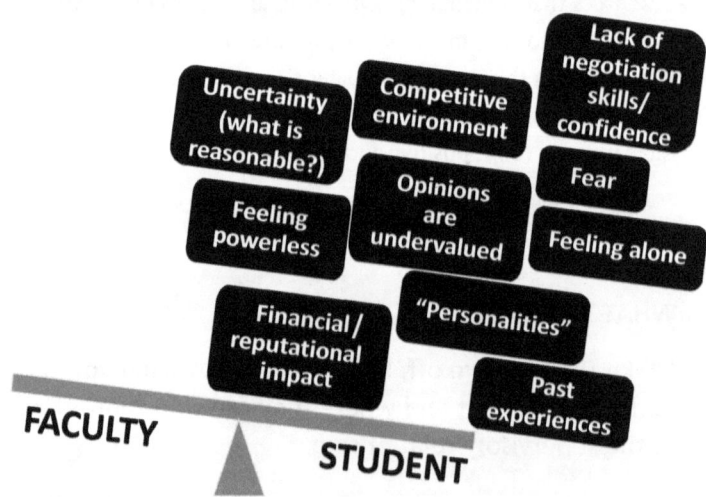

Figure 10. Slide from Grad CRC "Getting the Most from Your Supervision" workshop, 2019

In our conflict management workshops for grad students, we discussed the model of power developed by Robert Adler and Elliot Silverstein that includes four types of power: personal, organizational, information, and moral.[15] While participants were often familiar with other models of power, this model highlights two sources of power that grad students often do not realize they can work to increase:

- *Information power* (i.e., the power to be as well as or more well-informed than the person you are negotiating with). According to Adler and Silverstein, information is one of the sources of power "that provides the greatest opportunity to shift the dynamics of a negotiation."[16]
- *Personal power* (i.e., just because a tenured faculty member is an expert in their research domain and has financial security/secure position with the department doesn't mean they are expert negotiators). As one workshop participant declared, "Learning that I DO have some power in this inherently imbalanced student–supervisor relationship was important."

WHAT YOU CAN DO

Q. What challenges would you put on the faculty side of this "challenges negotiating with students" image?

! In a negotiation you can only control you – how you prepare for a conversation, how you act during a conversation, when you walk away, and what you do next. What anyone else does or doesn't do is out of your control. Focusing on what is in your control can be empowering.

! If a student seems overwhelmed with a particular situation or conflict on top of the many moving parts of grad school, help them to simply "swim through the big pond" by encouraging them to be proactive about conflict resolution and to consider and focus on the best approach for them in the moment (rather than all the possible "*what-ifs ...?*")

! "With great power comes great responsibility."[17] Helping student to increase their information power... in advance of an important conversation shifts the perception that as a

> faculty member you hold all the power. For example, if you know what policies, processes, or resources apply to the situation at hand, send links in advance.

Listen to Get More than Information

No doubt you have heard many times about the importance of "active listening" for effective communication. It is a way of listening that can and should be practiced because it "requires effective use of verbal and nonverbal communication, as well as mental and emotional discipline."[18] When we feel that someone is listening to us, we feel like we are developing trust and rapport with the listener; we feel understood, respected, valued, and appreciated.

For managing graduate conflict, active listening can also:

- de-escalate a situation
- make students feel more relaxed and able to share their concerns
- provide opportunities for clarification (e.g., different phrases may mean different things to different people, or words may be used for impact rather than meaning)
- mean that students are more willing to listen[19]
- lay the groundwork for problem-solving

Consider that our way of communicating is informed by context (who, where, when), culture (values/beliefs, norms, and practices), perspective (how do I view a situation before and during a conversation), and our interests and goals (what do I want to achieve from this interaction?). This means that there is a lot for us to listen for. It also means that there could be a lot at stake for the person we are talking to, and we need to consider how we demonstrate that we are listening. Peer advisor Tony (MPH) reflected, "Empathy, compassion, and communal empowerment are important ingredients to support graduate students who may find themselves in a hard situation. Sometimes all it takes is someone who is willing to listen for a person to feel less alone in managing their conflict in ways that they feel are best for them."

WHAT YOU CAN DO

! Discuss with a colleague the questions we asked participants in our workshops:

Q1. *How can we tell if someone is listening?*

Q2. *Is the "look" of listening universal?*

Q3. *How would listening change if there isn't any "look" available (i.e., text/email)?*

! Consider challenges and opportunities of trying to engage in active listening online. Drawing from her post–COVID-19 research, Professor Karin Wahl-Jorgensen (Cardiff University, UK) notes that "the very sparseness of the Zoom environment facilitate[ed] 'active listening.' In the absence of other stimuli, I was able to fully concentrate on reading my interviewees' verbal and non-verbal cues. Here, it is important to note that the practice of active listening is a privilege at any time and especially in the middle of the pandemic."[20]

! A picture can be worth a thousand words (even a quick doodle). In coaching conversations, I might sketch out what I was hearing to see if a visualization might help the

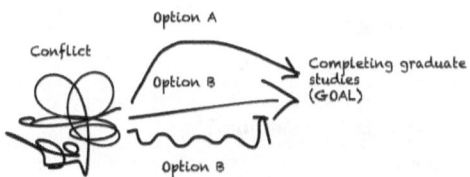

person get a problem "out of their head" and onto paper. Remember, the quality of the drawing is far less important than the act of making a conflict into something tangible (an image on paper), which has the benefit of visually separating the conflict from the person who had been thinking about it.

TIP SHEET: SIX CRITICAL LISTENING TIPS FROM THE FBI AND MIT

> 1. *Ask open-ended questions* and make encouraging verbal ("um-hmm") and non-verbal responses (nod). This is a way to ensure you are getting the whole story.
>
>> "What happened next?" "And then what?"
>>
>> "Tell me more about X."
>>
>> "Can you give me more details about Y [concern]?"

> 2. *Listen for and respond to emotional cues.*
>
>> "So, you were pretty angry after that happened."
>>
>> "You seem really unhappy about their comments."

> 3. *Reflect back what the speaker is saying.*
>
>> SPEAKER: "I was really upset by the committee's feedback."
>>
>> LISTENER: "Sounds like the committee's feedback made you upset."

> 4. *Pause.*
>
>> Leave room for silence – speakers tend to fill a pause if there is more information that needs to be shared.

> 5. *Maintain personal boundaries* and use "I" statements (sparingly) to name difficult behaviors.
>
>> "I feel uncomfortable [emotion] when you use obscenities/swear words [behavior] because I think it takes us away from the purpose of this conversation [reason]."

> 6. *Summarize and try to capture what might be most important to the speaker (interests).* This is a way to check accuracy and encourage the speaker to correct you.
>
>> "You've described a really complex set of issues. Let me see if I've understood correctly."
>>
>> "What I hear you saying is [paraphrase]. Is that right?"
>>
>> "You mentioned concerns about A, B, and C, and it sounds like the most critical one for you is B. Is that right?"
>>
>> "It seems important to you that [X or Y happens] – is that accurate?"

> **Sources/Resources**
>
> Vincent A. Dalfonzo and Michele L. Deitrick, "Focus on Training: An Evaluation Tool for Crisis Negotiators," *FBI Law Enforcement Bulletin (LEB)*, 9 October 2015, https://leb.fbi.gov/2015/october/focus-on-training-an-evaluation-tool-for-crisis-negotiators.
>
> Carol Orme-Johnson and Mark Cason-Snow, "Basic Mediation Training: Trainer's Manual," Mediation@MIT, 2002, https://www.yumpu.com/en/document/read/49769309/basic-mediation-training-trainers-manual-campus-conflict-.

Answer More Often with a Question

Negotiation research suggests that asking more questions can result in better individual performance in a negotiation.[21] Why not use this tool more often when working with students and colleagues to resolve conflicts? During our workshops, we would challenge participants to practice responding in everyday conversations with a question rather than a comment and to use open-ended questions rather than being content with "yes/no" answers. Here are some things to keep in mind when you are asking questions:

- Tone matters.
- Both open-ended and closed (pointed) questions are useful.
- Follow up questions ("Can you tell me more about [what you just mentioned]?" "And what else?") help build rapport.
- Final questions ("Is there anything we still need to talk about?") can leave a lasting impression.[22]

CLOSED (YES / NO)	OPEN
"Are you okay?"	"How was your day?"
"Is this deadline reasonable?"	"What are your thoughts on this deadline?"
"Do you understand next steps?"	"Can you do a quick summary of next steps?"

WHAT YOU CAN DO

! Practice asking more open-ended questions with your friends and family. See if, and how, it makes a difference in your interactions. Here are a few examples of open-ended questions that are focused on underlying interests:

- What is important to you about [PARAPHRASE THEIR POSITION]?
- You mentioned [PARAPHRASE], can you tell me more about that?
- What bothers (or interests) you most about [SPECIFIC DETAIL]?

! When negotiating (trying to come to a resolution) with a student or colleague, ask ONE more question. Issues can be complex and layered – dig beneath positions to uncover interests and test assumptions.

! Build your own library of great questions and ways to ask them. Here is some inspiration:

- In their HBR podcast, "Ask Better Questions," Leslie K. John and Alison Wood Brooks talk about optimistic and pessimistic assumption questions, "You are going to be able to meet our deadline, right?" versus "You aren't going to be able to meet the deadline, are you?"[23]

- As set out in the University of Waterloo's "Question Strategies," there is a distinction between structured questions ("What are some of your objectives in this chapter in relation to the research framework?") and unstructured questions ("What's going on in this chapter?").[24]

ROLE PLAY: REFLECTIVE QUESTIONING[25]

Time Required. 20–30 minutes

Instructions. In pairs, one person is the student, and the other person is a faculty member who the student has contacted for support. The student will read the story, and then record three questions asked by the other person (responding in between – make up the answers!). Switch roles after the first role play. At the end of the role play, the pairs can discuss the questions that were asked, share how they felt being asked these questions, and identify any additional questions that could have been asked.

READY? ACTION!

STUDENT: My supervisor expects to see us in the lab on weekends, makes dismissive comments about our efforts, and points out that long days are the only way to get ahead in this field.

1. _____
2. _____
3. _____

STUDENT: The few times I have met my supervisor, they have failed to read what I've sent them, and they just drill me with challenging questions. Everyone in our department (faculty included) knows that they are a terrible supervisor/professor, but no one has attempted to intervene in any way.

1. _____
2. _____
3. _____

STUDENT: My supervisor is really intense; at times, they have sent very harsh emails and been very hard on me verbally in front of other students. I know I'm not the only grad student who gets called out, but I'm feeling less and less confident about my ability to complete the research.

1. _____
2. _____
3. _____

Reframe as a Joint Problem to Solve

While disagreement is a normal part of the supervisory relationship, it can be frustrating to know where to start when it seems like your interests do not align with your student's interests. Reframing the problem as one that requires joint effort can create "buy-in" into the problem-solving (i.e., we are in this together) and help ensure that any solution that emerges is viewed as legitimate. An initial discussion can provide information to frame the problem as an "How do we/can we ...?" problem. For example, consider a situation where a PhD student isn't making significant progress on writing their thesis. The supervisor flags this as a concern, and the student seems defensive. The supervisor could initially frame the problem as:

> "How do we [make some writing progress]?"

Further discussion and inquiry can bring clarity and specificity to the question based on both the supervisor's and the student's interests:

> "How can we [best make some writing progress PROBLEM] given [your need to focus other obligations at the present time, aka STUDENT INTEREST] and [keeping in mind time to completion deadlines, aka SUPERVISOR INTEREST]?"

WHAT YOU CAN DO

! At the outset, ask, "How do we want to share responsibility for setting the agenda for conversations, summarizing discussion points, and keeping track of action items?"

Focus on the Future

We all hold onto memories of past injustices – feelings and thoughts related to situations when we have been or believe we have been wronged. So, if we have had prior difficult interactions with someone or were involved in similar circumstances that didn't go as we had hoped, ties to the past can hinder attempts to think strategically about how to approach a present conflict and build mutually agreeable solutions for the future.

Conflict coaching works with individuals to reorient them toward the future. This is distinct from therapy or counseling which may include deep explorations into past experiences and their impact. As peer advisor Margeaux (PhD English/Gender Diversity Studies) noted, "I think that in academia there's a real fear of not always knowing the answers or what the 'right' answer for a given situation is. But [conflict coaching] embraces that moment where you may not know the right answer and turns that moment into an opportunity for dialogue where together we can come up with myriad possible solutions."

We found it was helpful to remind the people who came to us for support about the limits of our role and mandate – it gave them the choice about whether to continue with a conflict coaching future focus or to seek out other supports, or in many cases, they opted to do both concurrently.

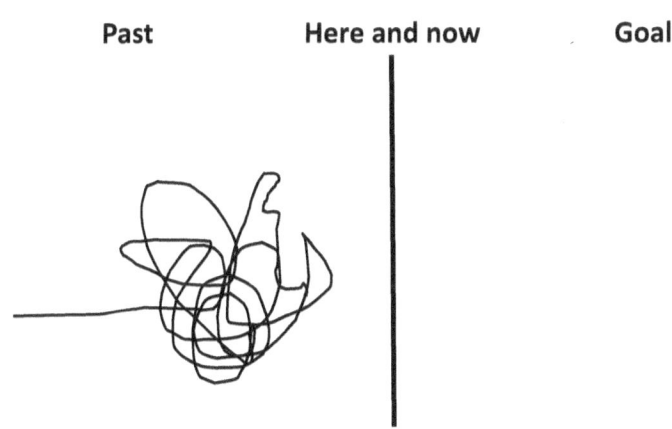

Figure 11. Slide from Grad CRC "Conflict Management for Supervisors" workshop, 2017

> **WHAT YOU CAN DO**
>
> ! Here are some questions to reorient conversations toward the *future:*
>
> - What issue is most important to you?
> - What are some things you could try?
> - What other options do you have?
> - Have you thought about the pros and cons of this idea?
> - What would make this option work better for you?

Move beyond "Difficult"

We often heard comments like these from students:

- "My supervisor is *difficult*."
- "I find it *difficult* to talk to my supervisor."

In the first example, it helps to separate the "person from the problem"[26] and focus on the specific behaviors that are happening and that seem difficult (the problem) – as opposed to labeling the person as "difficult." I am not sure how to brainstorm options for how to make someone else *less difficult*, but I can certainly brainstorm options for dealing with difficult behaviors (e.g., ways to have conversations or strategies for staying level-headed during conversations when difficult behaviors arise).

As a first step, try to learn more about the issue:

- "When you say, '*my supervisor is difficult*' what do you mean?"
- "Tell me more about why you '*find it difficult to talk to*' your supervisor."

Consider that there may be a number of reasons why someone might seem to be difficult to talk to. Perhaps acting in this way has worked for them in the past, or maybe they like to prepare for conversations and find being put on the spot is stressful. Or perhaps, like so many of us, they are busy and juggling multiple priorities, and unaware or unappreciative of the impact of their words and actions.

It is that last point that I found useful in coaching – reminding people (and reminding myself!) that sometimes what they are experiencing may have very little to do with them and the situation at hand and has more to do with what is going on with the other person. Opportunities to engage in shifts in perspective normally happen later in a conversation; that is, only after someone has shared their story are they open to considering the other person's story.

WHAT YOU CAN DO

! Think about how you can mitigate your own possible role in conflict. One method of prevention is modeling: "Instructors [should] follow the same rules that they expect their students to follow (e.g., be well prepared, deal with assignments in a timely manner, be respectful and civil, and welcome diverse points of view)."[27]

! If you find yourself labeling people or behaviors as "difficult", pause, and take a moment to familiarize yourself with the policies, guidelines, and support offices before taking steps to address the concerning behavior.

! Consider getting a "second opinion" from one of the university's support offices by asking questions anonymously:

- "Hi, I'm a faculty member – I'd rather not give my name or department at this time. Is it possible to talk with you about some behavior that I find [worrying/strange]?"

! If you decide to address the issues directly with the individual:

- Know your boundaries and review the tips on page 196.
- Be specific about which behaviors are the issue and whether it falls under a particular policy or guideline or if it relates to one of your personal boundaries or an

> unwritten departmental expectation. (Note: Being able to refer to the policy – online or on paper – can be very helpful in starting a conversation about a specific behavior because the policy is external to you and the other person.)

Exercise Cognitive Flexibility

In their article, "Individual and Organizational Factors Promoting Successful Responses to Workplace Conflict," Debra Gilin Oore, Michael Leiter, and Diane LeBlanc write: "A cognitive ability to move flexibly through various perspectives on the conflict situation, or more broadly, to 'zoom out' from conflict, helps individuals resolve conflict."[28] We used perspective reframing as a conflict coaching tool to reveal potential pathways to effective communication.

When someone is able to see that other people have their own perspectives on a conflict, they may be able to appreciate that these different perspectives may be creating barriers to resolution of a conflict. Cognitive flexibility can help people to achieve a "psychological distance from interpersonal conflict" that lets them see beyond "their own biased viewpoints," helps them "focus on their highest-priority conflict issues," and enables them to generate their own "creative, out-of-the-box solutions to seemingly irreconcilable differences."[29]

Importantly, acknowledging the existence of another perspective does not mean that the person has to agree with that other perspective. In addition, perspective reframing does not mean that the individual will now want to engage in discussion with the other person – especially if their perspective is viewed as harmful or disrespectful. In such circumstances, in order to resolve a conflict, one option is to involve a trusted third party to facilitate a conversation between the different perspectives [WHO AND HOW].

Where conversation is possible, it may help to start by acknowledging the other person's perspective before asking them to consider the validity of another perspective. As Stephen Dubner notes in his Freakonomics podcast, Blaise Pascal made the argument back in the seventeenth century that this is a more effective approach than simply telling someone that their perspective is wrong; Pascal wrote, "Now, no one is offended at not seeing everything; but one does not like to be mistaken."[30]

WHAT YOU CAN DO

! If a discussion doesn't seem to be getting anywhere, it may be because the conversation is focused on a very narrow issue or a specific point of view. Considering another (third-party) perspective may help move the conversation into more productive territory:

- "What if we step back and look at [problem X] from a [department/industry/academic field] perspective? Have we missed anything?"

Switch to a Bigger Picture View

A bigger picture or "bird's-eye view" discussion can help you and your graduate students with time management and productivity. The results of a 2007 Australian study[31] that looked at the importance of various time management behaviors (being organized, avoiding distraction, planning and prioritizing, having a clear goal and purpose) suggest that it may be more helpful to revisit long-term goals and reflect upon the purpose of your research, rather than to clear your desk and empty your inbox.

WHAT YOU CAN DO

! If a potential source of conflict relates to lack of productivity or to poor time management, instead of asking specific task-oriented questions like:

- Have you cleared your schedule for writing next week?
- How are you going to organize your research so you can find files more effectively?

> ! Encourage students to shift to a big-picture view by asking questions like:
>
> - What's motivating you?
> - How is what you are working on now related to your research plan?
> - What is your highest priority and why?

Consider Timing

Effective conflict management is about knowing when to actively engage to resolve an issue, when to seek more information, when to pause, and when to simply ask questions rather than offer solutions. In conflict coaching, we tried not overwhelming students with too many referrals or too much information and "not rushing to talk about solutions too quickly, but to fully hear the student's story first" (Megan, MEd Counselling Psychology).

> **WHAT YOU CAN DO**
>
> ! Build time into key meetings to let stories unfold.
>
> ! Pause before problem-solving. Look for cues that the other person is ready to move from storytelling into problem-solving. Alternatively, simply ask:
>
> - "Is there anything else you'd like to add before we start talking about options?"

Acknowledge Complexity

Complexity is why effective approaches to managing conflict can be time consuming, and why it can be useful to be familiar with a range of possible approaches and strategies. It may be equally important to acknowledge and highlight complexity in order to have more productive discussions about how to resolve a conflict.

Research from the Difficult Conversations Lab (Columbia University) suggests that thinking about issues "in simplistic terms: wrong or right, truth or lie, good or bad," tends to result in people picking sides, attacking, and defending.[32] However, if information is instead reframed as "a variety of related but complicated sub-issues, then people feel, think, and behave differently because there is more to process."[33]

Many of the decisional shortcuts ("heuristics")[34] that we use to manage complex situations can also lead to "snap judgments" or unfair categorizations or assumptions in the moment ("They are a liar"; "If they can't do this task, they must be lazy/incompetent"). For more effective conflict resolution, we also want to slow down in order to observe and challenge our shortcut tendencies and to see and understand the complexity.

WHAT YOU CAN DO

! Consider the following versions (A and B) of a student describing an issue to their supervisor: version A frames the issue in terms of right/wrong, and version B frames the issue as more complex:

A. "You lied to me. I was supposed to schedule my defense for three months from now, and now you are saying it is going to be at least five months out. This delay is wrong, and you know it."

B. "I think there is a problem. I thought I was going to be defending in three months, and you are saying it is going to be at least five months. I know that there are many moving parts here in terms of who is involved, schedules, priorities, and academic requirements. There is so much to consider, and I want to talk about what might be possible since I've been working hard to meet the earlier deadline, and I've put in place some plans that rely on that timeframe."

Q. Can you think of any questions you could ask a student who came to you with version A in order to help them see the complexity of their concern?

! According to research, what you do before a conversation can prime the conversation for complexity. Listen to these podcast conversations about the importance of complexity and the power of pre-conversations: "Embrace Complexity to Overcome Polarization: Discussing a Way Out with Dr. Peter Coleman of Columbia University,"[35] and Amanda Ripley's "Complicating the Narratives"[36] – a discussion of complexity in journalism when reporting on conflicts.

Use Positive and Negative Messaging

In the past, I've used the classic "carrots and sticks" metaphor (incentives/disincentives, positives/negatives) when trying to encourage someone to consider what might motivate another person to do or not do something. Motivation is complex; thinking carefully about when to use "carrots" and when to rely on "sticks" can be key. According to research by Dr. Tali Sharot, fear or negative feedback is one way to motivate people to stop doing something while hope or positive feedback is a "better motivator, on average, for motivating action."[37] In particular, when we are experiencing a situation negatively, we may feel like it is appropriate to respond in kind, and that isn't always the most effective response. For example, I heard questions like, "Isn't there a way to force someone to do X [or stop doing Y]?"

In the university context, it can sometimes be hard to determine what a faculty "stick" might look like (especially for tenured faculty), whereas "carrots" can be more easily cultivated. I recall a discussion with one of the vice-deans at the graduate school about what types of "sticks" might be available to get faculty (in particular the ones that need it most!) to participate in professional development training. Many could also have been framed as "carrots":

- formal letters (reprimand/praise) that might impact progress through academic ranks
- monetary awards (don't get/get)
- requirement for formal reviews (have/don't have)

From one of our faculty workshops, we had the following request: "We would have liked advice on how to impress upon students the seriousness of a situation." Perhaps this is an instance where using clear positive and negative messaging could be effective.

Consider this example where a faculty member has already made several attempts to engage a grad student in a discussion about their PhD progress and the need for a timeline, after expressing both curiosity and concern. The faculty member decides it is time to put something in writing, using positive or hopeful messaging, in order to motivate the student to *start* developing a timeline and confirm a day/time to review the timeline together.

> From: SUPERVISOR
> To: STUDENT
> Re: PhD Academic Progress – Your timeline
>
> Hi STUDENT,
> We have had a few conversations [DATES] about your academic progress, which is important to me as your supervisor and is essential for reaching your goal of obtaining your PhD. Please see [POLICY LINK] for the required timeframe. We talked about how important it is for you to put together a timeline to outline your research goals for the next six months. We looked at the handbook [LINK] which has information on how to prepare a timeline and why it is important for PhD students. We also agreed to talk before [DATE] to review your timeline. I wanted to check in to see if you needed any more information and to book a time/date for our meeting.
> Sincerely, your SUPERVISOR

And if there was no response from the student, the supervisor might opt for a positive or a negative approach in their follow up email. Here is an example of a negative approach – because the supervisor wants the student to *stop* avoiding the issue. Note the importance of setting out for the student what happens next:

From: SUPERVISOR
To: STUDENT
Re: PhD Academic Progress – URGENT

Hi STUDENT,

I emailed you on [DATE] about the timetable for your research goals for the next six months and you failed to respond. We have already discussed my concerns on several occasions. By failing to provide this timetable and not responding to my email, you have put your academic progress at risk and I'm very concerned that you will not be able to get back on track. The policy [LINK] is clear about the consequences for PhD students who fail to make satisfactory academic progress. As your supervisor, I'm required to [NEXT STEPS in POLICY]. Please note that I will be doing so at the end of next week if I don't hear back from you. It is time to stop avoiding and take action. Sincerely, your SUPERVISOR

WHAT YOU CAN DO

! If you promote being proactive about conflict, consider messaging that is hopeful and positive.

! Discuss the following three situations with a colleague.

1. A faculty supervisor who is concerned about a PhD student's lack of engagement in the research.

2. A department chair who wants to motivate faculty members to attend professional development sessions.

3. A student who has reached out to their advisor numerous times for feedback and hasn't had any response.

Q1. Would you recommend "carrots" or "sticks"? Provide one or two examples for each.

Q2. Is there a current challenging situation where you could try to communicate using positive messaging (perhaps refer to carrots) or negative messaging (perhaps refer to sticks)?

Keep Process Top of Mind

 Here are five excellent reasons why it is important to focus on the process of resolving a conflict rather than on the outcome (the "how" rather than the "what"):

1. *It creates opportunities for "buy-in."* If students are given an opportunity to participate in a decision-making process (or one that creates a set of standards or obligations), they are more likely to accept and abide by an outcome (even a less favored one!).

2. *Students may not be ready yet.* We aren't always our best selves when we are in conflict, and it can take time to share a story before problem-solving can take place. Students will find it easier to listen and problem solve when they feel heard, and this means hearing your questions too!

3. *It allows you to test assumptions.* Do you assume that grad students prefer free-flowing problem-solving or a more directive solutions-oriented structure? Focusing on process allows you to test assumptions.

4. *It can help to take the pressure off.* A focus on process is different from a focus on finding solutions. By focusing on trying to understand a student's interests and priorities and on asking questions and clarifying information rather than solving the student's problem, you are respecting the student's problem-solving journey.

5. *A fair process is the basis for fair decision-making.* If, in the end, you will be responsible for making a decision, your decision and reasons will need to stand up to possible future scrutiny as well as the process by which you came to your decision (i.e., the process).

Negotiate in a Way That Is Respectful and Inclusive

While it can be effective to take a strong stance in favor of one's own interests, good negotiators generally avoid emotional attacks and are less aggressive in advocating against other people's ideas and interests.[38] Treating others poorly in the context of a negotiation, may "signal a lack of empathy and perhaps less willingness to come to some agreement."[39]

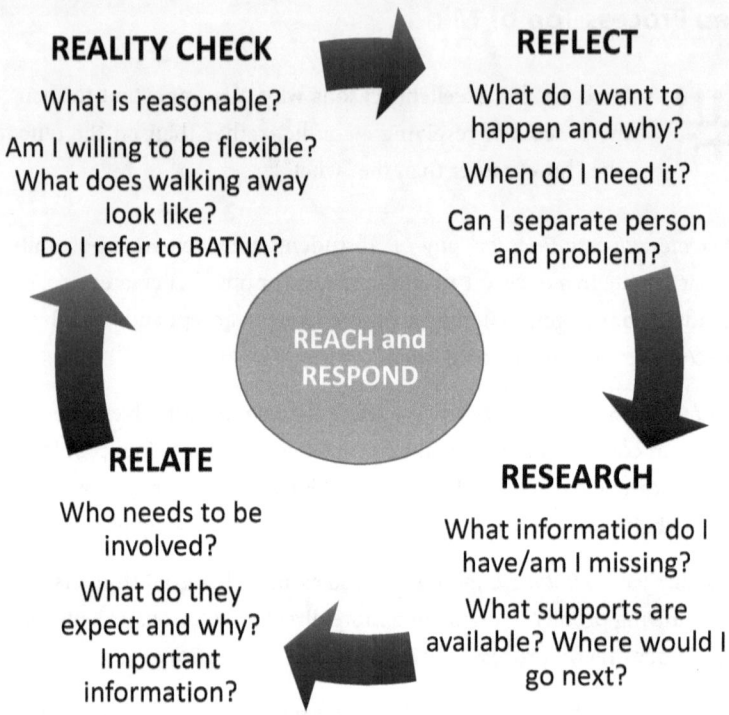

Figure 12. 6 Rs – Slide from "Conflict Resolution Fundamentals" workshop (part of Graduate Professional Skills series)

In developing a conflict resolution workshop series, I combined many of the negotiation recommendations and research findings that are outlined in this book into a six Rs cycle. The first four Rs (Reflect, Research, Relate, and Reality Check), in the outer cycle (in no strict order), relate to what happens before the negotiation, and the final two Rs (Reach and Respond), in the inner cycle, relate to what happens in the actual negotiation.

- *Reflect.* Consider positions, interests, and possible approaches to the conflict. What do you want to happen and why? How would you consider your relationship with the person separately from the issue that you're trying to resolve? Consider timing.
- *Research.* Information is powerful. What questions do you need to ask to get missing information? Consider the systems in which the conflict exists – what barriers and inequities might exist, and what potential impact do they

have (on you as faculty and on your student)? What supports/resources are available?

- *Relate.* Consider your interests and priorities in relation to what the other person's interests and priorities might be. What approach are you taking and why (e.g., hard negotiation or cooperative negotiation, or both)?[40] How does power (at an individual or systemic level) impact this negotiation?

- *Reality check.* What is a reasonable outcome? What happens if no agreement can be reached (i.e., your "Plan-B" or BATNA [Best Alternative to a Negotiated Agreement])?[41] Be cognizant of feeling pressured into an agreement by exhaustion or because significant time and energy has already invested in trying to resolve an issue. Consider what walking away might actually look like. Are there costs/benefits of taking one approach over another?

- *Reach.* Research suggests that effective negotiators make persuasive and "lofty goal"[42] offers – they reach for what they want even if achieving that is unlikely.[43]

- *Respond.* It is equally important to respond to others' offers while impressing upon the other side the validity of your own arguments.

Self-Evaluate: What Could I Do Better …

Here is one of my favorite examples of feedback from a conflict prevention workshop that I ran several years ago in a master's class at the invitation of the instructor (i.e., it was a captive audience of over forty students) with two peer advisor co-facilitators:

> "Honestly you guys do a great job despite your limitations. Like conflict resolution stuff is so insanely boring and it's just common sense, but you guys try really hard to use activities to make this boring topic actually interesting which is really great."

The feedback was refreshingly honest and a signal that while we seemed to be on the right track, we still had work to do to get grad students to appreciate the important strategic considerations behind "common sense" approaches to managing conflict.

For coaching feedback, we relied on an anonymous online survey (very few responses), on recording comments we heard after coaching conversations as part of our data entry, and we also engaged in self-evaluation. Through debriefing (primarily between co-coaches), sharing challenges and successes at team meetings, and annual 360 degree reviews, we tried to listen openly to observations about our work, including criticism and acknowledge where there might be room for improvement.

My work with the graduate peer advisor team gave me a deeper appreciation of how useful it can be to engage in experiential "in the field" reflection.

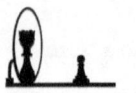

Each conflict that we tried to help others resolve or manage gave us an experience that we learned from. We developed skills that might help us resolve our next issue with greater understanding and appreciation of alternative perspectives. The peer advisors (as well as all of the participants in our workshops) were encouraged to take the strategies and tools that they were learning and use and share them in the real world (i.e., off campus).

We practiced, in a real way, the skills we were asking others to use – and our own commitment to self-reflection and continuous improvement made our program stronger. As you try various strategies and approaches to managing conflict with your graduate students, listen to feedback (if provided), be open to doing things differently, share your own challenges and successes with colleagues (mindful of privacy) and listen to their perspectives, and importantly: self-assess.

WHAT YOU CAN DO

! Try the "Your Supervisory Practice: Self-Assessment" tool[44] created by Maria Gardiner and Hugh Kearns, researcher-practitioners in cognitive behavioral coaching for higher education.

! Reflect on a supervisory (or non-supervisory) situation. Deidra Faye Jackson (University of Mississippi in Oxford), recommends asking simple questions like:

- What worked well?
- What can I focus on next time?
- Where can I improve or enhance my skills and abilities?[45]

... And What Am I Doing Well? (Be Kind to Yourself)

It is important for our mental wellness that we take time to acknowledge what we are already doing well in our work.[46] Consider and celebrate what you are already doing to prevent and manage conflict with your graduate students. If you read the tips in the "What You Can Do" boxes and think, "I'm already doing that" or "That seems easy enough to try," that's great! The best responses and approaches to conflict will be those that are authentic, respectful, and mindful of the nuances of a particular situation. As I would tell the peer advisors during training – make these tools your own – break them apart, rebuild them, be accurate, and be yourself.

Consider the things that grad students told us that they really liked about their supervisors and note how they coincide with grad conflict hotspots:

- supportive, kind, listen
- available, responsive, and make time for regular check-ins
- give sound advice and provide honest critical feedback
- facilitate networking, share information about jobs, and provide reference letters
- share calls for papers, facilitate involvement in research projects/co-publishing
- support grant writing, share information about funding
- identify relevant readings
- work through problems together

How many of these are you doing?

What Can Departments or Institutions Do to Support Conflict Management?

As peer advisor Sam (MA Public Health) observed, "[While I was doing outreach for the Grad CRC,] I found that there was much resistance to our services from staff and administrators who, at times, seemed to feel threatened by our presence as a supportive advising service." While there are dozens of ways for faculty as individuals to manage conflict and build early resolution competency, sustaining a conflict management shift from avoidance to action requires engagement and buy-in at the departmental and institutional levels. In this way, the responsibility for managing conflict lies with everyone from front-line departmental staff to senior institutional leadership. Effective conflict management will necessarily involve responding to individual issues as they arise as well as building capacity across a system to prevent or manage future issues.

Whether there is interest in and support for building a comprehensive conflict management program or just for putting together an online session about managing expectations in supervision, it is important to start somewhere. Building a sense of shared responsibility for managing conflict can start with a simple message: *conflict = opportunity.*

To start, institutions can leverage the post-COVID-19 recognition and appreciation of front-line workers and look at what is happening on the front lines of graduate conflict management. Is there sufficient support, resources, and training so that conflicts are being addressed early and effectively? Research out of Queen Margaret University in the UK examined various models of alternative dispute resolution, including Ombudsman Ontario's "issue-based approach" that grants front-line ombuds caseworkers sufficient freedom to bring about flexible and creative solutions to problems. The study concluded that:

- An organization that empowers front-line/early intervention personnel with discretionary powers may encourage the earlier resolution of issues ...

As long as ...

- front-line personnel are well-trained and qualified to ensure that their discretion is exercised properly and fairly.[1]

Engaging with grad students in the heat of the moment and being able to brainstorm fair and viable solutions is a challenging and multi-faceted task. Perhaps contrary to conventional university conflict management design where complex matters may be funneled upwards within the institution, early resolution for graduate conflicts may be better achieved by ensuring that highly qualified front-line staff (i.e., training) have wide discretion about how to resolve issues – especially complex ones. Improving supervisory relationships while acknowledging power imbalances "must arrive from an institution-wide cultural shift" (Nelson, MSc Institute for Medical Science).

WHAT YOU CAN DO

! Start small and track successes and don't be afraid to fail and reassess. There is power in small wins.[2] Think about what you could do right now.

! Conduct a conflict management initiative "pre-mortem."[3] Imagine what could go wrong with a new initiative in your department:

Q1. What happens if there is an increase in complaints coming to the department's attention?

Q2. What if you discover that conflict is rampant among faculty members and grad students?

! Get faculty talking about conflict = opportunity by learning about Rachel Botsman's theory of building a "trust

> stack" to span the gap between the people, the organization, and a new idea (conflict management), as outlined in "The 3 Steps of Building Trust in New Ideas and Businesses."[4]
>
> Q1. What would a trust stack look like in your department?
>
> Q2. Using Botsman's insights, how would you build trust into (familiarity with and enthusiasm for!) the idea of conflict management?

Encourage Training and Other Professional Development

There would generally be an increase in the number of faculty coming to me for individual coaching after we ran a training session in their department or if they attended one that ran centrally on campus. In other words, workshops are gateways to individual problem-solving (at least for those faculty who value professional development).

Supporting faculty conflict management training signals to faculty (and to students) that their department appreciates the challenges facing graduate students and supervisors and is committed to helping to resolve these issues. From a faculty member who attended one of our supervision workshops in 2019 we heard, "The workshop made me exercise seeing things from a student's perspective (which we all should do, but never practice)."

Peer advisor Nelson (MSc Institute for Medical Science) noted that the increasing number of graduate chairs and faculty members who were reaching out to set up workshops or training for their students was "a huge step in the right direction in ameliorating a culture where a hapless graduate student fears the repercussion of approaching or challenging their erudite professors." Our service was helping to form lines of communication and connection between graduate students and faculty in both academic and administrative roles.

WHAT YOU CAN DO

! We found that faculty attendance would vary widely depending on the topic, day/time of year, how sessions were advertised (e.g., word of mouth, invitation from the department, or email from our office), or whether our session was being offered as part of a regular meeting or run as a special session. Like sessions for grad students, we tried to incentivize faculty with lunch or snacks and capture their attention with fun titles.

Q. *What works to bring faculty together to learn in your department?*

! Here are three things faculty liked about a one hour lunch and learn session we ran entitled "We Need to Chat … Pitfalls and Rewards of Informal Meetings":

1. *Structured discussion:* "We liked that there was lots of time for discussion among attendees, that the discussion had structure, and that the facilitators kept the meeting on track."

2. *Specific scenarios:* "We were happy to be able to discuss several specific scenarios (real-to-life examples) and we wanted more time to talk about our own current concerns and to brainstorm options."

3. *Handouts:* "We loved that you provided a handout (paper) – please send in electronic form, including resources, the five pitfalls handout, and the reminders (re: meeting agendas and keeping good records of conversations)."

! When developing faculty training or putting together a workshop resources list, it is good practice to look for contributions from a diverse group of authors. For example, if you are including resources related to supporting grad students with disabilities, consider whether any of the articles/guides were written by people living with a disability.[5]

! Sometimes if we ran a student workshop, faculty might email in advance to ask to join. In my view, it is important that if a workshop has been advertised for grad students, it should be for students. Having faculty in attendance will always change the dynamic in the room (a consideration the facilitators would manage on the spot, if a faculty member showed up at a session). Inquiries from faculty would often lead to us running sessions specifically for faculty, or a joint student/faculty session.

Build a Faculty Coaching Team

One of the only, and certainly the most comprehensive, faculty initiatives I encountered was a "graduate advisory (dream) team"[6]. Faculty leadership in one of the university's larger science departments saw that there were increasing numbers of students escalating concerns, and so in 2019 they recruited  fourteen additional faculty members who would be trained and made available to subsets of students within the department, thus sharing the load. I was invited to participate in the dream team's inaugural full-day training, and I provided a ninety-minute session on conflict coaching. They were even given monogrammed baseball hats!

A faculty coaching team may be able to offer students a sounding board for concerns – many times we found students were not looking for specific solutions, but for information, strategies, and perspective. In addition to building capacity to help students, I expect that this graduate advisory team was also providing support to one another, and perhaps to other faculty members in the department; similar to the levels of support that existed within our peer advisor team.

A faculty coaching team will ideally be a diverse group, including junior/senior faculty with different identities, backgrounds, and viewpoints. For the peer advisor team, I also looked for indication that the graduate student was a good listener (or willing to learn) and a team player with an interest in conflict resolution. Here are excerpts from the peer advisors' job description:

> We welcome applications from individuals with varied life experiences and identities, and from various academic programs. Team members will be selected from various graduate programs/units and backgrounds.

> In this role, the G2G peer advisors (Grad-to-Grad) must be self-motivated team players and role models for best practices in conflict prevention within the graduate community.

It is also important to manage expectations about who you are looking for and what the role involves in terms of time and commitment. For example, for the peer advisor role, I specified that:

> There is an intensive and mandatory thirty-five hour in-person training commitment for the position, in addition to regular bi-weekly team meetings/in-service training over the year. After training, the peer advisors manage their own flexible schedules, providing part-time coaching, outreach, and training (six to eight hours per week) to their peers within their departments and across the university.

WHAT YOU CAN DO

! When you recruit, articulate the benefits of participating in a faculty coaching initiative (i.e., what is your sales pitch for why faculty should want to join, why this type of initiative matters, or why this activity might be professionally beneficial within the department? (for someone who has tenure, or is/is not looking for tenure)?):

> Be part of a diverse team of faculty that is committed to helping manage conflict more effectively in the department – get to know your colleagues' conflict management styles!
>
> Join the first-ever faculty advisory team – your chair will be there!

! How you recruit impacts who you reach and who becomes interested. Consider:

- *Language/Formatting*. Are you using welcoming and inclusive language?

- *Skills/Experience.* What do faculty coaches need coming into the role versus what they can learn in the role?

- *Advertising platforms.* Using different platforms (email, social media, website, job board, or printed copies) can help you reach a wider audience.

! A great reference is *Working towards Inclusion: Equitable Practices for Hiring Student Staff and New Professionals*, written by Sania Hameed and Mary Stefanidis for the Canadian Association of College & University Student Services.[7]

Q1. *Outside of a faculty coaching team, what opportunities are there to share with faculty colleagues what you learn about supporting graduate students and about related policies, processes, or resources?*

Q2. *How are best practices recorded and shared among colleagues?*

Consider Peer Support

Below are some of the comments we received from grad students who talked with the peer advisors:

- "[Talking to a peer] is the best way to prepare for a difficult discussion with your supervisor/committee! Feeling best prepared now and learned something for life!"
- "I really enjoyed my experience with my peer advisor. I found her knowledgeable about the resources available at the university, encouraging, and supportive. It was especially nice to just have someone I could talk to about my experience, and I could tell that she genuinely wanted to help me."
- "I really appreciate all of the time you put into listening and providing me with strategies and resources."

There is enormous value in using peers on the front line of conflict management, including the potential "to improve mental health and build resilience."[8]

What Can Departments or Institutions Do to Support Conflict Management?   235

Figure 13. Grad CRC graduate student peer advisor teams, 2015–20

The peer advisors observed that while grad students might be intimidated to connect and talk with people in their department, the diversity of the peer team allowed students to feel more comfortable in reaching out for assistance with a conflict. Although in general, I provided support to faculty and staff, on occasion, faculty would also connect with the peers. After her second year in the peer advisor role, Amika (PhD Health Informatics) observed, "I realized that what staff and faculty sought was not different from students – a confidential and nonjudgmental space where they could identify their interests, consider new positions, and strategize on how to move forward in a manner that preserves their integrity and relationships."

We tried to meet individuals "where they were at" in terms of physical location[9] and how far they were along with the conflict resolution. In our peer-to-peer coaching model, individuals could have one or several informal and confidential conversations with one or multiple members of our team. It often came as a surprise that we did not keep notes or files on conversations (whether they were quick five-minute chats or emotional two-hour – or longer – discussions), and that we didn't ask anyone for their name, student ID, or any other personal information to access our service. Every conversation was an opportunity to help someone organize their thoughts, prioritize their goals, recognize relevant policies and constraints, learn some conflict management skills, and utilize (if they were not already) the many services available at the university.

Some of the other benefits of using trained graduate peer advisors for front-line conflict management at a university include:

- They expand capacity and fill in gaps that may exist in supporting and connecting students to campus resources as they navigate challenging issues in graduate school.

- They are credible and trusted (they are grad students too!). While facilitating a conflict resolution training workshop or providing individual conflict coaching, they connect in ways that staff and faculty can't.
- They benefit from the advising sessions as coaches (professional skills for employability of PhD/master's students) as much as the students they coach (learning skills and strategies, and feeling heard by someone who understands).
- They are capable and committed individuals who feel strongly about supporting their fellow students and enjoy collaborating with professional staff and engaging proactively with faculty.

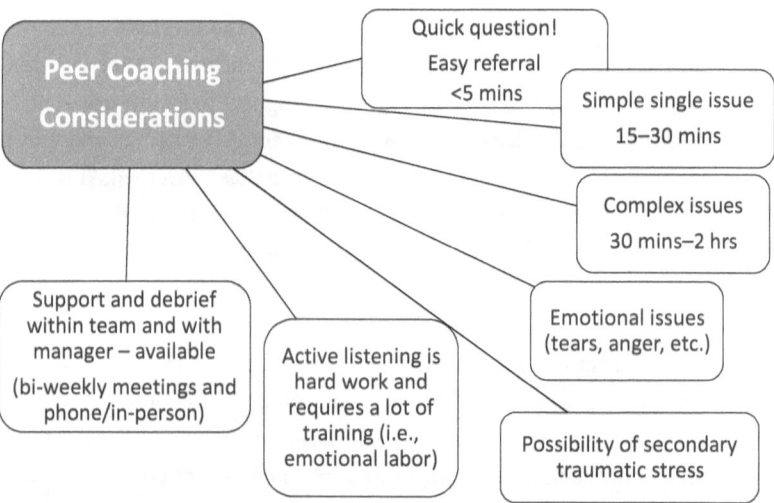

Figure 14. Grad CRC slide from "Peer Coaching" workshop for Osgoode Mediation Clinic participants, 2017

As colleagues have mentioned to me over the years, peer programs are common, but our peer support was extraordinary. Perhaps this is because of the level of training required, but it was also due to the remarkable team compositions year over year, and their enthusiasm for conflict resolution (seven students in our first year, and fifteen in our final year). Our team was, as one peer noted, "diverse by design." This started with recruitment – after our first year, the senior peer advisors helped to advertise positions by participating widely in orientation activities while new positions were open. It was important to reach out widely and hire individuals from different departments/faculty; from sciences, arts, and engineering, to those pursuing a PhD or a master's degree, to different identities, perspectives, backgrounds, and experiences.[10] As two peer advisors noted, "When joining the team, it [diversity] was the first thing I personally noticed, and it made me feel safe" (Lynie, MI Library and Information Science), and "It's honestly beautiful to feel that I can be myself in a safe and healthy work environment, and that I can be part of a team that cares so deeply about the impact of our work on our peers and the campus community!" (Tony, MA Public Health).

What else does it take to build a great peer program?

- Willingness to let the peers inform the type of support that is being offered and how connections are made with peers. Every year the peers provided feedback on the program and, in doing so, they informed its next iteration.

- Intense training, in-service training, and ongoing support. In our model, current team members mentored new team members and helped to facilitate new staff training and onboarding.

- Active management and supervision. Being mindful of the possibility of secondary stress.[11]

In the end, while I have amazing things to say about working with graduate peers, the peer advisors themselves are the best advocates for a peer support initiative:

> "I loved being a peer advisor. Having the opportunity to listen deeply, strategize and work through conflicts that graduate students have on a one-to-one basis has been incredibly rewarding." (Kimberly, PhD Social Justice Education)

> "In addition to gaining conflict resolution skills, my interpersonal skills have been greatly refined! I have learned to work together in a team, either on presentations or co-coaching a student appointment. But the most surprising skill I've gained is how much more compassionate and kind I have become toward others." (Anuya, PhD Psychology)

"My work as a peer advisor positively shaped my entire experience as a graduate student. I have found an essential support system among my colleagues, developed the confidence to navigate the challenges of grad school, and have become equipped to help other students overcome obstacles in their own programs. Engaging with the diverse experiences of my colleagues and the students who use our service continues to broaden my point of view on and off campus." (Rebecca, MEd OISE)

Building the Grad CRC Peer Team Timeline – First Year Pilot
September–December 2015
• Consultation (relationship building/information gathering) • Draft Grad CRC terms of reference; outline peer team program objectives, goals, coaching model, and guiding principles • Assessment and data collection, storage, and application; confidentiality and safety protocols; consultation with university privacy lawyer • Pilot report prepared for partners; discussion (end of October) • Peer training developed; learning objectives; partners for training; training schedule • Preparation to advertise/hire peer team (job description, responsibilities, hours); start with smaller team (5–7 students); recruit peers
January 2016
• Formal training/onboarding for peers – 40 hrs • Launch – Grad CRC open for student, staff, and faculty consultation; start promoting services • Test survey/application for inputting assessment data
February–May 2016
• Informal weekly meetings – discuss issues/share knowledge • Formal monthly training; continuing professional development • Check in regularly with peers about how things are going; suggestions/modifications • Peers meet with students (drop-in, appointments, facilitated group meetings) • Offer workshops/sessions for students, faculty, and staff
June 2016
• Peers write personal reflections; 360 interviews • Initial full data assessment – What works? changes? expansion? • Determine whether to extend existing peer contracts to December 2016 (for those not graduating) • Hiring and training of new peers – timing/any changes needed?
July–August 2016
• Hiring – target departments/student groups for potential peers? • Determine how peers/Grad CRC will be involved in orientation? • Report for partners on 6 months (January–June 2016)

Know When to Bring in an External Third Party

Involving an external third-party neutral, such as a mediator, a conciliator, or a facilitator,[12] can help people find their way to a mutually agreeable resolution to a conflict. Sometimes a university will have an on-campus mediation service or an internal ombuds who may mediate or facilitate in appropriate circumstances; however, more often universities will simply have designated individuals or offices with mandates to assist faculty or students to resolve issues (what I would call an "internal neutral"). If an internal neutral is going to be involved in a conflict, their role and the limitations of their role should be clear. Here are three questions to ask:

1. Does the internal neutral have a role in any decision-making process related to the conflict? (The answer should be NO.)

2. Does the internal neutral have any training or experience as a mediator or facilitator? (The answer should be YES.)

3. Will participants view the person as impartial/neutral no matter what happens during/after the process? (Again, the answer should be YES.)

If the answers are not as above, it may be more appropriate to consider bringing in an external third-party neutral. I recall speaking with one chair who seemed completely dedicated to the grad students in their department, yet they did not feel it was appropriate for them to be in the middle of a particular student-to-student dispute.

Here are four questions to ask in determining whether hiring an external third-party neutral is an appropriate course of action:

1. Is there a conflict that is having an impact on the individuals involved, the department, and the institution (and perhaps beyond)?

2. Have the individuals involved already tried to resolve the conflict themselves, unsuccessfully?

3. Are the individuals likely to consent to participating in a mediation/facilitated process? What factors might be influencing their decision to participate? (For example, timing; understanding of what a mediation/facilitation process will involve; preferences for mediators/facilitators with subject matter expertise, or particular background, experience, or identities.)

4. Will the costs of engaging an external professional be acceptable to participants or the department/institution, and will there be a significant cost if the issue is not resolved? (Consider the possibility and costs of legal recourse.)

Over four and a half years, requests for referrals to external third-party mediators/facilitators were rare, and in my experience, the reality of "mediation" as an option was quite different from what was stated on most campuses. In other words, just because an institution says that "mediation can or should take place is not sufficient for a mediated solution to actually occur."[13] At times I could identify opportunities for external mediation or restorative conversations, but because of cost and unfamiliarity – or where there was a perception that involving a third-party neutral would result in a loss of control over a situation – they were not often implemented. Most of the time the individuals we were coaching wanted to try to resolve their issues on their own using the strategies we discussed.

Here is an example of when I recommended hiring a third party: A department administrator had contacted me about an interpersonal conflict between two graduate students in a lab who had previously been involved romantically (the conflict). I understood the students were "open" to any conflict resolution process that might help them to continue to work together, but they hadn't been able to resolve their issues themselves. They needed to work together given their research interests (consent). I was told that the department would be willing to pay for a professional external mediator because the students seemed unable to "get past" their issues, and the option of doing nothing was potentially detrimental to the students, the research, and the department. There were no free mediation services on campus.

> **WHAT YOU CAN DO**
>
> ! Most mediators and ADR practitioners are willing to having a brief free conversation to explain their background, experience, approach, and availability. Ask about rates and incidental fees up front, just as you would for any service (e.g., an electrician or a mechanic).
>
> ! At some universities (or in some cities), there are also free community mediation services that may be appropriate to consider.

Look at Online Guided Conflict Resolution Pathways

A conflict resolution guided pathway (which I refer to as a "resolution pathway") is a "choose your own resolution" opportunity. It is a flexible, self-directed road map for navigating a system such as a university. Normally, virtual access is available twenty-four-seven from anywhere a student has internet access. Possible interventions (mediation, external decision-maker/arbitration) are outlined at various stages.

Some educational institutions use guided pathways in academic advising,[14] and there are online dispute resolution systems that allow individuals to explore options for resolving issues outside of the court system, for example:[15]

- "Steps to Justice" guided pathways for legal information and forms re: family law, housing, and powers of attorney for Ontario
- "Civil Resolution Tribunal Solution Explorer" provides customized legal information and options for various civil law disputes in British Columbia

A resolution pathway may be a way to deliver some of the information conflict coaches might provide at an early stage, for example:

- information about resources, processes, and policies
- self-help strategies
- opportunities to explore options and next steps for self-identified goals
- printable/saveable summary of the pathway that can be used by the student as a plan of action

While a resolution pathway may sound ideal, there are important considerations/challenges, including:

- *Cost.* Building a system from scratch or using an online dispute resolution provider will have a lot of up-front costs.

- *Accuracy (content developed by experts, peers, etc.).* A guided pathway must be cohesive, actually helpful (tested with real students!) and updated regularly.

- *Confidentiality.* How and how much information is collected and stored.

- *Limitations.* A conflict resolution guided pathway is unlikely to be a replacement for person-to-person interactions – instead it should be seen as a complement.

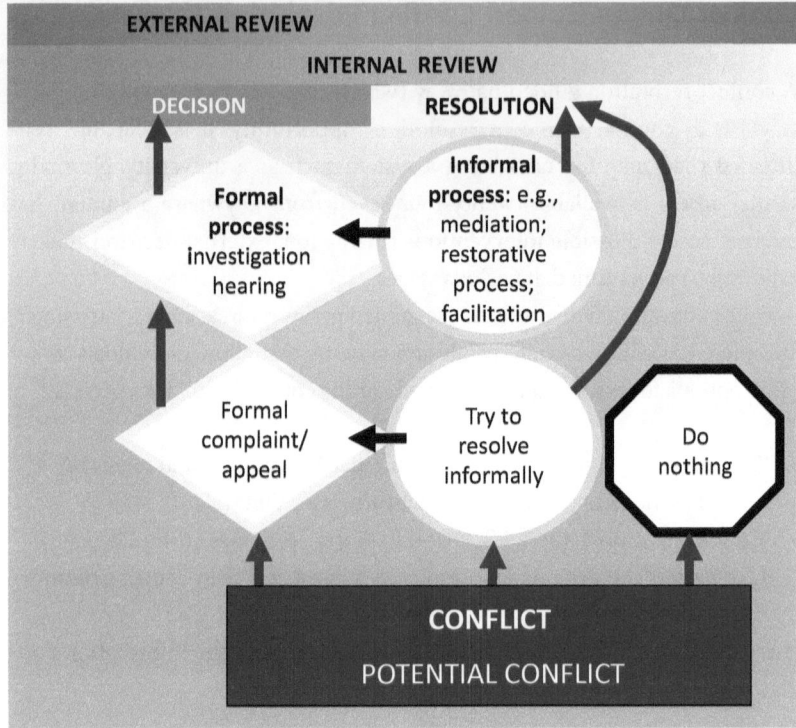

Figure 15. Flow chart showing typical pathways for conflict resolution within post-secondary institutions

Live Up to Institutional Promises

Shining a light into the shadowy corners of graduate school to illuminate potential conflict can require a great deal of "administrative courage."[16] If after reading this book you are convinced that the right approach is to develop a comprehensive conflict management program, pause, and then consider that if you build it, they will come. As I noted in an earlier chapter, there is a desire among members of the graduate community to learn how to manage conflict earlier and more effectively, and by filling a need, you will be building trust between grad students and the institution/department, between faculty and the institution/department.

Be aware that when an institution or department makes promises to the members of its community to provide certain types of support or mechanisms for resolving serious issues, and then fails to live up to those promises, there can be a sense of "institutional betrayal." This term is often used by survivors of sexual violence to describe their experiences with institutional processes and official commitments that overpromised and under-delivered.[17] This sense of institutional betrayal can be heard in statements such as these which we heard in our conversations:

- "Why should I trust the university?"
- "I went to [university service] last year and it was a terrible experience – why would I go back to them now?"
- "My department says it cares about grad students but that isn't true. I know students who have complained to the chair, and nothing happened."

WHAT YOU CAN DO

! Building trust is essential. Spend time finding out what your community needs and what is realistic to provide. We know from conversations with faculty and staff that they are often disillusioned by what has happened in the past (or not happened), and this has a dampening effect on their willingness to address current conflicts.

! Be transparent about what came before, even if it wasn't a success (e.g., a workshop series that was canceled due to COVID-19; a department peer mentor program that was recommended but never implemented). Explain why it is important to try again and consider whether there might be a need to apologize for taking so long to get this far.

! Be clear about current realities and constraints, including timelines for future action. Explain how (and over how long) the process will unfold. Students, faculty, and faculty in administrative positions can have very different perceptions of time and of what is an appropriate pace of action. What seems like an average time frame to make a decision or implement a new initiative might seem like excessive delay to a grad student who has been waiting for the decision or advocating for the initiative, or incredibly fast to a faculty member whose research timeline spans decades.

What Do We Do When Conflict Isn't Resolved?

The reality is that not every grad school problem has a solution, and not every difficult supervisory situation has a happy ending. Conflict management does not always equal conflict resolution or full resolution of all of the issues that might be involved in a complex conflict. Individuals may choose to avoid, defer, compromise, escalate, or otherwise deal with a particular conflict rather than try to bring it to a resolution. From my experience, regardless of whether a conflict is resolved or not, moving forward after there has been a conflict requires even more work than the attempts at resolution.

We found that sometimes individuals were seeking an apology that was unlikely to ever come, or were questioning whether they could forgive, or were wondering if rebuilding trust was going to be possible. A lot has been written on the role of apologies,[1] forgiveness,[2] and trust in moving past conflict – and that work is worthy of another book to explore its role in the graduate context.

Instead, to end this book I will share insights from our conversations about why graduate conflicts are not always resolvable.

Advice Doesn't Always Lead to Resolution

A faculty member once asked me with some frustration after a workshop: "What can I do if a grad student doesn't take my advice?"[3] My answer was, "It depends." It depends on the consequences of not taking the advice, on whether the student has enough information to assess the pros and cons of taking the advice (now, later, or never), and on whether the situation warrants intervention by the faculty member.

Even though faculty advice may be coming from a place of good intention (i.e., trying to help the student), the student may not feel that it meets their interests and needs (i.e., they don't think the advice works for them and their specific circumstances), or they may not be ready to hear advice (i.e., they aren't ready to hear or aren't open to problem-solving), or they don't understand why the advice was given (i.e., they don't acknowledge any issue). Ultimately, absent concerns about capacity, the choice is theirs to make, regardless of whether a faculty member feels that is the best course of action. Accepting this and not ruminating about whether the student might have taken your advice if you had presented it differently is part of moving forward after a conflict.

There Needs to Be a Different Process

If there were no attempts to resolve a conflict using a clearly outlined process (formal or informal) or if there are concerns that the process did not unfold properly or fairly, you may want to ask: "Should we re-engage using a different process?" If the answer is "maybe," consider the following questions:

- Is it the right/fair/reasonable thing to do in the circumstances?
- Are we able to commit time/energy necessary to revisit the past?
- Is anything likely to change in terms of the outcome?
- Is there an opportunity to create new processes that will be restorative and fair?

Whether or not there is another attempt made to resolve the conflict, it is important to look critically at the original conflict resolution processes to assess:

- What did we do well?
- What could we do better?
- How do we make sure this doesn't happen next time or with other students?

It is important to remember that a different process doesn't mean it has to be a formal or legalistic process – for example, instead of an unstructured discussion, there could be a facilitated discussion or mediation. Cheryl Foy, university secretary and general counsel at Ontario Tech University, puts it like this:

> If, in times of conflict, we avoid the conflict by engaging in formal processes that essentially "kick the can down the road," our workplaces won't get better. We won't get better at resolving conflict. If we can't do

it internally, how can we be models for the type of conflict resolution we want to see out in the world? How can we be leaders for our students?[4]

It Is Simply Time to Move On

When a relationship between a student and a supervisor (or a committee member) is broken, and restoring trust and respectful academic interactions is not possible, it can make sense to cut ties.[5] As the Honorable Justice Winkler observed about conflict, "Sometimes we need to state our disagreements, appreciate our differences, and move on."[6] In coaching, we heard from grad students who wanted to change supervisors because their supervisor had "lost faith" in their work or their committee members had "suddenly turned on them."

While respecting their perspectives on the situation, we talked about the realities of moving on – that doing so might not be easy or without consequences in terms of academic/research progress and potential long-term impacts as well. Even if there isn't an ongoing relationship between individuals who have had a conflict, academia can be a "small world" situation – and individuals may find themselves together again in similar or other circumstances such as in the lab, in the department, in the field, or as potential future references, colleagues, connecters, or co-authors. The mechanics (who, how, when) of ending a supervisory or a committee relationship and of how the individuals feel throughout the process (respect, kindness) are both critical.

Often we found it was helpful for students when the peer advisors outlined a range of possible options for them, even if they had come in to talk about "How do I change supervisors?" or "What happens if I leave grad school?" Students told us they found it helpful to consider their suggested option as one of a range of options (e.g., taking a leave of absence, changing to a master's, leaving the PhD program, continuing to work with the same supervisor, or changing supervisors).

It Can Make More Sense to Agree to Disagree

Most of the time, individuals were coming to talk with us before they had made significant efforts to try and resolve an issue; although, we also had conversations where despite best efforts, resolution wasn't happening. As Cinnie Noble notes, even "if no agreement seems to be possible, the choice remains to maintain our opposing views and consider how to move forward regardless."[7] Consider the following:

- *What are our shared interests and how do we focus on these moving forward?* Attempt to highlight, even at a very big picture level, where there are common interests. Frame the discussion about what might work for the future rather than what didn't work in the past.
- *What do we need to do to create a "better" supervisory relationship (nuts and bolts)?* Try to brainstorm what "better" might look like, and then together outline or create diagrams to illustrate the various elements.
- *What should happen if we disagree in the future?* Here there is a recognition that conflict is going to happen, and together you are building a plan to address that inevitability. Outline processes or communication strategies that you both agree to use (e.g., whether you will involve a third-party neutral to help facilitate future conflicts). Keep in mind that if there is a fair process, any outcome of that process will more likely be seen as legitimate (15).

If there is at least a willingness to contemplate a state of agreeable disagreement, trying to answer these questions (together!) can help to support the relationship moving forward.

ROLE PLAY: SWITCHING SUPERSTAR SUPERVISORS

Time Required. 30 minutes = 5 prep / 15 role play / 10 debrief

Instructions. In pairs, one person plays the role of a PhD/master's student and the other plays the role of a graduate coordinator/chair (i.e., the graduate support faculty member within your department). Each person has confidential background information, and the student has additional information that they can share throughout the role play. You will have five minutes to prepare (get into character). Feel free to ad lib and add additional details to make this role play more realistic (i.e., you can go off script). After five minutes, we will call Ready? Action! and read the role play introduction aloud to set the stage. You will have fifteen minutes to act out the scene. At the end we will have a debrief discussion with the larger group.

Debrief Questions for Group Discussion:

- What did the coordinator do well?
- Were there any great questions?
- Was there anything that the coordinator could have done differently?

READY? ACTION! Read aloud: The student has arrived for their appointment with the graduate coordinator (virtual or in person). The coordinator welcomes them and invites them to share why they've booked the meeting/why they wanted to talk. The student begins to share their story.

SHARE WITH COORDINATOR ONLY Confidential Background. You are relatively new to this administrative role, although you are not new to being a faculty/supervisor. You understand your role to include listening, asking open-ended questions, and supporting grad students so that they can resolve their own issues.

SHARE WITH STUDENT ONLY Confidential Background. The past four months have been extraordinarily stressful, and you are very close to giving up on your "PhD dream." Nothing is worth this amount of stress. You are somewhat melodramatic and express your anger/sadness/frustration in waves as you recount various parts of your story. PAUSE often while you share your story and wait for the coordinator to ask questions/say something. You don't have to share everything at once.

STUDENT Details to Share Immediately. I feel like the supervisory relationship has immense potential for abuse because of the massive power imbalance. No one person in my life has had so much control and power over my professional development and outcomes as my supervisor. I feel like my supervisor has me doing things for their professional advancement that are borderline unethical, but I don't feel like I can really say no because of the power dynamic. Everything came to a boiling point last week. I need to switch supervisors. Can I do that? [PAUSE].

STUDENT Details to Share if Asked What Happened. There was an incident in the office last week – the supervisor was unbelievably angry about some of the data I'd been analyzing but this time I wasn't alone with the supervisor – other students were there so other people can confirm what happened. I've been told many times before by this pseudo-supervisor that I'm supposed to get certain results, and anything less is unacceptable. Since it is their stellar research reputation that drew me to the department in the first place, I really don't have any choice! Nothing in the data was fitting together the way it should have. I was trying to ask my supervisor about the inconsistencies, but they just yelled at me that it was clearly all my fault things weren't working and that I'd just have to work harder if I wanted to stay in their research group.

STUDENT Details to Share if Asked about Trying to Resolve the Conflict. I talked about this a little with my family, but they don't understand the depth of the problem. This goes to the very heart of my supervisor's current research! Since the incident, I've talked to a few other students. Turns out that it isn't just me – others have concerns about the data but they are afraid to speak up.

STUDENT Details to Share if Asked about Emotions/Feelings. I'm worried that if I do nothing, I'll lose years of my life to feeling bad, paralyzed by uncertainty. I'm convinced I've ruined my academic career because there is no way that I will be able to defend in four years with this supervisor. In fact, there is no way I want to spend another hour (let alone another five years!) in this department.

STUDENT Details to Share if Given Silence to Fill. I really do love the research I've been doing and feel so lucky to be in graduate school. My friends have told me that without a good recommendation from my supervisor I will never get a good academic job. Isn't there anyone who can do something about this? Isn't there any way to just switch supervisors? I've always dreamed of being referred to as "Dr.," and it would make my family really proud – I am the first in my family to go to university. There is no way that I want to quit my PhD, and the other members of my committee seem nice and are also experts in this area – although they don't have the "superstar" reputation and funding to match.

END OF ROLE PLAY *Move to Debrief.*

Notes

From the Author

1 Some of the documents that informed the creation of the Graduate Conflict Resolution Centre (Grad CRC) at the University of Toronto (UofT) included:
   - University of Toronto, *Report of the Provostial Advisory Committee on Student Mental Health* (Toronto: University of Toronto, 2014), https://www.provost.utoronto.ca/wp-content/uploads/sites/155/2018/03/Report-on-Student-Mental-Health.pdf;
   - University of Toronto Office of the Ombudsperson, *Report of the U of T University Ombudsperson* (Toronto: University of Toronto, 2013–2014), https://governingcouncil.utoronto.ca/annual-reports-and-administrative-responses;
   - University of Toronto Graduate Students' Union (UTGSU), *Harassment, Discrimination & Abuse Report* (2011);
   - "Canadian Graduate and Professional Student Survey (CGPSS) – Canadian Report," Fall 2013, https://www.dropbox.com/s/3jxs0fncka089t1/EN_CANADA_CGPSS_2013_REPORTS.xlsx.

   Note the results for the CGPSS question of whether their thesis/research advisor "overall, performed the role well" has remained relatively unchanged: 11.8 percent (2019) versus 11.7 percent (2013) of students disagreed/strongly disagreed with that statement.

2 Robyn A. Jacobson, "Managing Conflicts and Resolving Disputes Involving Students on University Campuses: The Present and the Future" (PhD diss., York University, 2012), 369–422, http://managingconflict.ca/wp-content/uploads/2010/01/Robyn-Jacobson-Dissertation1.pdf. According to Ms. Jacobson's PhD research, "The most essential place on university campuses for the management of conflict and resolution of disputes is a Conflict Management and Dispute Resolution Resource Centre" (469). She notes that many conflict management centers emerge with support and then are unceremoniously shut down. Trust, success, and usage are not always enough. Ms. Jacobson's 2012 research is the "first research that analyzes what Ontario universities are presently doing to manage conflict and resolve disputes involving students" (iv).

Who Wants to Talk about Grad School Conflict?

1 Grad CRC Annual Reports and 2019/2020 statistics provided to program partners.
2 We kept track of who we were speaking to (PhD and master's students, faculty, staff, other, faculty/department, year of study) and for how long (5 minutes to 2 plus hours), as well as the issues that were discussed, whether the individual was upset, what they were looking for from our service (information, advice, talk to peer, advocacy, other), and whether we made a referral. In this book, all of the case studies, examples, and excerpts from coaching conversations are based on actual conversations with graduate students, faculty, and staff between 2016 and 2020, with edits and compilations made to protect confidentiality and for illustrative purposes.
3 Luc Simon, "Canadian Graduate and Professional Student Survey (CGPSS) – 2019 Update," CGPSS, accessed 26 November 2021, https://cags.ca/cgpss. Raw data retrieved from Centre de recherche et d'intervention sur l'éducation et la vie au travail (CRIEVAT), *Canadian Graduate Professional Student Survey 2019 Summary Report – All Students,* accessed 26 November 2021, https://cags.ca/cgpss.
4 Corinne Pask-Aubé, *Canadian Graduate and Professional Student Survey (CGPSS) 2019 Aggregate Report* (Toronto: University of Toronto Planning & Budget Office, 2019), 3, 5, https://www.sgs.utoronto.ca/about/measuring-our-performance/cgpss. Out of 17,627 registered graduate students, the response rate was 34.3 percent.
5 Simon, "Canadian Graduate and Professional Student Survey," 11.
6 *Canadian Graduate and Professional Student Survey 2019 Summary Report – All Students,* accessed 26 November 2021, https://cags.ca/cgpss.

The *Canadian Graduate and Professional Student Survey* also reported: Q. 3-9-3: 13.3 percent ranked faculty grad student relationship as "fair" or "poor" (5); Q. 7-13-6: 11.8 percent disagreed or strongly disagreed that their advisor overall performed the role well (8); and Q. 7-13-3: 8.2 percent disagreed or strongly disagreed that "My advisor gave me constructive feedback on my work" (8). Results for the university are as follows: 16.1 percent reported faculty grad student relationship as "fair" or "poor" (15); 12.7 percent disagreed or strongly disagreed that their advisor overall performed the role well (46), 8.4 percent disagreed or strongly disagreed that "My advisor gave me constructive feedback on my work" (46).

Pask-Aubé, *Canadian Graduate and Professional Student Survey (CGPSS) 2019 Aggregate Report noted*: "Results for U of T are as follows: 16.1 percent reported faculty grad student relationship as "fair" or "poor" (15); 12.7 percent disagreed or strongly disagreed that their advisor overall performed the role well (46), 8.4 percent disagreed or strongly disagreed that "My advisor gave me constructive feedback on my work" (46).
7 For example, see the "Setting Expectations and Resolving Conflicts" workshops presented at Council of Graduate Schools (CGS) meetings and member

universities starting in 1997 in Karen L. Klomparens et al., *Setting Expectations & Resolving Conflicts in Graduate Education* (Washington, DC: Council of Graduate Schools, 2008).

8 Professor Bruce Shore, professor emeritus from McGill University, Canada, offers his advice for graduate advisors from an advisor's perspective: *The Graduate Advisor Handbook: A Student-Centered Approach* (Chicago: University of Chicago Press, 2014).

9 Jennifer E. Beer and Eileen Stief, *The Mediator's Handbook* (Gabriola Island, BC: Friends Conflict Resolution Programs/New Society Publishers, 1997), 11.

10 Safa (MSc Medical Biophysics, now MDPhD) worked with the Grad CRC on behalf of the Medical BioPhysics Graduate Students Association (MBPGSA) Mental Health & Wellness Committee, https://medbio.utoronto.ca/mental-health-mbp-faculty.

11 Medical BioPhysics Graduate Students Association (MBPGSA) Mental Health & Wellness Committee, "MBP Faculty Tip Sheet," University of Toronto, accessed 15 November 2021, https://medbio.utoronto.ca/mental-health-mbp-faculty.

12 For example, Kathleen Kauth, "Fight, Flight, or Freeze … Conflict Responses Are Very Personal," *Mediate.com,* 30 July 2021, https://mediate.com/fight-flight-or-freeze-conflict-responses-are-very-personal.

13 This recommendation is from James Nester, "How to Breathe Better and Why It Matters, Especially in a Pandemic," *CBC Radio*, 12 April 2021, www.cbc.ca/radio.

14 Belisa Vranich, author and psychologist, quoted in Lesley Alderman, "Breathe. Exhale. Repeat: The Benefits of Controlled Breathing," *The New York Times,* 9 November 2016, https://www.nytimes.com/2016/11/09/well/mind/breathe-exhale-repeat-the-benefits-of-controlled-breathing.html.

15 "Reducing Stress Through Deep Breathing (1 of 3)," John Hopkins Rheumatology, 25 January 2018, video, 0:03:00, https://youtu.be/Wemm-i6XHr8; "Box Breathing Relaxation Technique: How to Calm Feelings of Stress or Anxiety," Sunnybrook Hospital, 5 October 2020, video, 0:02:47, https://youtu.be/tEmt1Znux58.

16 At a September 2021 international virtual conference for ombuds in higher education (ACCOUO/ENOHE), some of my colleagues noted that they had seen greater collegiality and consultation, at least between faculty and administration on their campuses, as a result of the move to online communication. That said, there is evidence that COVID-19 exposed and exacerbated inequities for graduate students, as discussed by two PhD students in this webinar: "How Is COVID-19 Impacting Graduate Students in Canada?" Evidence for Democracy/Toronto Science Policy Network (TSPN), 27 August 2020, webinar, 0:58:34, https://www.youtube.com/watch?v=kkaTdaEvOz4&t=28s; and as discussed in this article by Megan Zahneis, "For Many Graduate Students, COVID-19 Pandemic Highlights Inequities," *Chronicle of Higher Education,* 26 March 2020, https://www.chronicle.com/article/for-many-graduate-students-covid-19-pandemic-highlights-inequities.

17 Marc Edward Fincher, "Navigating the New Normal: Strategic Higher Education Leadership in the Post-Covid Shutdown World," in *Handbook of Research on the Changing Role of College and University Leadership*, ed. Michael T. Miller and G. David Gearhart (Hershey, PA: IGI Global Books, 2021), 129. The author is from Mississippi State University.

18 Ontario Confederation of University Faculty Association (OCUFA), "OCUFA 2020 Study: COVID-19 and the Impact on University Life and Education," November 2020, https://ocufa.on.ca/assets/OCUFA-2020-Faculty-Student-Survey-opt.pdf.

19 Edward Keenan, "The Pandemic Has Made Us All So Full of Rage. What Happens if We Never Get Over It?," *Toronto Star,* 4 September 2021, https://www.thestar.com/news/world/2021/09/04/the-pandemic-has-made-us-all-so-full-of-rage-what-happens-if-we-never-get-over-it.html; Scott Schieman, Matthew Zhou, and Jasmine Kang, "Yes, People Do Seem Angrier Thanks to the COVID-19 Pandemic," *Toronto Star,* 5 July 2021, https://www.thestar.com/life/2021/07/05/yes-people-do-seem-angrier-thanks-to-the-covid-19-pandemic.html.

20 Mindi Thompson, "Advice for Faculty Members in a Turbulent Time," *Inside Higher Ed Advice* (blog), 19 March 2020, https://www.insidehighered.com/advice/2020/03/19/how-faculty-members-can-best-cope-stresses-covid-19-opinion.

21 "Communicating with Patients Experiencing Distress and Anger," *University Health Network - Princess Margaret Hospital,* 28 January 2021, https://www.uhn.ca/PrincessMargaret/Education/Communicating_Distress_Anger/Pages/respond_anger.aspx (link expired).

22 "Anger Management: 10 Tips to Tame Your Temper," *Mayo Clinic Healthy Lifestyle* (blog), 29 February 2020, https://www.mayoclinic.org/healthy-lifestyle/adult-health/in-depth/anger-management/art-20045434.

23 Kathryn Mannie, "U of T Professors, Faculty Sign Open Letter Calling for Written Apology on UTM Handcuffing," *Varsity*, 1 December 2019, https://thevarsity.ca/2019/12/01; Rosalind Hampton, Vannina Sztainbok, and Beverly Bain, "Open Letter: President Gertler, Defund and Abolish Campus Police," *Varsity,* 24 August 2020, https://thevarsity.ca/2020/08/24; Lwanga Musisi, "Op-Ed: Cops Off Campus – What Does It Actually Mean?," *Varsity*, 2 March 2021, https://thevarsity.ca/2021/03/01.

24 In December 2020, the Chief Commissioner for the Ontario Human Rights Commission (OHRC) wrote to all Ontario college and university presidents and principals about media reports and calls from students and student groups that highlight the fact that "Indigenous, Black and racialized students are experiencing significant concerns of discrimination, xenophobia and targeting on campuses and in academic environments across Ontario." Chief Commissioner, "Letter to Universities and Colleges on Racism and other Human Rights Concerns," OHRC, 18 December 2020, www.ohrc.on.ca/en/news_centre/letter-universities-and-colleges-racism-and-other-human-rights-concerns. In April

2021, the Chief Commissioner wrote again, emphasizing that from the student perspective, institutional administrators and internal complaints processes (both formal and informal), "had failed to effect change." Chief Commissioner, "Letter to Universities and Colleges on Actions to Address Systemic Discrimination," OHRC, 14 April 2021, www.ohrc.on.ca/en/news_centre/letter-universities-and-colleges-actions-address-systemic-discrimination.

25 Bob Blankenberger and Adam M. Williams, "COVID and the Impact on Higher Education: The Essential Role of Integrity and Accountability," *Administrative Theory & Praxis* 42, no. 3 (2020): 404–23, https://www.tandfonline.com/doi/full/10.1080/10841806.2020.1771907.

26 As defined by Professor Kimberlé Crenshaw (Columbia Law School), "Intersectionality is a lens through which you can see where power comes and collides, where it interlocks and intersects. It's not simply that there's a race problem here, a gender problem here, and a class or LBGTQ problem there. Many times, that framework erases what happens to people who are subject to all of these things." Featured Quote, https://www.law.columbia.edu/faculty/kimberle-w-crenshaw.

27 Sometimes referred to as BIPOC (Black, Indigenous, People of Colour).

28 "Anti-Black Racism – Definition and History," *Black Health Alliance*, accessed 2 November 2021, https://blackhealthalliance.ca/home/antiblack-racism/; "Glossary – Anti-Indigenous Racism," *Government of Ontario*, accessed 2 November 2021, https://www.ontario.ca/document/data-standards-identification-and-monitoring-systemic-racism/glossary; "Addressing Anti-Asian Racism," *Government of Canada*, last date modified 29 October 2021, https://www.canada.ca/en/canadian-heritage/campaigns/asian-heritage-month/anti-asian-racism.html.

29 Dr. Jane Freeman, Director Graduate Centre for Academic Communication, University of Toronto.

30 For example, at the University of Toronto there were several specialized tri-campus equity and inclusion offices that faculty could contact, including the Anti-Racism and Cultural Diversity Office and the Office of Indigenous Initiatives, https://people.utoronto.ca/inclusion/equity-offices/.

31 Brian Arao and Kristi Clemens, "From Safe Spaces to Brave Spaces: A New Way to Frame Dialogue around Diversity and Social Justice," in *The Art of Effective Facilitation: Reflection from Social Justice Educators*, ed. Lisa M. Landreman (Sterling, VA: Stylus Publications, 2013), 135. See also Heather M. Ross, "Challenging Conversations – Safe Spaces vs. Brave Spaces," *University of Saskatchewan Educatus* (blog), 8 June 2021, https://words.usask.ca/gmcte/2021/06/08; and Irshad Manji, "White Fragility Is Not the Answer. Honest Diversity Is," *Heterodoxacademy* (blog), 7 July 2020, https://heterodoxacademy.org/podcast/episode-14-white-fragility-is-not-the-answer-honest-diversity-is.

32 University of California San Francisco Office of the Ombuds, "Brave Conversations: 5 Step Tipsheet," accessed 2 November 2021, https://ombuds.ucsf.edu/communication-tools.

33 Kimberlé Crenshaw, "What Is Intersectionality?" National Association of Independent Schools, 22 June 2018, video, 0:01:54, https://youtu.be/ViDtnfQ9FHc.
34 Robin Everall, "Graduate Student Mental Health and Wellness Report" (Edmonton: University of Alberta, 2018), 13, https://cloudfront.ualberta.ca/-/media/gradstudies/about/faculty-and-staff/resources-for-supervisors-and-graduate-coordinators/20181128_graduate-student-mental-health-wellness-report.pdf.

Why Do Grad Students Avoid Conflict?

1 See Hugh Kearns, "Research Intelligence: How to Overcome Academic Imposter Syndrome," *Times Higher Education,* 18 July 2019, https://www.timeshighereducation.com/research-intelligence/research-intelligence-how-overcome-academic-imposter-syndrome; Kristopher Gies, "Responding to Uncertainty through a Growth Mindset," Career Advice, *University Affairs,* 13 July 2020, https://www.universityaffairs.ca/career-advice/responsibilities-may-include/responding-to-uncertainty-through-a-growth-mindset; Colleen Flaherty, "Mental Health Crisis for Grad Students," *Inside Higher Ed,* 6 March 2018, https://www.insidehighered.com/news/2018/03/06/new-study-says-graduate-students-mental-health-crisis; Caitlyn Blake-Hedges, "We're All Frauds: Managing Imposter Syndrome in Grad School," *American Society for Cell Biology* (blog), 30 March 2018, https://www.ascb.org/careers/frauds-managing-imposter-syndrome-grad-school/.
2 Elizabeth Cox, "What Is Imposter Syndrome and How Can You Combat It?," TED-Ed, 28 August 2018, video, 0:04:19, https://ed.ted.com/lessons/what-is-imposter-syndrome-and-how-can-you-combat-it-elizabeth-cox.
3 Isabel Rodriguez, "Imposter Syndrome: An Intersectional Approach," *Zenerations* (blog), 8 September 2020, https://zenerations.org/2020/09/08/imposter-syndrome-an-intersectional-approach/ (link expired).
4 "Identity in Academia: The Relationship between the Imposter Syndrome and Intersectionality," *Graduate Women in STEM U Mass Amherst* (blog), 31 August 2015, https://blogs.umass.edu/gwis/2015/08/31.
5 Quin Parker, "5 Professors Share Their Experiences of Imposter Syndrome," *Top Hat* (blog), 25 March 2019, https://tophat.com/blog/imposter-syndrome-academia/.
6 As author Stephen Dubner notes, "Until you can admit what you don't know, it's virtually impossible to learn what you need to. Because if you think you already have all the answers, you won't go looking for them." Stephen Dubner, "The Three Hardest Words in the English Language," *Freakonomics* (blog), 15 May 2014, transcript of podcast, https://freakonomics.com/2014/05/15/the-three-hardest-words-in-the-english-language.
7 Stephen Dubner and Steve Levitt, "The Three Hardest Words in the English Language," 15 May 2014, *Freakonomics,* podcast, 31:11, https://freakonomics.com/podcast/the-three-hardest-words-in-the-english-language.

Why Is Conflict Something Faculty Should Manage?

1 Quote is from *Tran v. University of Western Ontario et al.*, 2016 ONSC 1781, paragraph 80 (Canlii), https://canlii.ca/t/gnpl8. Justice Dunphy is commenting on the issue of academic discretion.
2 Susan A. Holton, "And Now ... the Answers! How to Deal with Conflict in Higher Education," *New Directions for Higher Education* 92 (1995): 79–89, http://dx.doi.org/10.1002/he.36919959213.
3 Note: I generally use the term "universities" in this book because in Canada only universities offer graduate-level degrees. Please also read "college" where appropriate.
4 Jacobson, "Managing Conflictsand Resolving Disputes," 56–64.
5 Holton, "And Now... the Answers!," 88.
6 Ramina Swanson, "Stop, Collaborate and Listen ... The Cost of Conflict in the Workplace," *From Science to Practice* 2, no. 1 (2016): 15–17, http://www.vanguard.edu/uploaded/Academics/Graduate/Organizational_Psychology/From-Science-Practice_Vol-2-Issue-104.pdf.
7 See "Presenteeism" in Canadian Mental Health Association, Ontario (CMHA Ontario) and Dalla Lana School of Public Health U of T, *Workplace Mental Health Promotion: A How-To Guide*, 28–30, accessed 15 November 2022, https://toronto.cmha.ca/help-for-employers.
8 As noted by Justice Dunphy in *Tran v. University of Western Ontario*, even with a range of formal and informal internal processes, "universities are not as such immune from civil suit." Nevertheless, "it is also true that the civil court system is singularly ill-suited to act as an all-purpose appellate tribunal of its actions" (80). In addition, in Ontario, students can go to the provincial ombudsman who oversees post-secondary institutions. Ontario Ombudsman, *2020–2021 Annual Report: Trends in Post-Secondary* (Toronto: Ontario Ombudsman, 2021), https://www.ombudsman.on.ca/resources/reports-and-case-summaries/annual-reports. It can, however, be difficult (i.e., time consuming and expensive) for the courts to determine if the issues should be left to a university's "academic discretion" or subject to judicial oversight. See *Lam v. University of Western Ontario*, 2017 ONSC 6933 (CanLII), 27–32, http://canlii.ca/t/hp39v.
9 Anne Mullens, "When Students Sue," Features, *University Affairs*, 7 April 2008, accessed 4 November 2021, https://www.universityaffairs.ca/features/feature-article/when-students-sue/.
10 Amanda C. Nellis et al., "Productive Conflict in Supervision," *Vistas 1* (2012), https://www.counseling.org/Resources/Library/VISTAS/2012_Vol_1_67-104/2_2012-ACA-PDFs/Article_81.pdf.
11 Yasmeen Wafai, "Why Difficult Conversations Can Actually Be a Good Thing," *Yes! Solutions Journalism*, 11 July 2019, https://www.yesmagazine.org/social-justice/2019/07/11/hard-conversations-solve-conflicts.
12 ADR (sometimes referred to as "appropriate dispute resolution") normally refers to ways of settling disputes outside of the courtroom (e.g., negotiation,

mediation, or arbitration), whereas "dispute resolution" and "conflict resolution" normally refer to any means of resolving disagreements, including legal action.
13 Kay Guccione, *Trust Me! Building and Breaking Professional Trust in Doctoral Student Supervisor Relationships* (London: Leadership Foundation for Higher Education, 2018), https://www.advance-he.ac.uk/knowledge-hub/trust-me-building-and-breaking-professional-trust-doctoral-student-supervisor.
14 Gary T. Furlong, *The Conflict Resolution Toolbox: Models & Maps for Analyzing, Diagnosing & Resolving Conflict* (New York: Wiley, 2005), 142–6.
15 My understanding is that the original version of the orange parable is from Roger Fisher, William Ury, and Bruce Patton, *Getting to Yes: Negotiating Agreement without Giving In*, 2nd ed. (New York: Penguin, 1991).
16 Matthew Mossanen et al., "A Practical Approach to Conflict Management for Program Directors," *Journal of Graduate Medical Education* 6, no. 2 (2014): 345–6, https://www.ncbi.nlm.nih.gov/pmc/articles/PMC4054741/. There are other conflict models, for example, Ron Kraybill, "Style Matters: The Kraybill Conflict Style Inventory," 27 July 2011, https://www.slideshare.net/Riverhouse/style-matters-conflict-style-inventory.
17 David R. Dunaetz, "*Personality and Conflict Style: Effects on Membership Duration in Voluntary Associations*," OSF Preprints, 2 March 2009, 12, https://osf.io/z8b24/.
18 Jacobson, "Managing Conflicts and Resolving Disputes," 424.

What Does Graduate Conflict Management Involve?

1 In this book I do not make a distinction between a "dispute" and a "conflict."
2 The G2G training, and our promotion and educational materials invited individuals to talk with us by using this Albert Einstein–inspired tagline: "Conflict = opportunity? Ask us how."
3 Ontario Regulation 131/16 sets out the requirements for college and university sexual violence policies as well as the process by which these policies should be established and published. O.Reg. 131/16 Sexual Violence at Colleges and Universities under the *Ministry of Training, Colleges and Universities Act*, R.S.O. 1990, c. M.19, https://www.ontario.ca/laws/regulation/160131. See also https://news.ontario.ca/en/release/60131/ontario-strengthens-sexual-violence-and-harassment-policies-at-postsecondary-institutions.
4 There may also be recourse at the provincial (e.g., Ontario Ombudsman) or state level. Many university and college ombuds offices are members of the Association of Canadian College and University Ombudspersons (ACCUO), http://accuo.ca/, the International Ombudsman Association (IOA), https://ioa.memberclicks.net/, or the European Network of Ombudsmen in Higher Education (ENOHE), https://www.enohe.net/.
5 Jacobson, "Managing Conflicts and Resolving Disputes," 36.
6 Klomparens et al., *Setting Expectations & Resolving Conflicts*, 11.
7 As an articling student I was told by a senior litigation partner to "Never, ever, hide mistakes." He told us he wanted to hear about every error, even the small

ones, because small problems had the tendency to grow in the shadows – and become much harder to resolve when they were eventually (and they would be) found out. I followed this advice and invited the members of my team to come to me with small concerns or questions. For me, the time spent managing "small stuff" was time well spent in preventing larger issues from disrupting or compromising our reputation and good work.

8 "Dispute Resolution Mechanisms (with Flowchart)," *University of Guelph, 2022–2023 Academic Calendar,* accessed 2 November 2021, https://calendar.uoguelph.ca/graduate-calendar/general-information/policy-responsibilities-advisors-committees-student-mediation-procedures/dispute-resolution-mechanisms/.
9 Fisher, Ury, and Patton, *Getting to Yes.*
10 Katie Shonk, "Principled Negotiation: Focus on Interests to Create Value," *Harvard Program on Negotiation* (blog), 1 February 2021, www.pon.harvard.edu/daily/negotiation-skills-daily/principled-negotiation-focus-interests-create-value/.
11 Chris Provis, "Interests vs. Positions: A Critique of the Distinction," *Negotiation Journal* 12, no. 4 (1996): 305–23, https://doi.org/10.1111/j.1571-9979.1996.tb00105.x.
12 For a more in-depth application of an interest-based approach to resolving interpersonal supervisory conflict, see Klomparens et al., *Setting Expectations & Resolving Conflicts,* 34–57.
13 Natalie Sharpe, ed., "Fairness Is Everyone's Concern: A Sampling of Practices and Resources on Cultivating Fairness," Association of Canadian College and University Ombudspersons (ACCUO), May 2015, http://accuo.ca/wp-content/uploads/2017/07/FairnessGuide2015.pdf.
14 Equity, as well as "equity, diversity, and inclusion" (EDI or DEI, and sometimes DEIJ, J = justice), are terms that are widely used on Canadian university campuses, although they are "complex and often contested terms, in both meaning and enactment." Melissa Guenter and Merli Tamtik, "Policy Analysis of Equity, Diversity and Inclusion Strategies in Canadian University – How Far Have We Come?," *Canadian Journal of Higher Education* 49, no. 3 (2019): 42, https://journals.sfu.ca/cjhe/index.php/cjhe/article/view/188529. I like this definition from DEI strategist Arthur Chan: "Diversity is a fact. Equity is a choice. Inclusion is an action. Belonging is an outcome," LinkedIn, https://www.linkedin.com/in/arthurpchan/.
15 "Principles of Good Complaint Handling," *Parliamentary and Health Service Ombudsman,* accessed 3 November 2021, https://www.ombudsman.org.uk/about-us/our-principles/principles-good-complaint-handling.
16 David De Cremer and Steven L. Blader, "Why Do People Care About Procedural Fairness? The Importance of Belongingness in Responding and Attending to Procedures," *European Journal of Social Psychology* 36, no. 2 (2005): 212, http://dx.doi.org/10.1002/ejsp.290.
17 Sharpe, ed., "Fairness Is Everyone's Concern," 6–9.
18 Sharpe, ed., "Fairness Is Everyone's Concern," 9. Thank you to Martine Conway, Ombudsperson University of Ottawa, for her thoughtful comments on the evolution of the fairness triangle – a discussion that I look forward to continuing!

19 De Cremer and Blader, "Why Do People Care About Procedural Fairness?" 223–4.
20 Kimberly Papillion, "The Neuroscience of Decision-Making: Are We Foul or Fair?" TEDxNashvilleWomen, 22 April 2019, video, 0:16:02, https://youtu.be/aCWYkZ5i-gE.
21 David Kestenbaum, Michael Lewis, and Heidi Schreck, "No Fair – Act 1," 5 April 2019, *This American Life*, podcast, at 13:18 (of 62:21), https://www.thisamericanlife.org/672/no-fair.
22 Nora Farrell, "Administrative Fairness Checklist for Decision-Makers," Ryerson University Office of the Ombudsperson, November 2002, https://www.torontomu.ca/content/dam/ombudsperson/documents/Administrative%20Fairness%20checklist.pdf.
23 "Fairness by Design: An Administrative Fairness Self-Assessment Guide," British Columbia Ombudsperson, 16 July 2019, https://bcombudsperson.ca/guide/fairness-by-design-an-administrative-fairness-self-assessment-guide/.
24 Grad CRC data 2016–19 from annual reports: 40 percent PhD, 33 percent master's, and 8 percent unspecified graduate students.
25 Heather McGhee Peggs, "July 1, 2017–June 2018 Grad CRC Insights Report," U of T Graduate Conflict Resolution Centre, 2018.
26 Ijeoma Oleo, *So You Want to Talk about Race* (Seattle, WA: Seal Press, 2019). For anyone interested in a very readable economic perspective on racism, I also recommend Heather McGhee, *The Sum of Us – What Racism Costs Everyone and How We Can Prosper Together* (New York: One World, 2021). See also Sheila Cote-Meek, "Speaking Out on the Inequities in Academia," Opinion, *University Affairs*, 27 August 2020, http://www.universityaffairs.ca/opinion/from-the-admin-chair/speaking-out-on-the-inequities-in-academia/. Dr. Cote-Meek notes, "The intersecting layers of multiple identities further impact how people are viewed and treated in society and in the academy."
27 As former peer advisor Lynie Awywen (MI, Library and Information Science) observes, in 2020 many universities across North America issued "solidarity statements" in response to "protests against anti-Black racism and racial violence [taking] place in the United States, Canada, and countries around the world." See "U of T Expresses Solidarity with the Black Community," *U of T News*, 2 June 2020, https://www.utoronto.ca/news/u-t-expresses-solidarity-black-community.
28 Chris Gill et al., *Models of Alternative Dispute Resolution ADR: A Report for the Legal Ombudsman* (Edinburgh: Queen Margaret University, Consumer Insight Centre, 2014), https://www.researchgate.net/publication/269401391_Models_of_Alternative_Dispute_Resolution_ADR.
29 Robin Amadei, "Conflict Coaching," *Mediate.com*, March 2011, https://mediate.com/conflict-coaching.
30 Scott Shank, "Potential Identities: A Case Study of Professional Coach-Client Communication" (MA thesis, University of Western Michigan, 2015), https://scholarworks.wmich.edu/honors_theses/2535.
31 Nirmala Hariharan, "The Faculty Series: What Does It Take to Be a Mentor?'" *Naturejobs* (blog), 1 February 2016, http://blogs.nature.com/naturejobs/2016/02/01/the-faculty-series-what-does-it-take-to-be-a-mentor/.

32 Herminia Ibarra and Anne Scoular, "The Leader as Coach," *Harvard Business Review,* November-December 2019, https://hbr.org/2019/11/the-leader-as-coach.
33 From faculty training in 2019 for the first-ever Molecular Genetics Graduate Advisory (Dream) Team at U of T: https://moleculargenetics.utoronto.ca/always-here-help-grad.
34 As defined by Canada's largest mental health teaching hospital and world-renowned research center, the *Centre for Addiction and Mental Health* (CAMH): "Trauma is the lasting emotional response that often results from living through a distressing event. Experiencing a traumatic event can harm a person's sense of safety, sense of self, and ability to regulate emotions and navigate relationships." "Trauma," *CAMH*, accessed 3 November 2021, https://www.camh.ca/en/health-info/mental-illness-and-addiction-index/trauma.
35 Consider for example, the decision of Ryerson University in Toronto, Canada to engage in a process to change the name of the university as recommended by a task force charged to "examine and more fully understand Egerton Ryerson's relationship with Indigenous Peoples, his links to the education system in Ontario, and his role in the development of residential schools in Canada, as well as to interpret these findings in both their historical and modern context." Standing Strong (Mash Koh Wee Kah Pooh Win) Task Force, *Standing Strong Report and Recommendations* (Toronto: Ryerson University, 2021), https://www.torontomu.ca/content/dam/next-chapter/Report/SSTF-report-and-recommendations-Aug_24_FINAL.pdf.
36 Roseann Martin (Elder), "Trauma Informed and Culturally Appropriate Approaches in the Workplace," Native Women's Association of Canada, April 2019, http://www.nwac.ca/wp-content/uploads/2019/04/Final-Trauma-Informed-Culturally-Appropriate-Approaches-in-the-Workplace-Final.pdf.
37 I extend my appreciation to staff of the 519 (https://www.the519.org) in Toronto, Ontario, who ran a session for the peer advisors about ways to interact with students in a trauma-informed manner. See also Monique Tello, "Trauma-Informed Care: What It Is, and Why It's Important," *Harvard Health Publishing* (blog), 16 October 2018, https://www.health.harvard.edu/blog/trauma-informed-care-what-it-is-and-why-its-important-2018101613562.
38 "Conflict Management for Instructors," Centre for Teaching Excellence, University of Waterloo, accessed 3 November 2021, https://uwaterloo.ca/centre-for-teaching-excellence/teaching-resources/teaching-tips.
39 Ted Wachtel, "Defining Restorative," International Institute for Restorative Practices (IIRP) Graduate School, accessed 3 November 2021, https://www.iirp.edu/images/pdf/Defining-Restorative_Nov-2016.pdf.
40 "Restorative Justice: What Is Restorative Justice?," Government of Canada, Department of Justice, last modified 10 December 2021, https://www.justice.gc.ca/eng/cj-jp/rj-jr/index.html.
41 "What Is Justice? Reflections on Restorative Justice," Alberta Civil Liberties Association, accessed 3 November 2021, https://www.aclrc.com/what-is-justice-reflections-on-restorative-justice.

42 Mary Leung, "The Origins of Restorative Justice," Canadian Forum on Civil Justice, 1999, www.cfcj-fcjc.org/sites/default/files/docs/hosted/17445-restorative_justice.pdf.
43 Wachtel, "Defining Restorative."
44 Here are examples of universities using restorative approaches: Australia: "Restorative Communities," *Victoria University of Wellington*, accessed 3 November 2021, https://www.wgtn.ac.nz/students/support/student-interest-and-conflict-resolution/restorative-communities (restorative approaches for student misconduct issues); Canada: "Restorative Justice and the Residence Community Standards," *University of Alberta*, accessed 3November 2021, https://www.ualberta.ca/residence/current-residents/community-expectations/restorative-justice.html (restorative approaches to residence issues), and Jennifer J. Llewellyn, Jacob MacIsaac, and Melissa Mackay (on behalf of participants), *Report from the Restorative Justice Process at the Faculty of Dentistry* (Halifax: Dalhousie University, May 2015), https://cdn.dal.ca/content/dam/dalhousie/pdf/cultureofrespect/RJ2015-Report.pdf; and the United States: "Restorative Justice," *University of Michigan Office of Student Conflict Resolution (OSCR)*, accessed 3 November 2021, https://oscr.umich.edu/RestorativeJustice.
45 Truth and Reconciliation Commission (TRC), *Truth and Reconciliation Commission of Canada: Calls to Action* (Ottawa: TRC, 2015), https://www2.gov.bc.ca/assets/gov/british-columbians-our-governments/indigenous-people/aboriginal-peoples-documents/calls_to_action_english2.pdf; Sarah Treleaven, "How Canadian Universities Are Responding to the TRC's Calls to Action," *Maclean's*, 7 December 2018, https://www.macleans.ca/education/how-canadian-universities-are-responding-to-the-trcs-calls-to-action/; Ian Munroe, "Where Truth and Reconciliation Stand at Canadian Universities," *University Affairs*, 19 August 2021, https://www.universityaffairs.ca/features/feature-article/where-truth-and-reconciliation-stand-at-canadian-universities/.
46 Previous discoveries of marked and unmarked graves at residential schools were documented as part of the TRC process, and discoveries of additional burial sites are ongoing. For more information on residential schools and the 2021 discoveries, see "Residential School History," *National Centre for Truth and Reconciliation*, accessed 5 November 2021, https://nctr.ca/education/teaching-resources/residential-school-history/; "Tk'emlúps te Secwépemc Release Final Report on Unmarked Graves at Former Kamloops Residential school," *CBC Radio-Canada*, 15 July 2021, https://ici.radio-canada.ca/rci/en/news/1809374/tkemlups-te-secwepemc-release-final-report-on-unmarked-graves-at-former-kamloops-residential-school.
47 See specifically, TRC Calls to Action #24, #27, #28, #57, #62, and #92.
48 David R. Karp, *The Little Book of Restorative Justice for Colleges & Universities: Repairing Harm and Rebuilding Trust in Response to Student Misconduct* (New York: Good Books, 2013), 25.
49 Wachtel, "Defining Restorative."
50 Tony Case, *Restorative Justice Learning Debrief* (Halifax: Dalhousie University, 2017), 21, https://cdn.dal.ca/content/dam/dalhousie/pdf/dentistry

/DENT_Oct2017Learning%20Debrief.pdf. Case notes that Dalhousie already has knowledge, understanding, and expertise related to RJ/RA that could be enhanced, but "without the skill and leadership of the internal practitioners, there is no safe and supportive engagement of participants and no behavioural change possible or community evolution and development."

51 Argyle Communications Inc., *Appendix B: What We Learned – Engagement Overview and Analysis* (Toronto: Ryerson University Standing Strong (Mash Koh Wee Kah Pooh Win) Task Force, 2021), 5, https://www.torontomu.ca/content/dam/next-chapter/Report/Appendix-B-What-we-learned-Aug-17.pdf.

52 Ann Smith and Lesley Spencer, "Restorative Practice: Emotional Intelligence in the Workplace," *Princess Alice Hospice*, accessed 3 November 2021, http://www.pah.org.uk/wp-content/uploads/2019/11/pah_jm_A0_restorative_practice__NO_PHOTO_OCT19.pdf.

53 Lindsey C. Pointer, "Q&A Facilitating Circles Online," *Lindsey Pointer* (blog), 28 March 2020, https://lindseypointer.com/2020/03/28/qa-facilitating-circles-online/.

54 Gina Baral Abrams and Joshua Wachtel, "During the COVID-19 Crisis, Restorative Practices Can Help," International Institute for Restorative Practices (IIRP) Graduate School, 24 March 2020, https://www.iirp.edu/news/during-the-covid-19-crisis-restorative-practices-can-help.

55 For example, Chelsea Vowel's commentary on the Canadian Association of University Teachers (CAUT) Territorial Acknowledgment Guide: Chelsea Vowel, "Beyond Territorial Acknowledgments," *âpihtawikosisân* (blog), 23 September 2016, https://apihtawikosisan.com/2016/09/beyond-territorial-acknowledgments/.

56 Inspired by *Trauma-informed: The Trauma Toolkit, 2nd ed.* (Winnipeg: Klinic Community Health Centre, 2013), https://trauma-informed.ca/wp-content/uploads/2013/10/Trauma-informed_Toolkit.pdf.

57 At the time we used a platform that required us to set up two separate accounts so that the peer advisors could log in simultaneously and join on a video call.

58 "How Tech Is Impacting the Workforce of Tomorrow," *Randstad USA*, accessed 17 November 2021, https://insights.randstadusa.com/how-tech-is-impacting-the-workforce-of-tomorrow.

59 Justin Kruger et al., "Egocentrism Over E-mail: Can We Communicate as Well as We Think?," *Journal Personal Social Psychology* 89, no. 6 (2005): 925–36, https://www.researchgate.net/publication/7378566_Egocentrism_over_e-mail_Can_we_communicate_as_well_as_we_think.

60 See, for example, this guide for staying safer online: Consumer Reports, "Security Planner; Keep Your Data Secure with a Personalized Plan," accessed 23 November 2021, https://securityplanner.consumerreports.org.

61 For example, see: University of Toronto, "Cyber-Aggression at the University of Toronto," accessed 4 November 2021, http://www.viceprovoststudents.utoronto.ca/wp-content/uploads/SLC2552_Cyber-Bullying_AODA.pdf.

62 Inger Mewburn, "How to Email Your Supervisor (or the Tyranny of Tiny Tasks and What You Can Do about It," *The Thesis Whisperer* (blog), 23 March 2016,

https://thesiswhisperer.com/2016/03/23/how-to-email-your-supervisor-or-the-tyranny-of-tiny-tasks-and-what-you-can-do-about-it/.
63 *Oxford Learners Dictionaries*, s.v. "informal," accessed 23 November 2021, https://www.oxfordlearnersdictionaries.com/us/definition/english/informal?q=informal.
64 Farrell, "Administrative Fairness Checklist."
65 Nathan Rambukkana "Open Letter from Nathan Rambukkana to Lindsay Shepherd," Wilfrid Laurier University, 21 November 2017, https://wlu.ca/news/spotlights/2017/nov/open-letter-to-my-ta-lindsay-shepherd.html (site discontinued). See also Safina Husein, "Breaking: President of Laurier Issues Apology Regarding Lindsey Shepherd," *The Cord*, 21 November 2017, https://thecord.ca/breaking-president-of-laurier-issues-apology-regarding-lindsey-shepherd/.
66 Fisher, Ury, and Patton, *Getting to Yes*.
67 "The Power of Listening Circles," IIRP Graduate School, 29 October 2020, video, 0:59:39, https://www.youtube.com/watch?v=wTEe_-nlZGk.
68 "Fairness by Design: An Administrative Fairness Self-Assessment Guide," British Columbia Ombudsperson, https://bcombudsperson.ca/guide/fairness-by-design-an-administrative-fairness-self-assessment-guide.
69 Thanks to Garvin De Four (then U of T Assistant Ombudsperson) for running this session with me and to Helen Slade (then Coordinator, Student Academic Progress), for her comments on the workshop handout.

If It's Not My Conflict, How Can I Help?

1 Michael I. Norton, Daniel Mochon, and Dan Ariely, "The IKEA Effect: When Labor Leads to Love," *Journal of Consumer Psychology* 22, no. 3 (2012): 453–40, doi: 10.1016/j.jcps.2011.08.002. Fairness has also been linked to durability of outcomes of negotiations, see Daniel Druckman and Lynn Wagner, "Justice and Fairness in Negotiation," *Group Decision and Negotiation* 26 (2017): 9–17, https://link.springer.com/content/pdf/10.1007/s10726-016-9496-4.pdf.
2 Aimé Avolonto, "Letter from a Black Colleague," *Teaching While Black* (blog), 8 April 2021, https://www.teachingwhileblack.ca/post/letter-from-a-black-colleague. Professor Avolonto filed a claim with the Ontario Human Rights Tribunal in June 2018, which is, as of November 2021, still in process.
3 Libby Mahaffy, "A Person with a Conflict Is Like a Hurricane," MIT, 17 January 2015, video, 0:02:27, https://www.youtube.com/watch?v=66qQRMfW1Xg.
4 "Microaggressions & Allyship," Temerty Faculty of Medicine, University of Toronto, accessed 4 November 2021, https://temertymedicine.utoronto.ca/microaggressions-and-allyship. See also "A Guide to Responding to Microaggressions," University of Illinois Urbana Champaign, Grainger College of Engineering – Women in Engineering, accessed 4 November 2021, https://wie.engineering.illinois.edu/a-guide-to-responding-to-microaggressions/.
5 On other campuses, similar offices (or individuals who have similar roles and responsibilities) might have different names, for example, Office of Human

Rights, Equity and Inclusion Office, or Discrimination and Harassment Office.
6 As Ms. Awywen notes, concerns about anti-Black interactions with the police is a founding premise of the BLM (Black Lives Matter) movement, and on some campuses there are movements to get #CopsOffCampus, including at the University of Toronto. See Morgan Murray, "A Look Into the Cops Off Campus Movement," *The Strand* 63, Issue 8, 2 February 2021, https://thestrand.ca/a-look-into-the-cops-off-campus-movement/.
7 "Referrals," *University of Western Ontario*, accessed 4 November 2021, https://www.uwo.ca/health/enhance_wellness/others/referrals.html.
8 "Identify Assist Refer," University of Toronto, 2018, online training module, https://iar.utoronto.ca/main/education-module.
9 Elizabeth Dori Tunstall, "How Maya Angelou Made Me Feel," *The Conversation*, 29 May 2014, https://theconversation.com/how-maya-angelou-made-me-feel-27328.

CONFLICT #1 – Supervision

1 Jacobson, "Managing Conflicts and Resolving Disputes," 30. Ms. Jacobson also includes in the "most difficult to resolve disputes" category: mental health, misconduct, interpersonal and other, which includes political issues, unfair processes, financial issues, withdrawals, placements, unwillingness to resolve/lack of responsibility, ideology, culture, and academic accommodation.
2 For our graduate service, it is perhaps surprising that spring/summer were busy given this is the time of the year when courses have wrapped up (exam and essay time). However, this is looking at the calendar year through an undergraduate student lens. My theory is that summer was the one season in the all-year endeavor that is grad school when students could actually think about things that were bothering them. Supervisors were taking holidays, TA responsibilities were finished, and all that was left on the table was the actual graduate work (and whatever issues were holding that back).
3 Nana Lee, "Finding the Right Supervisor-Student Match," Career Advice, *University Affairs*, 7 February 2019, https://www.universityaffairs.ca/career-advice/graduate-matters/finding-the-right-supervisor-student-match/.
4 Kevin D. Haggerty and Aaron Doyle, *57 Ways to Screw Up in Grad School: Perverse Professional Lessons for Graduate Students* (Chicago: University of Chicago Press, 2015).
5 Katherine Fulgence, "A Theoretical Perspective on How Doctoral Supervisors Develop Supervision Skills," *International Journal of Doctoral Studies* 14 (2019): 721–39 at 733, https://doi.org/10.28945/4446.
6 Grad SERU (Graduate Student Experience in the Research University) was developed in 2014. In 2017, over 3,500 master's and doctoral students (20.7 percent of approximately 19,000 graduate students) participated in the survey at the University of Toronto. Grad SERU, *Results of the 2017 Graduate Student Experience in the Research University (gradSERU) Survey*, University of Toronto, 2018,

https://www.sgs.utoronto.ca/wp-content/uploads/sites/253/2019/09/UofT_gradSERU-report_2018_FINAL.pdf. For more information, see "grad SERU Survey," UC Berkley, accessed 8 November 2021, https://cshe.berkeley.edu/seru/about-seru/seru-surveys/gradseru-survey-design.

7 Shelley Rose Adrian-Taylor, Kimberly A. Noels, and Kurt Tischler, "Conflict Between International Graduate Students and Faculty Supervisors: Toward Effective Conflict Prevention and Management Strategies," *Journal of Studies in International Education* 11, no. 1 (2007): 90–117, https://www.researchgate.net/publication/249632033_Conflict_Between_International_Graduate_Students_and_Faculty_Supervisors_Toward_Effective_Conflict_Prevention_and_Management_Strategies.

8 Adrian-Taylor, Noels and Tischler, "Conflict Between International Graduate Students and Faculty Supervisors," 101–2.

9 Jeff Harry, "Stop Asking 'How Are You' & Replace It with This Question," Medium, 2 April 2020, https://jeffharryplays.medium.com/stop-asking-how-are-you-replace-it-with-this-question-9e6ac53013b8.

10 Modified from Jeff Haden, "10 Much Better Questions to Ask Than 'How Are You Doing?'" *Inc.*, 6 May 2020, https://www.inc.com/jeff-haden/10-much-better-questions-to-ask-than-how-are-you-doing.html.

11 "Personality," American Psychological Association, accessed November 8, 2021, https://www.apa.org/topics/personality.

12 Terry Gatfield, "An Investigation into PhD Supervisory Management Styles: Development of a Dynamic Conceptual Model and Its Managerial Implications," *Journal of Higher Education Policy and Management* 27, no. 3 (2005): 311–25, https://doi.org/10.1080/13600800500283585. See also "Supervision Guidelines for Faculty – Section 3: Supervisory Styles," School of Graduate Studies, University of Toronto, accessed 8 November 2021, https://www.sgs.utoronto.ca/resources-supports/supervision-guidelines/supervision-guidelines-for-faculty-section-3-supervisory-styles/.

13 Riikka Kyrö et al., "What Determines Supervision Style? Introducing the Key Players," Lund University Faculty of Engineering, 2019, https://portal.research.lu.se/portal/files/65822554/Kyro_etal2019_report_Whatdeterminessupervisionstyle_Introducingthekeyplayers.pdf.

14 Wiebke Bleidorn, "How Personality Traits Change Over Time," American Psychological Association – APA Journals Dialogue, 20 January 2020, video (audio only), 0:20:15, https://www.apa.org/pubs/highlights/podcasts/episode-30.

15 Josephine Due, Sofie Kobayashi, and Camilla Osterverg Rump, "To Lead the Way – Inspiration for PhD students and Their Supervisors," University of Copenhagen (2013), 26, https://healthsciences.ku.dk/phd/hoejrebokse/ku-brochure/KU_god_vejledning_UK_2013_web.pdf.

16 DeWitt Scott, "Grad School Personalities," *Inside Higher Ed* (gradhacker blog), 1 April 2016, https://www.insidehighered.com/blogs/gradhacker/grad-school-personalities.

CONFLICT #4 – Interpersonal Conflict (Not Supervisory)

1. Grad CRC Insights Reports 2016–2017, 2017–2018, 2018–2019.
2. Kate Cassidy, "Tuckman Revisited: Proposing a New Model of Group Development for Practitioners," *Journal of Experiential Education* 29, no. 3 (September 2007): 413–17, https://doi.org/10.1177/105382590702900318.
3. William A. Cunningham et al., "Conflict in Your Research Group? Here Are Four Strategies for Finding a Resolution," Careers, *Science*, 18 November 2019, https://www.science.org/content/article/conflict-your-research-group-here-are-four-strategies-finding-resolution.
4. N. Sharon Hill and Kathryn M. Bartol, "Five Ways to Improve Communication in Virtual Teams," *MIT Sloan Management Review*, 13 June 2018, https://sloanreview.mit.edu/article/five-ways-to-improve-communication-in-virtual-teams/.
5. "Group Work," *Kathryn Woodcock* (blog), 3 September 2021, https://woodcock.blog.ryerson.ca/category/current-students/groupwork/.
6. Thank you to Dianne Ashbourne, UofT Mississauga, for her input on common group work issues that we used to modify and create these case studies.

CONFLICT #5 – Research and Thesis

1. See Jacobson, "Managing Conflicts and Resolving Disputes," 115–21.
2. Canadian Association for Graduate Studies (CAGS), "A Guide to Intellectual Property for Graduate Students and Postdoctoral Scholars," *CAGS*, accessed 25 November 2021, http://www.cags.ca/documents/publications/working/Guide_Intellectual_Property.pdf.
3. CAGS, "A Guide to Intellectual Property," 17. Section VII – Dispute Resolution, advises students that as a first step, "you and your supervisor should first try to resolve any differences amicably."

CONFLICT #6 – Academic Progress

1. Colleen Flaherty, "What About Graduate Students," *Inside Higher Ed*, 7 April 2020, https://www.insidehighered.com/news/2020/04/07/graduate-students-seek-time-degree-and-funding-extensions-during-covid-19.
2. "Building an Effective Graduate Student-Supervisor Relationship," University of British Columbia Wellbeing Lab, accessed 5 November 2021, https://wellbeing.ubc.ca/building-effective-graduate-student-supervisor-relationship.
3. Nana Lee and Allan Kaplan, "Best Practices for Reducing Time to Completion," Career Advice, *University Affairs*, 23 May 2018, https://www.universityaffairs.ca/career-advice/career-advice-article/best-practices-for-reducing-time-to-completion/.
4. Hugh Kearns and Finn, "My Feedback Style (Self-Assessment)," Thinkwell, 2017, http://www.ithinkwell.com.au/resources/tools-for-the-supervisor.

5 Hugh Kearns, "What to Do with Writing Feedback," Oregon State University, 22 July 2015, video, 0:52:42, https://media.oregonstate.edu/media/t/0_4olw1c1u.
6 Ken Sterling, "Eliminate 'but' from our Vocabulary When Giving Feedback," *Inc.*, 24 October 2018, www.inc.com/ken-sterling/eliminate-but-from-your-vocabulary-when-giving-feedback.html/.
7 Hugh Kearns (@ithinkwellHugh) "Feedback needs to be specific," Twitter, 8 April 2019.

CONFLICT #7 – Family and Personal

1 In particular, we could refer students to the (free) services of the Osgoode Mediation Clinic at York University: https://www.osgoode.yorku.ca/community-clinics/osgoode-mediation-clinic/.
2 "How to Support Those Living with Suicide Loss," Canadian Association for Suicide Prevention, accessed 9 November 2021, https://suicideprevention.ca/support-for-people-living-with-loss/how-you-can-support-those-living-with-suicide-loss. I compiled these tips for the peer advisors after several students died by suicide on campus followed shortly thereafter by a tragic 2019 airplane disaster (Ukraine Flight 752), which claimed the lives of several graduate students from our university.

CONFLICT #8 – Health and Wellness/Accessibility

1 University of Toronto, "Student Mental Health Resource," accessed 12 November 2021, https://mentalhealth.utoronto.ca.
2 University of Toronto, "Identify Assist Refer" online modules (https://iar.utoronto.ca) are available to all U of T students, staff, and faculty, and are free and accessible to non-U of T members – select "Other." All of the Grad CRC peer advisors participated in this online training and a supplementary two-hour session on supporting mental health for students.
3 Chris Woolston, "PhDs: The Tortuous Truth," *Nature*, 13 November 2019, https://www.nature.com/articles/d41586-019-03459-7.
4 Chloe A. Hamza et al., "When Social Isolation Is Nothing New: A Longitudinal Study on Psychological Distress During COVID-19 Among University Students With and Without Pre-existing Mental Health Concerns," *Canadian Psychology* 62, no. 1 (2021): 20–30. https://doi.apa.org/fulltext/2020-66840-001.html.
5 Igor Chirikov et al., "Undergraduate and Graduate Students' Mental Health During the COVID-19 Pandemic," *UC Berkeley: Centre for Studies in Higher Education*, 2020, https://escholarship.org/uc/item/80k5d5hw.
6 Yorick Peterse et al., "Addressing Mental Health Crisis among Doctoral Researchers," *Public Library of Science PLOS* (blog), 31 July 2018, https://ecrcommunity.plos.org/2018/07/31/addressing-the-mental-health-crisis-among-doctoral-researchers-part-ii/.

7 Arielle Shanok and Nicole Benedicto Elden, eds., *Thriving in Graduate School: The Expert's Guide to Success and Wellness* (Maryland: Rowman & Littlefield, 2021).
8 Accessibility Services, *Demystifying Academic Accommodations,* University of Toronto, accessed 3 November 2021, https://studentlife.utoronto.ca/wp-content/uploads/AS-Demystifying-Academic-Accommodations-Booklet_July_2017_AODA-1.pdf; Accessibility Services St. George campus, *Accessibility Services Graduate and Professional Program Student Handbook,* University of Toronto, 2021–2022, https://studentlife.utoronto.ca/wp-content/uploads/AS-Graduate-and-Professional-Program-Student-Handbook.pdf.

CONFLICT #9 – Laboratories

1 Irene S. Levine, "Mind Matters: Managing Conflict in the Lab," *Science,* 23 September 2005, https://www.science.org/content/article/mind-matters-managing-conflict-lab.
2 Dr. Nana Lee (UofT biomedical sciences professor) pointed out this lighthearted version that was developed by Professor Patrick Schloss at the University of Michigan. See Pat Schloss, "Lab Social Contract," *Schloss Lab,* revised May 2019, http://www.schlosslab.org/lab_business/social_contract.html.
3 Benjamin Tsang, "Lab Conflict and How to Address It," *Nature* (blog), 9 March 2018, http://blogs.nature.com/naturejobs/2018/03/09/lab-conflict-and-how-to-address-it/.
4 Lewis Research Group, "Lewis Lab Equity, Diversity and Inclusion Statement," *University of Alberta,* accessed 16 November 2021, http://grad.biology.ualberta.ca/mlewis/lewis-lab-equity-diversity-and-inclusion-statement-2/.
5 For examples of Independent Development Plans (IDP), see https://myidp.sciencecareers.org/ (free access); www.imaginephd.com/ (sign-up required – for humanities and social sciences).

CONFLICT #10 – Career and Work

1 Depending on their interests and priorities at this time (i.e., money or happiness), some grad students might be interested in the following article: Emily C. Bianchi, "People Who Graduate during Recessions Earn less Money – but They're Happier," *Harvard Business Review,* 21 September 2018, https://hbr.org/2018/09/people-who-graduate-during-recessions-earn-less-money-but-theyre-happier.
2 Jen Polk, "Choose Your Words Wisely, Professors," *PhD to Life* (blog), 8 November 2021, https://fromphdtolife.com/2021/11/08/choose-your-words-wisely-professors/.
3 See, for example, this guide for graduate students in biomedical sciences: Nana Lee and Reinhart Reithmeier, *Success after Graduate School* (Toronto: NR Publishing, 2016).

4 Wendy Hall, "Writing Strong Letters of Recommendation," *University of British Columbia*, accessed 12 November 2021, https://www.grad.ubc.ca/sites/default/files/doc/page/faculty_writing_strong_letters_of_recommendation.pdf.
5 Michael Ernst, "How to Write a Letter of Recommendation," *Washington State University*, October 2002, https://homes.cs.washington.edu/~mernst/advice/write-recommendation.html.
6 Commission on the Status of Women, "Avoiding Gender Bias in Letter of Reference Writing," *University of Arizona*, accessed 12 November 2021, https://csw.arizona.edu/sites/default/files/avoiding_gender_bias_in_letter_of_reference_writing.pdf.
7 Nana Lee, "GPD 19 – Reframing Failure," University of Toronto, 28 February 2020, video, 0:05:55, https://www.youtube.com/watch?v=3xvGgL-AaMg.
8 Inspired by tales from the *University of Toronto History Internships* (blog), https://sites.utm.utoronto.ca/historyinternships/blog.

What Can Supervisors Do to Prevent Conflict?

1 Jonathan Wai, "The Demise of the "Big Picture Thinker" in Psychology," *Psychology Today (*blog), 31 July 2017, https://www.psychologytoday.com/ca/blog/finding-the-next-einstein/201707/the-demise-the-big-picture-thinker-in-psychology.
2 Fisher, Ury, and Patton, *Getting to Yes*.
3 Alan Sharland, "Communication & Conflict: 4 Word Build Activity," *Communication and Conflict Newsletter* #001, 2 January 2008, https://www.communicationandconflict.com/4-word-build.html. Depending on the size of the group, this activity would take 30–40 minutes: 15–20 minutes (giving between 1 and 5 minutes for each round), and a 15–20 minute debrief.
4 Lauren Friese and Rumeet Billan, "How to Lead Millennials," Rotman School of Management U of T, accessed 14 November 2021, https://www.rotman.utoronto.ca/ProfessionalDevelopment/Executive-Programs/FeaturedArticles/How-to-Lead-Millennials.
5 Madeline St. Amour, "Gen Z Open to Non-Traditional Education," *InsideHigherEd*, 25 June 2020, https://www.insidehighered.com/quicktakes/2020/06/25/report-gen-z-open-nontraditional-education.
6 "Executive Summary: The New Generation of Students – How Colleges Can Recruit, Teach, and Serve Gen Z," *Chronicle of Higher Education*, 2018, http://connect.chronicle.com/rs/931-EKA-218/images/NextGenStudents_ExecutiveSummary_v5%20_2019.pdf.
7 Nanda Dimitrov, *Western Guide to Mentoring Graduate Students Across Cultures* (London, ON: Western University Teaching Support Centre, 2009), https://ir.lib.uwo.ca/tsc-purple-guides/4/.
8 Due, Kobayashi, and Osterverg Rump, "To Lead the Way."
9 Kerry Patterson et al., *Crucial Accountability: Tools for Resolving Violated Expectations, Broken Commitments and Bad Behavior* (New York: McGraw-Hill, 2013), 24–8, 75–103.

10 University of Copenhagen Graduate School of Health and Medical Sciences, "Alignment of Expectations between the PhD Student and Supervisor – Discussion Sheet," accessed 14 November 2021, https://healthsciences.ku.dk/phd/apply/applying/before-submitting-the-phd-application/Expectation_alignment_between_supervisor_and_PhD_student_-_Discussion_sheet.pdf.
11 "Tools for the Supervisor," *Thinkwell*, accessed 17 November 2021, https://www.ithinkwell.com.au/resources/tools-for-the-supervisor.
12 "Tools to Give Your Student," *Thinkwell*, accessed 17 November 2021, https://www.ithinkwell.com.au/resources/tools-to-give-your-student.
13 Brené Brown, "Brené Brown at the Up Experience 2011," The UP Experience, 6 December 2012, video, 0:16:09, https://www.youtube.com/watch?v=JJo4qXbz4G4&list=PLrunGv2JGx52ej-e9R8OyfJMcRVGNBBXt.
14 Theresa Rogers and Jennifer Jakobi, "Webinar on Supervision in the COVID-19 Context," University of British Columbia, 26 May 2020, videos, https://www.grad.ubc.ca/faculty-staff/information-supervisors/webinar-supervision-covid-19-context; "Guidelines for Effective Remote Supervision," *University of Calgary*, March 2020, https://grad.ucalgary.ca/sites/default/files/teams/3/FGS%20Guidelines%20for%20Remote%20Supervision_March2020.pdf.
15 "What to Do: A Toolbox of Ideas That Have Worked: Boundaries," *Out of the Fog*, 3 December 2015, https://outofthefog.website/what-to-do-2/2015/12/3/boundaries.
16 Alexandra Sastre, "Setting Healthy Boundaries in Academia," Ideas on Fire, 18 April 2017, https://ideasonfire.net/setting-healthy-boundaries-in-academia/.
17 "Setting Boundaries as a Graduate Student," Grad Life Grind, 22 November 2020, video, 0:15:59, https://www.youtube.com/watch?v=AH8lKorubaU.
18 James Hayton, "The Basic Principles Every PhD Student Needs to Know," 2021, video, 1:09:13, https://www.youtube.com/watch?v=VrMwAOtB9S4
19 Colleen Flaherty, "My Professor Cares: Can 'Light-Touch, Targeted Feedback' to Students via Email Improve Their Perceptions of and Performance in a Class," *Inside Higher Ed*, 14 January 2019, https://www.insidehighered.com/news/2019/01/14/can-light-touch-targeted-feedback-students-improve-their-perceptions-and-performance, citing Scott Carrell and Michal Kurlaender, "My Professor Cares: Experimental Evidence on the Role of Faculty Engagement," NBER Working Paper No. w27312 (June 2020), https://faculty.econ.ucdavis.edu/faculty/scarrell/engagement2.pdf.
20 The concept of a "nudge" was developed by Richard Thaler and Cass Sunstein in their book, *Nudge: Improving Decisions about Health, Wealth, and Happiness* (New Haven, CT: Yale University Press, 2008).
21 Kim Manturuk, "Reclaiming the Nudge," *Inside Higher Ed*, 13 November 2019, https://www.insidehighered.com/digital-learning/views/2019/11/13/dont-give-nudge-it-can-still-help-students-opinion. Manturuk notes that while nudges have had mixed success in higher education, one example where it did work was at Georgia State University where "offering customized messages, instead of form letters, reminding students of pre-matriculation tasks

reduced the number of enrolled students who never showed up on campus by 21 percent."
22 Manturuk, "Reclaiming the Nudge."
23 Nudge4Solutions Lab, ideas42, and Heckscher Foundation for Children, *Nudges, Norms and New Solutions (May 2018)*, 41–68, https://nudge4.ideas42.org/wp-content/themes/nudge4/resources/downloads/NudgesNormsNewSolutions.pdf.
24 Nudge4Solutions et al., *Nudges, Norms and New Solutions*, 60–5.
25 Inspired by Art Markman, "Your Team Is Brainstorming All Wrong," *Harvard Business Review*, 18 May 2017, https://hbr.org/2017/05/your-team-is-brainstorming-all-wrong.
26 Mewburn, "How to Email Your Supervisor (or the Tyranny of Tiny Tasks and What You Can Do about It."

What Can Supervisors Do to Resolve Conflict?

1 Katherine Fulgence Swai, "A Theoretical Perspective on How Doctoral Supervisors Develop Supervision Skills," *International Journal of Doctoral Studies* 14, (2019): 721–39, https://www.informingscience.org/Publications/4446.
2 Amanda C. Nellis et al., "Productive Conflict in Supervision," American Counselling Association, 2011, https://www.counseling.org/Resources/Library/VISTAS/2012_Vol_1_67-104/2_2012-ACA-PDFs/Article_81.pdf.
3 Nellis et al., "Productive Conflict in Supervision."
4 Fazlollah Ahmadi, Aziz Shamsi, and Nooredin Mohammadi, "Using Intelligent Interaction to Manage Student – Supervisor Conflict: A Qualitative Study," *Journal of Educational Health Promotion* 9, no. 18 (2020), www.ncbi.nlm.nih.gov/pmc/articles/PMC7034219/.
5 Julie L. Brockman, Antonio A. Nunez, and Archana Basu, "Effectiveness of a Conflict Resolution Training Program in Changing Graduate Students Style of Managing Conflict with their Faculty Advisors," *Innovations in Higher Education* 35 (2010): 277–93, https://doi.org/10.1007/s10755-010-9142-z.
6 Adrian-Taylor, Noels, and Tischler, "Conflict between International Graduate Students and Faculty Supervisors," 101–2.
7 Chanel Lewis, "Radical Listening," TEDxDirigo, 15 December 2017, video, 0:07:47, https://www.ted.com/talks/chanel_lewis_listening_is_radical.
8 William Ury, "The Power of Listening," TEDX San Diego, 5 January 2015, video, 0:15:40, https://youtu.be/saXfavo1OQo.
9 Alison Wood Brooks "Get Excited: Reappraising Pre-Performance Anxiety as Excitement," *Journal of Experimental Psychology* 143, no. 3 (2014): 1144–58, https://www.apa.org/pubs/journals/releases/xge-a0035325.pdf.
10 Katy Milkman, "Season 6–1: A Bundle of Nerves," 3 August 2020, *Choiceology*, podcast, 0:37:47, https://www.schwab.com/resource-center/insights/content/choiceology-season-6-episode-1.
11 "Negotiation," Lexico, accessed 16 November 2021, https://www.lexico.com/definition/negotiation (link expired).

12 Honorable Warren K. Winkler, Chief Justice of Ontario (Canada), "Mediation with a Difference: Accepting 'No' in Dispute Resolution," Remarks at Osgoode Hall Law School, York University, 14 June 2012, https://www.ontariocourts.ca/coa/about-the-court/archives/2012-mediation-with-a-difference/.
13 Winkler, "Mediation with a Difference."
14 Robert S. Adler and Elliot M. Silverstein, "When David Meets Goliath: Dealing with Power Differentials in Negotiations," *Harvard Negotiation Law Review*, (Spring 2000), 3, https://www.hnlr.org/articles/archive/. Adler and Silverstein also talk about the key role of perceptions of power, which in the graduate context, leans heavily in favor of faculty and administrators.
15 Adler and Silverstein, "When David Meets Goliath," 6.
16 Adler and Silverstein, "When David Meets Goliath," 20. I also note a possible other source of power that faculty often cite as being held by students, social media power – where the power is in the ability to share information in a public forum.
17 Attributed to Voltaire (or Uncle Ben in Spiderman).
18 JoAnne Yates, "MIT Sloan Communication Program Teaching Note," MIT-OpenCourseware, 2010, https://ocw.mit.edu/courses/21w-732-science-writing-and-new-media-fall-2010/resources/mit21w_732f10_listening (link expired).
19 Ury, "The Power of Listening." Ury notes in his talk, "because I listened to him [President Hugo Chavez], he was more ready to listen to me."
20 Karin Wahl-Jorgensen, "The Affordances of Interview Research on Zoom: New Intimacies and Active Listening," *Communication, Culture and Critique* 14, no. 2 (2021): 375, https://doi.org/10.1093/ccc/tcab015.
21 Hillary Anger Elfenbein et al., "Why Are Some Negotiators Better than Others? Opening the Black Box of Bargaining Behaviors," *SSRN Electronic Journal*, May 2010, https://www.researchgate.net/publication/228181972_Why_are_Some_Negotiators_Better_than_Others_Opening_the_Black_Box_of_Bargaining_Behaviors.
22 Alison Wood Brooks and Leslie K. John, "Ask Better Questions," May 2018, *HRB IdeaCast,* podcast, 0:24:39, https://open.spotify.com/episode/2S4FLQ5OnuiWuwwFBILrz7.
23 Brooks and John, "Ask Better Questions."
24 Centre for Teaching Excellence, "Question Strategies," University of Waterloo, https://uwaterloo.ca/centre-for-teaching-excellence/teaching-resources/teaching-tips/alternatives-lecturing/questions/question-strategies.
25 Grad CRC Training 2019, inspired by issues described by graduate students in the UTGSU, *Harassment, Discrimination and Abuse Report*.
26 Fisher, Ury, and Patton, *Getting to Yes*.
27 Jacobson, "Managing Conflicts and Resolving Disputes," 309.
28 Debra Gilin Oore, Michael Leiter, and Diane LeBlanc, "Individual and Organizational Factors Promoting Successful Responses to Workplace Conflict," *Canadian Psychology* (2015): 302, https://www.researchgate.net/publication/282295599_Individual_and_Organizational_Factors_Promoting_Successful_Responses_to_Workplace_Conflict.

29 Oore, Leiter, and LeBlanc, "Individual and Organizational Factors."
30 "69: How Can You Convince Someone They're Wrong?," 3 October 2021, in *Freakonomics No Stupid Questions*, produced by Rebecca Lee Douglas, podcast, 0:37:49, https://freakonomics.com/podcast/nsq-pascal-rejection/.
31 Hugh Kearns and Maria Gardiner, "Is It Time Well Spent? The Relationship between Time Management Behaviours, Perceived Effectiveness and Work-Related Morale and Distress in a University Context," *Higher Education Research & Development* 26, no. 2 (2007): 235–47, https://citeseerx.ist.psu.edu/viewdoc/download?doi=10.1.1.1043.1341&rep=rep1&type=pdf.
32 Yasmeen Wafai, "Why Difficult Conversations Can Actually Be a Good Thing," *Yes Magazine* 11 July 2019, https://www.yesmagazine.org/social-justice/2019/07/11/hard-conversations-solve-conflicts. See also Advanced Consortium on Cooperation, Conflict, and Complexity, "Navigating Political Polarization in Times of Crisis: Lessons from the Difficult Conversations Lab," Columbia University, 28 September 2018, https://news.climate.columbia.edu/2018/09/28/navigating-political-polarization-times-crisis-lessons-difficult-conversations-lab/.
33 Wafai, "Why Difficult Conversations Can Actually Be a Good Thing."
34 Roy Lewicki and Chad Brinsfield, "Framing Trust: Trust as a Heuristic," in W.A. Donohue, R.G. Rogan, and S. Kaufman, eds., *Framing Matters: Perspectives on Negotiation Research and Practice in Communication* (New York: Peter Lang Publishing, 2011), https://www.researchgate.net/profile/Roy_Lewicki/publication/309107248_Framing_trust_trust_as_a_heuristic.
35 Peter Coleman, "Embrace Complexity to Overcome Polarization: Discussing a Way Out with Dr. Peter Coleman of Columbia University," 29 June 2021, in *Fluent Knowledge*, podcast, 0:29:02, https://fluentknowledge.com/shows/the-purple-principle/the-way-out.
36 Amanda Ripley, "Complicating the Narratives: What if Journalists Covered Controversial Issues Differently – Based on How Humans Actually Behave When They Are Polarized and Suspicious?," *Solutions Journalism*, 27 June 2018 (updated 11 January 2019), https://thewholestory.solutionsjournalism.org/complicating-the-narratives-b91ea06ddf63.
37 Shankar Vedantam, "Facts Aren't Enough: The Psychology of False Beliefs," 22 July 2019, in *Hidden Brain*, produced by NPR, podcast, 0:51:00 https://www.npr.org/transcripts/743195213.
38 Karen A. Hegtvedt, "The Talk of Negotiators: Shaping the Fairness of the Process and Outcome," in Kjell Törnblom and Riël Vermunt, eds., *Distributive and Procedural Justice: Research and Social Applications* (New York: Routledge, 2007), 159–82.
39 Hegtvedt, "The Talk of Negotiators," 176.
40 Markus M. Müller and Elisabeth Kals, *Interactions between Procedural Fairness and Outcome Favorability in Conflict Situations* (New York: Routledge, 2007), 128.
41 Fisher, Ury, and Patton, *Getting to Yes*.
42 Adler and Silverstein, "When David Meets Goliath," 15.
43 Elfenbein et al., "Why Are Some Negotiators Better than Others?," 17–18. According to the authors, better negotiators talk more, argue more, question more, consider more options, share more (feelings), and think in the long term.

44 Maria Gardiner and Hugh Kearns, "Your Supervisory Practice: Self-Assessment," Thinkwell, 2017, http://www.ithinkwell.com.au/resources/tools-for-the-supervisor.
45 Deidra Faye Jackson, "You Better Check Yourself: Shining a Soft Light Inward to Assess Where You Are and Where You Could Be," *Grad Hacker* (blog), *Inside Higher Ed*, 31 March 2019, https://www.insidehighered.com/blogs/gradhacker/you-better-check-yourself.
46 Katy Kamkar, "Overcoming Self-Doubt with Dr. Katy Kamkar," 12 November 2019, in *Power Up Your Presence*, podcast, 0:28:54, https://www.stitcher.com/show/power-up-your-presence/episode/007-over-coming-self-doubt-with-dr-katy-kamkar-65217426.

What Can Departments or Institutions Do to Support Conflict Management?

1 Gill et al., *Models of Alternative Dispute Resolution*, 34.
2 Teresa M. Amabile and Steven J. Kramer, "The Power of Small Wins," *Harvard Business Review,* May 2011, https://hbr.org/2011/05/the-power-of-small-wins.
3 Gary Klein, "Performing a Project PreMortem," *Harvard Business Review,* September 2007, https://hbr.org/2007/09/performing-a-project-premortem.
4 Rachel Botsman, "The 3 Steps of Building Trust in New Ideas and Businesses," Ideas.TED, 8 December 2017, https://ideas.ted.com/the-three-steps-of-building-trust-in-new-ideas-and-businesses/. Watch Rachel Botsman, "We've Stopped Trusting Institutions and Started Trusting Strangers," TED, 7 November 2016, video, 0:17:08, https://www.youtube.com/watch?v=GqGksNRYu8s.
5 While pursuing her master's degree, Ms. Awywen was a member of the Diversity Working Group in her faculty, this group audited each course syllabus in her master's stream and found most of the content selected was written by white authors, even on issues pertaining to students who identify as Black, racialized, LGBQT2S+, Indigenous, and living with a disability. This group provided additional or alternative resources from a more diverse/inclusive set of authors.
6 Molecular Genetics Graduate Advisory (Dream) Team, accessed 6 October 2022, https://moleculargenetics.utoronto.ca/always-here-help-grad.
7 Sania Hameed and Mary Stefanidis, *Working towards Inclusion: Equitable Practices for Hiring Student Staff and New Professionals,* prepared for the Canadian Association of College & University Student Services, 2021, https://www.cacuss.ca/files/Resources/P15_Working%20Towards%20Inclusion%20(final_2021).pdf
8 Rebecca R. Fried, Melanie-Anne P. Atkins, and Jennifer D. Irwin, "Breaking Grad: Building Resilience Among a Sample of Graduate Students Struggling with Stress and Anxiety via a Peer Coaching Model – An 8-Month Pilot Study," *International Journal of Evidence Based Coaching and Mentoring* 17, no. 2 (2019): 3–19, doi: 10.24384/sa09-av91. The authors noted the participants' positive experiences in the eight-month pilot peer coaching program at Western University.
9 The Grad CRC was not a physical "center" – it was just my office, a few bookable meeting/training rooms, and by 2019–20, fourteen PhD and master's student

peer advisors spread out over three campuses. The peer advisors hosted daily drop-ins in grad lounges or cafés, or students could book an appointment online at a central location or elsewhere on campus upon request (including by phone or Skype). We went to where the students were rather than requiring them to come to us.

10 Hameed and Stefanidis's *Working towards Inclusion* would have been a great resource to have as a reference while I was recruiting the Grad CRC peer advisors: https://www.cacuss.ca/files/Resources/P15_Working%20Towards%20Inclusion%20(final_2021).pdf.

11 Casey Warren Phillips, "Secondary Traumatic Stress and Student Leader Paraprofessionals" (PhD diss., partial fulfillment, Nippising University, 2016), https://tspace.library.utoronto.ca/bitstream/1807/92713/1/PhillipsDissertation-FINALCOPYDec2016.pdf.

12 Mediators may also be members of a professional organization such as ADRIC (Alternative Dispute Resolution Institute Canada) or NACM (National Association of Certified Mediators) and they often have a particular type of mediation training: e.g., community-based mediation, interest-based mediation, family mediation. The terms mediator and conciliator are often used interchangeably, although sometimes a "conciliator" refers to a government-appointed neutral, and a "mediator" to a neutral chosen by the parties.

13 Jacobson, "Managing Conflicts and Resolving Disputes," 379.

14 Davis Jenkins and Sung-Woo Cho, "Get With the Program ... and Finish It: Building Guided Pathways to Accelerate Student Completion," PDF file, Community College Research Centre – Teachers College, Columbia University, CCRC Working Paper No. 66, January 2014, https://ccrc.tc.columbia.edu/media/k2/attachments/get-with-the-program-and-finish-it-2.pdf.

15 "Steps to Justice: Your Guide to Law in Ontario: Guided Pathways," Community Legal Education Ontario, accessed 30 November 2021, https://stepstojustice.ca/guided-pathways-home/; "British Columbia Civil Resolution Tribunal Solution Explorer," Civil Resolution Tribunal, accessed 30 November 2021, https://civilresolutionbc.ca/solution-explorer/.

16 Karla M. Satchwell, "The Administrative Courage of Academic Deans," in Michael Manley-Casimir and Alesha D. Moffat, eds., *Administrative Discretion in Education* (Edmonton, AB: Brush Education, 2012), 172–90.

17 Jennifer J. Freyd, "Institutional Betrayal and Institutional Courage," University of Oregon, last updated 2 November 2021, https://dynamic.uoregon.edu/jjf/institutionalbetrayal/.

What Do We Do When Conflict Isn't Resolved?

1 For an overview of what makes a good apology, see British Columbia Ombudsperson, "Quick Tips on Apologies: What Are the Elements of an Effective Apology?" accessed 14 November 2021, https://bcombudsperson.ca/assets/media/Quick-Tips-Apology.pdf.

2 Brooke Deterline, "The Power of Forgiveness at work," *Greater Good Magazine*, 26 August 2016, http://greatergood.berkeley.edu/article/item/the_power_of_forgiveness_at_work; Ayca Delibalta, Ezgi Caglar, and Sinem Evin Akbay, "Forgiveness and Forgiveness Flexibility among University Students: An Experimental Study," *World Journal of Education* 10, no. 4 (2020), https://files.eric.ed.gov/fulltext/EJ1265387.pdf.
3 The opposite can be true – where a student takes faculty advice without considering whether that advice meets their interests, for example, because this is what they have done in the past, for cultural reasons, because of perceptions of power, or because of fear. See Erica Ly, "The Intimidation: Parent. Teacher. Boss. The Power Difference," *New College* (blog), 12 January 2017, https://www.newcollege.utoronto.ca/student-blog/parent-teacher-boss-power-difference (link expired).
4 Cheryl Foy, "Creating a Respectful Workplace? Don't Start with the Law," *University Affairs*, 9 November 2020, https://www.universityaffairs.ca/opinion/legally-speaking/creating-a-respectful-workplace-dont-start-with-the-law/.
5 Abby Young-Powell, "When the Relationship with Your PhD Supervisor Turns Toxic," *The Guardian*, 22 January 2018, https://www.theguardian.com/education/2018/jan/22/when-the-relationship-with-your-phd-supervisor-turns-toxic.
6 Winkler, "Mediation with a Difference."
7 Cinnie Nobel, *Conflict Mastery Questions to Guide You* (Toronto: CINERGY Coaching, 2014), 126. Ms. Nobel is a Canadian lawyer and conflict coach.

Index

Tables and figures are indicated by a letter following the page number: "t" for tables and "f" for figures.

academic progress, 132–40
accommodation, 33
accomodating disabilities, 152–6
active listening: effort required, 236f; importance of, 201–2, 206; resources, 66, 76, 201–2; tips on, 207–8, *see also* asking questions
Adler, Robert, 204–5
alternative dispute resolution (ADR). *See* conflict resolution
ambush: avoiding, 73, *see also* informal meetings
anger, 62–3
appeals, 113, *see also* conflict escalation
"Ask Better Questions" podcast (John & Brooks), 210
asking questions: about interests, 47–8; about patterns, 23–4; for clarification, 81–3, 185; as follow-up after referral, 89; to gauge mental health, 102–3; to manage expectations, 101; in negotiations, 209–12; reflective questioning, 30, 211–12; in response to strong emotions, 13, *see also* active listening
assumptions, 23–4
authorship, 127, 128–9, *see also* intellectual property (IP)
avoidance. *See* conflict avoidance

BATNA (Best Alternative to a Negotiated Agreement), 225
Botsman, Rachel, 229–30
boundaries, 61, 193–6
brave spaces, 15–16
breathing/pausing, 10, 11, 70, 71
Brooks, Alison Wood, 202, 210
Brown, Brené, 185

campus conflict. *See* conflict
campus police/security, 14
career concerns, 165–72
carrots vs. sticks, 220–2
case studies: academic progress, 136–7; on boundaries, 195; career and work concerns, 167–9; competitive colleague, 116; dealing with diversity, 55–8; family problems, 142–3, 147, 149; getting clarification, 83; grads under pressure, 103; group conflict, 120–3; health concerns, 112; lab conflict, 161–2; medical problems and disabilities, 155–6; mental health concerns, 134, 135, 136, 156; mismatched expectations, 187; personality conflicts, 105–6; positions vs. interests, 49–50; reactions to supervisor feedback, 35–6, 38–9; remote supervision, 192–3; research concerns, 127–8;

case studies (*cont.*)
responding to emotion, 62–3, 81, 87; switching supervisors, 178–9; using case studies with grad students, 198–9, *see also* role plays and skits
check-ins, 197–9
cognitive flexibility, 216–18
collaboration, 33–4
Columbia University, Difficult Conversations Lab, 219
compassion fatigue, 13–14
competition, 33
compromise, 33
confidentiality, 78, 81, 235
conflict: authorship-related, 127, 128–9; cost of, 28–30; data on, 3–5, 9f, 25t, 53–4, 84; effect of current events, 12–15; emotions involved in, 10, 62–3, 83–7; in groups, 119–23, 157–64; impact of, 3, 10; involving members of marginalized groups, 54–5; positive side of, 3, 28, 41, 44–5, 228, 229–30; research on, 219; timing of, 16–20, 95; types of, 7–9; unintentionally escalating, 36–8, *see also* conflict hotspots
conflict avoidance: alternatives to, 27, 32–6; bringing in third person, 36–8; institutionalized, 228; problems caused by, 29; reasons for, 21–6, 203
conflict calendar, 19–20
conflict coaching: described, 58–60; online vs. in-person, 12, 68; therapy vs., 213; training in, 230, 231–4, *see also* conflict resolution; Grad CRC (Conflict Resolution Centre)
conflict escalation: formal, 110–14, 124; unintentional, 36–8
conflict hotspots, 7–9, 93–172; academic progress, 132–40; career and work, 165–72; disability, 152–6; family issues, 134, 141–6, 147; formal escalation, 110–14, 124; grief and loss, 147–9; housing, 146–7; interpersonal non-supervisory, 115–24; intrapersonal challenges, 107–10; laboratories, 157–65; mental health, 150–2, 156; most common, 7–9, 93–5; research and thesis, 125–31; supervision, 95–106, 127–8, 153–4
conflict management: carrots vs. sticks, 220–2; conflict avoidance, 22–7; dealing with emotions, 13, 62–3, 83–7, 147–9; effective, 40–1, 44–5; empowering students, 79–81; fairness, 50–3, 77; helping students access services, 87–92, 110–14, 142; helping students with career concerns, 165–72; importance of, 28–32; inclusion issues, 15–16, 52–8, 152–4; informal, 32, 43, 72–8, 113; at institutional level, 34, 42, 228–43; intentionality in, 34; interpersonal conflict, 104–6, 116–24, 146–7; intrapersonal challenges, 107–9; in laboratories, 158–64; mental health concerns, 134–5, 142, 150–2; Nudge4 Lab recommendations, 197–8; online, 68–71, 241; openness to discussing small concerns, 42–3; outside help with, 216, 217, 239–40; positions vs. interests, 32–3, 45–50; post-conflict planning, 247; power imbalances, 203–6; process vs. outcome, 223; research on, 200; role of trust in, 31; safety concerns, 81–3; self-assessment, 225–7; self-care, 10–11, 13–14; for supervisors, 101–3, 173–99; supporting academic progress, 132–40; time needed for, 25–6; timing of, 218
conflict management exercises: "Can you just…?", 194; 4-Word Build, 180–2; referrals quiz, 91; Shared

Index   281

Responsibilities, 184, 186f, *see also* case studies; role plays and skits
conflict management resources: articles, 66, 104, 120, 133, 167, 229–30; blogs, 13, 25, 59, 133, 166, 199; books and guides, 32, 97–8, 127, 152, 234; checklists and forms, 53, 114, 184, 226; FAQs, 129; podcasts, 53, 202, 210, 220; videos on mental health, 11, 25, 195; videos on supervision, 53, 86, 104, 133, 167, 201–2, *see also* tip sheets
conflict management techniques: creating conflict calendar, 19–20; drawing the conflict, 207; embracing complexity, 218–20; negotiating, 45–50, 223–5; perspective reframing, 212–23; restorative approaches, 63–7, 75; thinking strategically, 6–7, 10–11; TK model, 33–5; trauma-informed approaches, 60–3, 67, 85–7, *see also* active listening; asking questions
conflict prevention: active mindset, 27; checking in, 197–9; coaching, 58–60; intellectual property issues, 126–9, 161; in laboratories, 160–2; research and thesis issues, 126–8; roles and responsibilities, 101, 183–90; setting boundaries, 193–6; for supervisors, 173–83, 190–3; valuing negative feedback, 5–7, 98–9
conflict resolution: barriers to, 23, 29, 87, 216; bringing in third parties, 216, 217, 239–40; customized, 44; early resolution, 58–60, 228–9; in higher education, 41–3; as not always possible, 40, 202–3, 244–50; online guided pathways, 241, 242f; openness to, 201–2; positive outcomes of, 30–1, 200; restorative approaches, 63–7, 75; studies of, 228–9, *see also* active listening; asking questions; conflict coaching; conflict management *headings*

conversations, difficult, 15–16, 22, 219
#CopsOffCampus, 14
COVID-19 pandemic: impact on conflict coaching, 11–13, 68; impact on grad students, 11, 12, 132, 151, 166; online interaction due to, 12, 207
Crenshaw, Kimberlé, 16
Crucial Accountability (Patterson et al.), 183–4

Dalhousie University, Restorative Justice Learning Debrief, 65
DEI (diversity, equity, and inclusion) statements, 159
difficult conversations, 15–16, 22, 219
Difficult Conversations Lab (Columbia University), 219
disability, 152–6
discomfort as information, 15, 44
discrimination, 14–15, 55–8, 86, 88
dispute resolution. *See* conflict resolution
diversity: among peer advisors, 236–7; inclusion issues, 15–16, 52–8, 152–4; resources, 234; in training materials, 231, *see also* marginalized groups
Doyle, Aaron, 97–8

early resolution, 58–60, 228–9
EDI (equity, diversity, and inclusion) statements, 159
Elden, Nicole Benedicto, 152
"Eliminate 'but' from Your Vocabulary When Giving Feedback" (Sterling), 133
email: resources, 199; tone of, 83; using for check-ins, 199; using in conflict management, 68–9, 70–1, 74, 76
emotions: dealing with, 10–11, 13–14, 62–3, 83–7, 147–9, 202; related

to supervision, 84, 95–7; setting emotional boundaries, 196
equality/equity, 51–2, 159
escalation, formal, 110–14, 124
escalation, unintentional, 36–8
expectations, clarifying, 97–8, 101, 183–90

faculty: avoiding conflict, 26–7; imposter syndrome, 26; lab-related concerns, 157–8; making referrals, 87–8; training in conflict coaching, 230, 231–4; work-related concerns, 165, *see also* supervision
faculty coaching teams, 232–4
fairness, 50–3
fairness triangle, 51, 52f
family concerns, 134, 141–6, 147
FBI (Federal Bureau of Investigation), on active listening, 208
57 Ways to Screw Up in Grad School (Haggerty & Doyle), 97–8
Fisher, Roger, 45–7
Foy, Cheryl, 245–6

G2G (grad-to-grad). *See* peer advisors
Gardiner, Maria, 226
"Getting the Most from Your Supervisor" (workshop), 180–2, 204–5
Getting to Yes (Fisher et al.), 45–7
grad conflict. *See* conflict
Grad CRC (Conflict Resolution Centre): confidentiality, 235; conflicts discussed at, 7–8, 9f; data collected by, 3–5, 9f, 25t, 53–4, 84; "Faculty Conflict Coaching" workshop slides, 80f; "Getting the Most from Your Supervisor" workshop, 180–2, 204–5; online vs. in-person, 68; peer advisor feedback on, 237–8; "Peer Coaching" workshop slides, 236f;

staff threatened by existence of, 228; timeline, 238, *see also* conflict coaching; peer advisors
Grad SERU survey, 98–9
grad students: academic progress, 132–40; accessing services, 87, 89, 110–11, 142; avoiding conflict, 21–6; career concerns, 165–72; dealing with negative feedback, 138–40; faculty-free workshops for, 231–2; impact of COVID-19 on, 11, 12–13; international students, 54, 56–7; intrapersonal challenges, 107–10; lab-related concerns, 157–8; need to be heard, 7; on peer advisors, 234; pressures upon, 102–3, 132; relationships with supervisors, 4–6, 84, 95–7, 99–100; respecting autonomy of, 79–80; satisfaction with academic experience, 5–6; supporting mental health of, 9, 10; surveys and studies of, 5–6, 98–100, 228–9; taking leave of absence, 112, 114; timing of conflicts, 16–20, 95, *see also* conflict hotspots
grief and loss, 147–9
group work, 119–23
Guccione, Kay, 32

Haggerty, Kevin, 97–8
health and wellness issues, 9, 112, 135–6, 152–6, *see also* COVID-19 pandemic; mental health
heuristics, 219
hotspots. *See* conflict hotspots
housing, 146–7

identity. *See* marginalized groups
imposter syndrome, 24, 25, 26
Indigenous approaches. *See* restorative approaches

"Individual and Organizational Factors Promoting Successful Responses" (Oore et al.), 216
informal meetings, 72–8
information power, 205–6
"institutional betrayal," 242–3
institutions: bringing in third parties, 216, 217, 239–40; building coaching teams, 232–4; conflict management training, 230–2; effective conflict management, 34, 42, 228–30; formal processes, 72, 110–14; peer support, 234–8; trust in, 242–3; using online guided pathways, 241, 242f
intellectual property (IP), 126–9, 161
interests vs. positions, 32–3, 45–50
interpersonal conflict, 104–6, 115–24, 146–7
interpersonal trust, 32
intersectionality, 14–16, 24, 25, 53–5, 204, *see also* diversity; marginalized groups
interventions, "light touch," 197–9
intrapersonal conflict, 107–10
isolation: COVID-19 leading to, 11, 12, 151; imposter syndrome leading to, 24; mini-case study, 142

Jackson, Deidra Faye, 226
Jacobson, Robyn, 34
John, Leslie K., 210

Kearns, Hugh, 133, 138, 226
Kilmann, Ralph H., 33

laboratories, 64, 157–65
land acknowledgment activities, 66
leaves of absence, 112, 114
LeBlanc, Diane, 216
Lee, Nana, 167
Leiter, Michael, 216
Levine, Irene S., 158
Lewis Lab (University of Alberta), 159

Lewis Research Group, 159
"light touch" interventions, 197–9
listening circles, 76

Manturuk, Kim, 197
marginalized groups: conflicts involving members of, 53–8; dealing fairly with, 51–2, 159; discrimination against, 14–15, 55–8, 86, 88; imposter syndrome, 24, 25; intersectionality, 14–16, 24, 25, 53–5, 204, *see also* diversity
Mayo Clinic, 14
mediation, 113, 216, 217, 239–40, *see also* conflict coaching; conflict resolution
meditation, 10, 11
meetings, 72–8; building trust in, 74–5, 76
mental health: compassion fatigue, 13; as conflict hotspot, 150–2, 156; gauging, 102–3; grudges, 14; impact of conflict on, 3, 10; isolation, 142; mini-case studies, 134, 135, 136, 156; pausing and breathing, 10, 11; stress, 134, 150–1; work/life balance, 9
Mental Health Framework (University of Toronto), 151
messaging, positive and negative, 220–2
microaggressions, 86
mini-case studies. *See* case studies
minority groups. *See* marginalized groups
MIT, on active listening, 208

national graduate survey (2019), 5–6
negotiating, 45–50, 209–12, 223–5
Noble, Cinnie, 246
Nudge4 Lab (University of Virginia), 197–8
nudges, 197–9

Oluo, Ijeoma, 55
ombuds, 41–2, 50, 113, 239
Ontario Human Rights Commission, Chief Commissioner of, 14
Oore, Debra Gilin, 216
open-ended questions. *See* asking questions
orange scenario, 32–3

pandemic. *See* COVID-19 pandemic
Pascal, Blaise, 216–17
Patterson, Kerry, 183–4
Patton, Bruce, 45–7
pausing, 10, 11, 70, 71
peer advisors: benefits of, 24, 234–6; diversity of, 236–7; on Grad CRC, 237–8; helping grads with thesis work, 125–6; job description, 232–3; making assumptions about identities, 54; recruiting, 236–7; training, 233
peer support programs, 234–8, *See also* Grad CRC (Conflict Resolution Centre)
personal power, 205
perspective reframing, 212–23
placements, work, 169
police, campus, 14
Polk, Jen, 166
positions vs. interests, 32–3, 45–50
post-conflict planning, 246–7
power: imbalances, 78, 88, 203–6; types of, 204–5
prejudice. *See* discrimination
pressure, 26, 102–3, 132, 134, 150–1
procedural fairness, 50–2
procedural trust, 32
publishing, 129–31

Queen Margaret University, research, 228–9
"Question Strategies" (University of Waterloo), 210

race. *See* marginalized groups
referrals, 87–92, 110–14, 142
reflective questioning, 30, 211–12, *see also* asking questions
reframing, 212–23
relational fairness, 51–2
reputation, concern for, 22
research and thesis issues, 126–8
response strategies. *See* conflict resolution
restorative approaches, 63–7, 75
Restorative Justice Learning Debrief (Dalhousie University), 65
retribution, fear of, 22
RJ (restorative justice), 63–4, 65
role plays and skits: career collision, 170–2; family priorities, 144–5; interpersonal problems, 116–18; lab overload, 163–4; publishing letdown, 129–31; reflective questioning, 211–12; switching supervisors, 248–50; time to prioritize, 188–90, *see also* case studies
roles and responsibilities, 101, 183–90
Ryerson University, 65

safe spaces, 15–16
self-evaluation, 225–7
Shanok, Arielle, 152
Sharot, Tali, 220
Silverstein, Elliot, 204–5
So You Want to Talk about Race (Oluo), 55
Standing Strong Task Force (Toronto Metropolitan University), 65
Sterling, Ken, 133
"storming," 119, 120–4
stress, 26, 102–3, 132, 134, 150–1
students. *See* grad students
substantive fairness, 51–2
supervision: as conflict hotspot, 93, 95–106, 127–8, 153–4, 155; effective supervision, 180–3; emotional

intensity around, 84, 95–7; feedback on, 35–6, 38–9; giving feedback as part of, 133, 138; grad student satisfaction with, 5–6, 178–9, 248–50; power dynamics, 101–2; preventing conflicts related to, 173–83; role of trust in, 32; styles of, 104–6; supervising remotely, 190–3, *see also* faculty
surveys and studies of grads, 5–6, 98–100, 228–9

territorial acknowledgment activities, 66
texting, using in conflict management, 69
thinking strategically, 6–7, 10–11
Thomas, Kenneth W., 33
Thomas-Kilmann (TK) model, 33–5
Thompson, Mindi, 13–14
Thriving in Graduate School (Shanok & Elden), 152
tip sheets: active listening, 208; "Brave Conversations," 15–16; dealing with negative feedback, 138; email best practices, 71; informal meetings, 78; "MBP Faculty Tip Sheet," 9; new to supervision, 175–7; nine steps (from informal to formal), 124; preventing lab conflict, 160–1; setting boundaries, 196; supervision early days, 175–7; trauma-informed questions, 67
TK model, 33–5
Toronto Metropolitan University, Standing Strong Task Force, 65
trauma-informed approaches, 60–3, 67, 85–7
trust: building, 31, 32, 74–5, 76; loss of due to conflict, 29; rebuilding post-conflict, 66–7; resources, 32, 229–30
Trust Me! (Guccione), 32
"trust stack," 229–30

Truth and Reconciliation Report (TRC), 63–4
Tuckman, Bruce, 119

uncertainty, dealing with, 27
uncomfortable conversations, 15–16, 22, 219
University of Alberta, Lewis Lab, 159
University of British Columbia, Wellbeing Lab, 132
University of California Davis, research at, 197
University of California San Francisco Office of the Ombuds, 15–16
University of Guelph 2021 Graduate Calendar, 43
University of Toronto: conflict with campus police, 14; Grad SERU survey, 98–9; Mental Health Framework, 151
University of Virginia, Nudge4 Lab, 197–8
University of Waterloo, "Question Strategies," 210
Ury, William, 45–7, 202

video calls: active listening on, 207; during pandemic, 12, 68; using in conflict management, 68–9, 70

Wahl-Jorgensen, Karin, 207
Wellbeing Lab (University of British Columbia), 132
Winkler, Warren K., Judge, 203, 246
work/life balance, 9
work placements, 169

Zoom. *See* video calls

Index created by Vivian Unger

About the Author

Heather McGhee Peggs has over twenty years of conflict management experience spanning corporate litigation, mediation, ombuds complaints-handling and investigations, conflict management training, and program development. Heather completed an undergraduate degree in sociology and politics (Queen's University) and received her LLB from the University of British Columbia. She was first recognized the power of alternative dispute resolution while co-mediating in the BC Provincial Small Claims Court in Vancouver. After graduating from law school she practiced corporate commercial litigation and then pursued her passion for informal dispute resolution to Toronto Metropolitan University (formerly Ryerson University) where she was the Assistant Ombudsperson.

As manager of the University of Toronto Graduate Conflict Resolution Centre (Grad CRC), Heather was an advocate for early resolution and positioning student staff "on the front lines" of conflict management in higher education. This book and the related online training she has developed for faculty (https://supervisingconflict.com) are a tribute to the graduate students who worked for and with the Grad CRC.

Heather is committed to continuing to learn and explore fair, effective, and equitable strategies for managing conflict in her role as Manager, Complaint Services at Ontario's Patient Ombudsman, and through her collaborations with ombuds colleagues (www.justequitable.ca). She resides in Toronto, Canada, with her family.

www.ingramcontent.com/pod-product-compliance
Lightning Source LLC
Chambersburg PA
CBHW030307080526
44584CB00012B/469